A COMPREHENSIVE STUDY OF FEMALE OFFENDERS

ABOUT THE AUTHOR

Doctor Martin Guevara Urbina is professor of sociology and criminal justice at Howard College. He has taught at New Mexico State University, Western Michigan University, and at the University of Wisconsin-Milwaukee as a tenured Associate Professor of Criminal Justice. Professor Urbina was awarded a Certificate of Recognition for Outstanding Teaching by Western Michigan University in 1999, and he was nominated for the 2002-2003 UWM Distinguished Undergraduate Teaching Award. His record includes 14 solo publications, 11 referred journal articles, and three books. Author of *Capital Punishment and Latino Offenders* (2003) and *Kylor's Adventure Through the Rain Forest: A Journey of Courage and Faith* (a children's book) Urbina has a children's book under review, and he is writing two academic books and two novels: *The Making of a Famous Writer* (fiction) *and Mi Vida: Between the Wind and the Rain, I looked up and Wept* (non-fiction). His work has been published in national and international academic journals, to include *Justice Quarterly, Social Justice,* and *Critical Criminology.* Urbina loves evening walks, and he is learning how to play classical guitar. His biggest delight: la lluvia!

A COMPREHENSIVE STUDY OF FEMALE OFFENDERS

Life Before, During, and After Incarceration

By

MARTIN GUEVARA URBINA, Ph.D.

Professor of Sociology and Criminal Justice
Howard College

CHARLES C THOMAS • PUBLISHER, LTD.
Springfield • Illinois • U.S.A.

Published and Distributed Throughout the World by

CHARLES C THOMAS • PUBLISHER, LTD.
2600 South First Street
Springfield, Illinois 62704

©2008 by CHARLES C THOMAS • PUBLISHER, LTD.

ISBN 978-0-398-07811-9 (hard)
ISBN 978-0-398-07812-6 (paper)

Library of Congress Catalog Card Number: 2008008613

With THOMAS BOOKS *careful attention is given to all details of man-
ufacturing and design. It is the Publisher's desire to present books that are satisfactory as to their physical qualities and artistic possibilities and appropriate for their particular use.* THOMAS BOOKS *will be true to those laws
of quality that assure a good name and good will.*

*Printed in the United States of America
CR-R-3*

Library of Congress Cataloging-in-Publication Data

Urbina, Martin G. (Martin Guevara), 1972-
A comprehensive study of female offenders : life before, during,
and after incarceration / by Martin Guevara Urbina.
p. cm.
Includes bibliographical references and index.
ISBN 978-0-398-07811-9 (hard) -- ISBN 978-0-398-07812-6 (pbk.)
1. Female offenders. 2. Female offenders--United States. 3. Women
prisoners. 4. Women prisoners--United States. I. Title.

HV6046.U73 2008
364.3'740973--dc22

2008008613

Por la gracia de los Dioses y las Diosas
Y
El apoyo de aquellos que me han protejedo y cobijado con tanto carino,
amor,
entusiasmo y respecto, he podido hacer realidad este proyecto academico
en el que deposito mi eterno amor y agradecimiento a ustedes
y espero que ustedes reciban en algun pequeno rincon
de su alma estas sencillas pero verdaderas palabras
de mi corazon y de mi alma!
* * *

Emily Suzanne Vermilya   *   Felipa Guevara Vertiz
Ustedes han sido mi bendicion!
-Martin "Nopalito"

For the grace of God, the Gods, and the Goddesses
And
The support of those who have protected and sheltered me with so much
affection, love,
enthusiasm, and respect, I have been able to make this academic project a
reality
in which I deposit my eternal love and gratitude to you
and I hope that you receive in some small corner
of your heart these simple but genuine words
of my heart and of my soul!
* * *

Emily Suzanne Vermilya   *   Felipa Guevara Vertiz
You have been my blessing!
-Martin "Nopalito"

PREFACE

Historically, scholars have investigated many facets of the American correctional system. The focus, however, has been primarily on adult male inmates. In fact, until recently, few empirical studies focused on women in prison, in part because people assumed that there was little variation between the prison experience of male and female offenders. In the last few years, though, a number of studies have demonstrated that there are fundamental differences between male and female prisoners in a never constant penal system.

While the application of a more holistic and sound investigated approach has resulted in groundbreaking discoveries, the experiences of female offenders continue to be far less studied (vis-à-vis their male counterparts), resulting in a shortsighted profile of female offenders in the American penal system. Only a decade ago, Barbara Owen noted in her classic study, *In the Mix* (1998:viii), that even though the prison population for both women and men has soared since the 1970's,

> [N]o American criminologist or sociologist has reported a full-length study of ethnographic research conducted in a women's prison. With the exception of journalist accounts of women's experiences in jails and prisons . . . and fictional accounts . . . there have been few academic, qualitative treatments of life in women's prisons.

Methodologically, existing studies generally fall into four categories: (1) the sample of participants is limited to a selected group of female inmates within a few facilities (normally one or two) and not the whole facility; (2) if entire facilities are selected, the sample is restricted to one or two state facilities and not the entire Department of Corrections; (3) studies tend to focus on African American and Caucasian inmates, giving little attention to other racial and ethnic groups, such as Latinas, Native Americans, and Hmong; and (4) in each case, studies tend to focus on specific issues such as safety or the relationship between inmates and correctional officers. Consequently, there has been a need for more comprehensive studies of female offenders for three fundamental reasons: (1) imperative research gaps remain to be bridged; (2) the female prison experience is not constant; and (3) prison rates for female offenders, especially minority offenders, have increased considerably in the last few years.

Seeking to avoid a partial or distorted description of life behind bars, a central goal of this book, then, is to provide a balance to the existing literature and research on female prisoners in the United States and, to an extent, abroad, focusing primarily (but not exclusively) on female offenders and using data gathered from the Wisconsin Department of Corrections, which has undergone drastic institutional changes since we entered the twenty-first century in 2000. With the objective of providing a holistic profile of the typical female prisoner, this book utilizes a comprehensive investigative approach by equating the experience of female offenders by the totality of circumstances within an historical, institutional, political, and ideological context. Likewise, instead of focusing on a selected group of inmates based on demographic factors, such as race, ethnicity, age, or size, every Wisconsin female prisoner who wished to participate in the investigation was included in the study. The critical objective is to offer an inclusive analysis of the things that are considered by female inmates to be the most significant before, during, and after their incarceration, as a way of better understanding the reasons that led to their first incarceration as well as subsequent incarcerations.

In sum, this book provides an in-depth perspective of the simultaneous interaction of historical, structural, religious, cultural, political, and ideological factors that shape and reshape the experiences of women before, during, and after their incarceration. Understanding the many challenges facing female inmates requires an appreciation of the relationship between inmates, correctional officers, and, by extension, society. This undertaking should also be viewed as a call not only for the American society but the International community to openly and honestly discuss and, hopefully, resolve a social and historical issue that continues to be persistent and, in a sense, embarrassing in a modern, wealthy, and democratic society. Finally, as we process into the twenty-first century, our mission is to go beyond the question of race, ethnicity, color, class, gender, crime, and prison to a level of safety, efficiency, and universal justice by providing a series of policy recommendations throughout the book, particularly in the concluding chapter and the Epilogue.

ACKNOWLEDGMENTS

Inevitably, it would have been impossible to conduct the research and write this book without the everlasting patience, advice, and unconditional support of many honest, loyal, and dedicated people. To begin with, my most sincere gratitude goes to the Milwaukee County House of Corrections and the Wisconsin Department of Corrections. In particular, of the Milwaukee County House of Corrections, I thank Jan Brylow and Lt. Lammers. With DOC, my thanks go to Kevyn Radcliffe, Marianne Cooke, Pamela Brandon, Anthony Streveler, Jodine Deppisch, William Pollard, Theodore Harig, Mary Dolan, Carrie Spranger, Lawrence Mahoney, Beverly Lewis-Moses, Sergeant Gipsin, and Sergeant Turluck. This book would never have come to fruition without their approval, assistance, perseverance, and sagacious advice during the early stages of the research investigation.

I would like to thank Debbie Evans for reviewing the questionnaire for language adequacy as well as Caitlen Daniels and Lana Kane for their valuable recommendations regarding the relationships between female inmates and their children. Y claro, my sincere appreciation goes to LeAnne Delsart for coordinating, with masterful skill, the logistics of the research project. Even during the most difficult moments of the lengthy research process, LeAnne managed to mobilize the research team in a positive direction.

I also extend my gratitude to my research assistants who participated in the data-gathering process: Jesse Fritz, Melissa McKay, Azael Brodhead, Rachel Dobrauc, Maria Rentas-Rodriguez, Kathleen Salmon, Kurt Mauer, Meighan Flannigan, and Scott Canevit. These research assistants not only expressed a sincere interest in the project, but indicated having gained, in addition to a memorial experience, a better understanding and an appreciation for the study of female offenders. I would like to thank Gloria Brumley and David Schmidt who cheerfully worked late hours assisting with final details. Adding more work to her tight schedule, Gloria Brumley insisted on getting things done to perfection, always with a polite smile and refreshing laugh.

Con carino, respecto y solidaridad, gracias al Doctor Adalberto Aguirre (University of California-Riverside), Doctor L. Thomas Winfree (New Mexico State University), Doctor Felipe de Ortego y Gasca (Western New Mexico University), Doctor Ruben Martinez (Michigan State University), Doctor Carl E. Pope (University of Wisconsin-Milwaukee), and Doctor Rick Ruddell (Eastern Kentucky University) for their words of wisdom, compassion, and love during uncertain and tearful moments. Not only am I forever indebted to you for never losing confidence in me, but for encouraging me to continue with my research and publication.

My profound appreciation also goes to Sara Nieling for coauthoring the Epilogue with me and for assisting with the editorial process the day before going into the hospital to give birth to her first child: Isabel Margaret Nieling. And, of course, I've like to acknowledge Doctors Barbara Bloom, Carl Pope, and Rick Ruddell, who reviewed the manuscript, for their divine kindness and wisdom. I am confident that their valuable recommendations have enriched the final product.

Mil gracias para Howard College for the analytical and emotional support. I am pleased and honored with the high level of professionalism, understanding, and compassion that I have received from my colleagues. In particular, I thank Doctor Cheryl Sparks, Terry Hansen, Doctor Amy Burchett, Doctor Jamie Park, Carol Hanes, Linda Conway, Javier Flores, Linda Keeney, Amber Buske, Cynthia Weeks, Erin MacKenzie, Julie Neal, and Cadet Bryant for their support and encouragement.

I'd like to say a special thanks to my publisher, Charles C Thomas, and its President, Michael Thomas, for being extremely patient, supportive, helpful, and understanding throughout the entire publishing process. His personality and charisma have been a real blessing. Al fin, I would like to acknowledge the heroic and, at times, magical efforts of all the people who contributed to the making of this book in one way or another. I'm well aware that seldom we have the honor and privilege to work with talented, honest, and loyal individuals, or better said, crusaders, who still believe, with great courage and faith, and who participate in the cause toward universal justice and peace.

Martin Guevara Urbina, Ph.D.
o simplemente, "Nopalito"

CONTENTS

TABLES

A COMPREHENSIVE STUDY OF
FEMALE OFFENDERS

Chapter 1

INTRODUCTION

The institutional experience of adult female offenders remains underresearched, and this chapter shows that certain significant research gaps remain to be bridged. Generally, criminologists and other investigators focus on documenting the overrepresentation of minorities throughout the American criminal justice system, but fail to analyze the prison experience by the totality of historical factors, events, issues, or circumstances. This kind of methodological approach is not, on its own, sufficient to fully capture the essence of institutional life. Instead, investigators need to place contemporary ideas, practices, and experiences in the context of the past and of broader ideas about gender, race, ethnicity, and the many factors that shape and reshape the prison experience. By providing an examination of prior prison investigations, explaining the format of the book, and briefly introducing the subsequent chapters, the author will demonstrate a new approach to the contemporary study of imprisonment.

THE NATURE OF PRIOR INVESTIGATIONS

Over the years scholars have investigated many facets of the U.S. correctional system. The focus, however, has been primarily on adult male inmates. In fact, until recently, few empirical studies focused on women in prison, in part because female offending was not defined as a significant social problem, and because some people assumed that there was little (or no) variation between male and female inmates (Belknap, 1996; Carlen, 1994; Rasche, 1974). In the last few years, though, a number of studies have not only demonstrated that there are significant differences between male and female prisoners, but that other significant issues have received little attention in academic literature, public discussion, and the media.

3

Several recent books have attempted to close these gaps in the empirical literature. Books which concentrate on adult female offenders include: Atwood (2000), Belknap (1996), Cook and Davies (1999), Girshick (1999), Kruttschnitt and Gartner (2004), Owen (1998), and Rierden (1997). Books which have focused upon the prison experiences of minority women include: Agozino (1997), Collins (1997), Díaz-Cotto (1996), and Mann (1993). Books focusing on the children of incarcerated parents include: Gabel and Johnston (1995), Seymour and Hairston (2001), Wright and Seymour (2000), and Travis and Waul (2003). Books documenting the historical development of punishment include: Myers (1998), Oshinsky (1997), and Ruddell (2004). Books describing the overrepresentation of minorities in the criminal justice system include: Beckett (1997), Mauer (1999), Miller (1996), Tonry (1995), and Urbina (2003a). Books that concentrate on the relationship between race and crime include: Hawkins (1998), Hudson (1996), Kennedy (1998), Messerschmidt (1997), Milovanovic and Schwartz (1999), and Urbina (2003a).

Although the relationship between prison, race, ethnicity, gender, and the complex multitude of intertwining factors varies from country to country, the widespread overrepresentation of minorities in penal systems everywhere suggests that ideas and perceptions of gender, race/ethnicity, and variation have become defining characteristics for prison systems (see Young, 2000; Zinn and Dill, 1994). Though, nowhere is this situation more apparent than in the U.S. where, for the first time in history, the penal population moved beyond two million in 1999. Of the total number of people incarcerated in U.S. state or federal correctional facilities, women constituted over 7 percent of the adult inmate population at the end of 2005. Since 1989, the numbers of African American prisoners have surpassed those of Caucasians, despite constituting only around 12.8 percent (38.3 million in 2006) of the general U.S. population. At the end of 2005, African Americans (non-Latinas/os) made up 39.5 percent and Latinas/os accounted for 20.2 percent of inmates sentenced to more than one year in prison. Currently, Latinas and Latinos constitute approximately 14.8 percent (44.2 million in 2006) of the total general population. Caucasians (non-Latinas/os), however, represented only 34.6 percent of inmates sentenced to more than one year in prison (Harrison and Beck, 2006; *Time*, 2006). In addition to these disproportionate numbers, minority women of all groups are filling the nation's prisons most rapidly of all racial and ethnic groups.

Thus, given the transformations that the correctional system undergoes to accommodate the new and additional demands of the inmate population, we argue that a comprehensive examination of female offenders will enhance our understanding of prison life in the U.S. Consider, for instance, the following issues. First, the prison system–as a whole–was originally designed to deal with the criminality of men (Maxey, 1986; Owen, 1998; Rierden, 1997; Rock, 1996). Therefore, given the increase of incarcerated women, female inmates confined to prisons are often enmeshed in a system that is ill-equipped to handle the specific needs of female offenders, the problems that brought them to prison and the challenges that women confront during their imprisonment. This rapid increase, for example, has affected the nature of the female prison population, the ways women serve their time, the delivery of programs and services, and the crowded conditions that affect housing, medical care, staffing, and security (Owen and Bloom, 1995a, 1995b). Oftentimes, however, critics fail to acknowledge that the correctional system is not only confronted with such increases, but with an extremely diverse and troubled population. Some policymakers do not realize that prisons are called on to deal with a set of complicated problems of women that society often ignores. The prison is then left to deal with the failures of society's local, state, and national institutions. People tend to expect too much from prisons and are frustrated and angry when a given situation is not remedied or solved cheaply and quickly. Second, investigators have claimed that some correctional systems have inadequate facilities to care for women with special needs–such as those who are pregnant or ill when they enter prison or become ill during their prison term (Schupak, 1986). Others are quick to note that the correctional system, at times working with limited resources, is faced with people who have numerous life-long problems (e.g., emotional and physical needs) when they enter prison. For instance, Andi Rierden (1997) suggests that social events (e.g., sexual and physical abuse) during childhood and/or adulthood influence a person's behavior. Barbara Owen (1998) and Lori Girshick (1999) claim that pre-prison experiences (i.e., histories of abuse, family and personal relationships, and economic marginality) affect the nature of women's response to prison. Similarly, Candace Kruttschnitt and Rosemary Gartner (2004) suggest that women's pre-sentence characteristics and experiences combined with the institutional environment in which they serve their sentence influence how they do their time in prison. Lastly, along with rapidly accelerating technology, changing population demographics, lengthening sentences, a graying inmate population as well as contemporary and critical issues, like HIV/AIDS, need further analysis.

Taken together, the existing literature suggests that while some things have not changed drastically, some things have changed significantly. While several classic works have been conducted and continue to serve as a frame of reference, significant gaps remain and need to be addressed (Belknap, 1996). The complexity of the matter itself suggests the need for more empirical research on women's experiences with crime and prison as well as their children and families (see Liebling, 1999). These are issues that society should be aware of and embrace, if we are to maintain a decent, efficient, and safe environment in prison and ultimately public safety for everybody.

In the hope of producing a sound and holistic final project, a series of classic studies will assist us in the process. Given the disproportionate numbers of women (and men) of color behind bars in the U.S. and other countries, it is of utmost urgency that the ways in which adult female offenders and their children interact be analyzed by the totality of issues, events, and circumstances. Rather than attempting to come up with one reason for variation (e.g., overrepresentation of people of color in prisons around the world), this book will present a variety of studies that suggest alternative ways of interpreting imprisonment as we move into the twenty-first century. It will build a framework of theoretical analysis within criminology and sociology to better understand the ideological ties between race, ethnicity, gender, and imprisonment. In order to accomplish this goal, the authors will draw on prior empirical research as well as literature from diverse fields of post-colonial, feminist theory, conflict theory, threat theory, ethnic/race studies, and globalization literature.

In this endeavor, the classic work of Jane Atwood in *Too Much Time: Women in Prison* (2000), Joanne Belknap in *The Invisible Woman: Gender, Crime, and Justice* (1996), Lori Girshick in *No Safe Haven: Stories of Women in Prison* (1999), Candace Kruttschnitt and Rosemary Gartner in *Marking Time in the Golden State: Women's Imprisonment in California* (2004), Barbara Owen in *In the Mix: Struggle and Survival in a Women's Prison* (1998), Andi Rierden in *The Farm: Life Inside a Women's Prison* (1997), Catherine Collins in *The Imprisonment of African American Women: Causes, Conditions and Future Implications* (1997), and Juanita

Diaz-Cotto in *Gender, Ethnicity and the State: Latina and Latino Prison Politics* (1996) will serve as a frame of reference to better understand the everyday experiences of female offenders in the U.S. correctional system. Additionally, this project builds on and extends some of the issues raised in Roy D. King and Mike Maguire's edited book *Prisons in Context* (1994) and Timothy J. Flanagan, James W. Marquart and Kenneth G. Adams' edited text *Incarcerated Criminals* (1998).

As for the controversial issue of race and ethnic variation, the work of cultural theorist Paul Gilroy, *The Black Atlantic: Modernity and Double Consciousness* (1993), and Martin Guevara Urbina, *Capital Punishment and Latino Offenders: Racial and Ethnic Differences in Death Sentences* (2003a), may provide a useful point of departure. According to Gilroy, ideas and ideologies of race and modernity are historically linked, and race, as we perceive it today, is a modern construct dating to the late eighteenth and nineteenth century, an era when the prison was invented (Acuna, 2004; Almaguer, 1994). Urbina argues that variation in punishment, particularly in modern times, is largely attributed to the threat that minority populations pose to mainstream America.

These propositions have critical implications for the field of criminal justice, criminology, and the entire American legal system. For instance, what if ideas of race (and ethnicity) which, as Gilroy suggests, are historically contingent and constructed, are necessary for the correctional system to "survive" and expand? Likewise, consider the implications if indeed variation in punishment is governed by threat differentials, as argued by Urbina. Could the United States, for example, sustain its current legal system, if one out of four African American men of a certain age were not under some form of incarceration or surveillance (Irwin and Austin, 1997; Tonry, 2004)? If incarceration rates continue, an African American male born in 2001 has a one in three chance of going to prison during his lifetime (Bonczar, 2003). Similarly, could the legal system survive and grow without the "new minority," Latinas and Latinos, who recently bypassed the African American population for the first time in history (Mandel, 1979; Urbina, 2007)? A Latino born in 2001 has a one in six chance of going to prison during his lifetime, while a Caucasian male has a one in seventeen chance of going to prison (Bonczar, 2003). Further, could the legal system survive and continue to grow without the newly "targeted" population, women, particularly African Americans (Mann, 1995; Richie, 1996)? The lifetime probability of going to prison among African American women (5.6%) is almost as high as for Caucasian men (5.9), Latinas (2.2%), and Caucasian females (0.9%) have a much lower lifetime chance of going to prison (Bonczar, 2003). And, would the criminal justice system survive, grow, and prosper without the "intergenerational connection," female offenders and their children, especially minority children? Would the system survive economically? Or, what if young Caucasian women (and men) were being imprisoned at the same rate? Would the American society support such practices of confinement? Lastly, what, if any, are the connections between modern imprisonment rates and historical practices of slavery, conquest, and colonialism (Acuna, 2004; Agozino, 1997; Almaguer, 1994; Bosworth and Flavin, 2007)? In short, just as it has been documented that punishment is an expression of historically contingent sensibilities (Garland, 1990), might it not be possible that ideas of race, of ethnicity, of difference, and of "other," play into the types of acts that we define as crimes and our strategies of when and how we respond to criminal behavior (Free, 2001; Urbina, 2007)?

By bridging the theoretical connections between race, ethnicity, gender, and imprisonment, and through documenting the historical interdependence of these concepts, this book seeks to provide a comprehensive analysis of the prison system. Empirically, by exploring the connections between adult female offenders and the children of incarcerated women, this book seeks to challenge current practices and views of the American prison system.

RATIONALE FOR WRITING THIS BOOK

While the existing literature in the area of corrections is extensive, the experiences of incarcerated women are by far less-studied, less-known, and thus there are certain research areas that deserve further examination (Atwood, 2000; Girshick, 1999; Kruttschnitt, Gartner, and Miller, 2000; Owen, 1998; Peugh and Belenko, 1999; Rierden, 1997). Existing books generally fall into three main fields. First, there are a handful of historical studies, generally produced in the United States that analyze the historical development of punishment in light of earlier race relations–i.e., "black and white" (Urbina, 2007). More commonly, books describe the overrepresentation of women (and men) of color (focusing primarily on African Americans) in the U.S. criminal justice system or elsewhere, or consider the relationship between race (and, on occasion, ethnicity) and offending and may include a chapter or two on prisons. Finally, some books concentrate solely on minority women (usually African Americans) in prison. Therefore, it is difficult to locate a comprehensive book that examines the challenges that female prisoners confront.

Methodologically, existing studies generally fall into four categories: (1) the sample of participants is limited to a selected group of inmates within one or two facilities; (2) if entire facilities are considered, the sample is restricted to one or two facilities (not the entire department of corrections); (3) studies tend to focus on adult female inmates or institutionalized girls; and (4) in each case, studies tend to focus on specific issues, like relationship with correctional officers, health issues, or drug issues. Hence, there is a need for more comprehensive studies of female offenders for five important reasons: (1) there are certain research gaps that need to be bridged; (2) the prison experience is not constant; (3) prison rates for female offenders, especially minority offenders, have increased drastically in the last two decades; (4) the links between the children of incarcerated mothers and their rise of future criminality need further investigation; and (5) issues like physical and mental health are becoming more critical. For instance, the Department of Correction in the state of Wisconsin, which tends to influence the rest of the country, has experienced some significant changes in the last ten years–e.g., prison rates of women tripled between 1997 and 2000, and state officials announced in 2000 that all female inmates institutionalized out of state were being brought back to Wisconsin. Yet, to our knowledge, no extensive study had been done on Wisconsin's incarcerated women prior to the current study.

A central objective of the current study, then, is to provide a balance to the existing literature and research on U.S. prisoners, focusing primarily (but not exclusively) on female offenders, using the Wisconsin Department of Corrections as an illustration.[1] In all, Wisconsin is unique for three essential reasons: (1) Wisconsin was the leading exporter of inmates; (2) Wisconsin incarcerates more African Americans per capita than any other state in the country, roughly three times as many inmates as the state of Minnesota; and (3) Wisconsin's correctional health care system is possibly one of the most chaotic in the country (*Milwaukee Journal Sentinel*, 2000a, 2002). Just as the devaluing of research interests deprives Caucasian female inmates of the dignity of contributing to theorizing about their lives, failing to conduct research on minority female prisoners deprives them of voicing their every day and every night experiences and concerns: physical and psychological well-being, dreams, goals, and desires. Particularly, considering the high probability of African American women to be involved in the criminal justice system at some point in their lives, the links between these two segments of society need to be investigated as finely as possible if we are to diminish the cycle of criminality in the United States.

Hence, instead of focusing on certain issues, the current study utilizes a detailed and comprehensive approach. Likewise, instead of limiting the sample to a specific group of inmates, the current study includes the entire Wisconsin Department of Corrections. That is, not only are we documenting the experiences of women in prison throughout the country (vis-à-vis the existing empirical literature), but we are investigating the entire Wisconsin correctional system to create a baseline for future investigations in other states.

In sum, this study will provide an in-depth perspective of the simultaneous interaction of historical, structural, and ideological forces that shape and reshape the experiences of women before, during, after their incarceration, particularly in Wisconsin. Understanding the many challenges facing both the correctional system and female inmates requires an appreciation of the relationship between inmates, correctional officers, and, by extension, society. For instance, at the same time that some society members demand that crime rates be reduced, little attention has been given to the issues confronting female prisoners after being released, which are likely to influence whether or not female prisoners end up back in prison. Such demand, though, should also be viewed as a call for society to come to grips with a fundamental dilemma that is vexing and persistent, but has remained silent for too long.

Rather than purporting to be a systematic treatment of the subject, this writing is explicitly anecdotal. As such, discussions, conclusions, and recommendations are contingent on the emotions, views, and perceptions of participating female prisoners. Hence, because the information was gathered from a nonscientifically chosen group of female inmates, this writing needs to be interpreted with caution. Our main goal is to provide a unique analysis of Wisconsin's female prisoners' (and elsewhere) everyday lives as the inmates themselves experience it (not a partial, or distorted description of prison life). The objective is to offer an inclusive and extensive analysis of the most meaningful aspects of the inmates' lives before, during, and after incarceration. Finally, our mission is to go beyond the question of race, ethnicity, color, class, gender, crime, and prison to a level of safety, efficiency, and universal justice. We should not be overburdened by the historical, economic, social, and political problems of the past, but energized by the possible prospects of the future.

FORMAT OF THE BOOK

In contrast to most existing studies, this book provides a comprehensive account of adult women in prison, paying particular attention to the experiences of female offenders before, during, and after their incarceration. The book is structured into ten chapters, each of which corresponds to a different body of historical, theoretical, and empirical work on female offenders and their subsequent incarceration.

In addition, it is important to understand how policies related to punishment are sometimes contingent upon broader transnational arrangements (Sanchez, 2007). Richard Bennett (2004:6), for instance, acknowledges the importance of understanding "crime that transcends. . . . borders and justice systems." Therefore, we further argue that it is also important to recognize that responses to crime may also be increasingly transnational. For example, some emerging social control policies, such as drug laws and anti-terrorism legislation, are the result of collaborative efforts that involve several countries, and are increasingly linked to foreign policy. As a consequence, some current imprisonment practices, like many economic and trade policies, seem to be global in nature.

CHAPTER OUTLINE

This book explores the lives of adult female offenders before, during, and after their incarceration. When possible, the first part of each chapter includes historical, theoretical, and prior empirical research about the issues under consideration. The second part of each chapter complement (or develop) these concepts through the current empirical research on the Wisconsin correctional system, referred from here on as the "Wisconsin Experience."

Chapter 2, "Leading Characteristics of the American Female Prisoner: A Twenty-First Century Profile," provides a detailed profile of the typical adult female offender in U.S. prisons in the twenty-first century. The first part of this chapter is divided into the following subsections: (1) the prison boom, (2) why the inmate population is significantly up, (3) a continuum of legal sanctions (including the drug legislation), (4) who goes to prison, (5) the cost of incarceration, and (6) what the public thinks. The second part of Chapter 2 reports the findings (i.e., demographic information, including family-related issues) of the Wisconsin experience.

Chapter 3, "The Lives of Female Prisoners Before Their Incarceration," provides a discussion of the lives of adult female offenders before their imprisonment. Examining the lives of incarcerated women prior to imprisonment is necessary to better understand what brought them to prison and how they cope with daily life inside correctional facilities. Barbara Owen (1998) documents that the life experiences that women bring into prison is important for how they will adapt to prison, how they will relate to other inmates and prison staff. Further, the combination of institutionalized greed, structural marginalization, and destructive personal choices are factors that often result in criminal behavior and consequently imprisonment. The historically explored race factor, then, is only one of the several influential factors governing the daily lives of incarcerated women. Candace Kruttschnitt, Rosemary Gartner, and Amy Miller (2000:696), for instance, report that a "woman's economic background seemed to have a much stronger effect on how she reacted to prison than did her race. Most of the women . . . came from impoverished backgrounds." The second part of Chapter 3 details the findings (e.g., information regarding family; alcohol and drug use; physical, sexual, verbal, and emotional abuse; and so forth) of the Wisconsin inmate population.

Chapter 4, "Inmates' Involvement with the Criminal Justice System," begins by providing a discussion of the history of prison inmates with the U.S. legal system. As noted by some scholars, female offenders were once viewed as maladjusted, misguided, and in need of assistance and treatment (Giallombardo, 1966), but female offenders are now viewed as dangerous, irredeemable, and in need of strict social control (Faith, 1993a; Merlo and Pollock, 2005). Together, these changes have resulted in a radical and rapid shift away from the rehabilitative and therapeutic goals that distinguished women's corrections from men's imprisonment for most of the twentieth century (Kruttschnitt, Gartner, and Miller 2000). Therefore, we need to understand the interaction of both historical and ideological factors that shape these changes. Chapter 4 then concludes by detailing demographic and offense-related characteristics of imprisoned women in Wisconsin, including prior criminal record, specific charges, plea bargaining, and type of attorney.

Chapter 5, "An Exploration of Female Prisons and the Women They Control," begins with the observation that the imprisonment of women in the U.S. has always been a different phenomenon than it has been for men. Women have traditionally been sent to prison for different reasons and once in prison, female inmates endure different conditions of incarceration (Simon and Landis, 1991). Nancy Kurshan (1992:331), for instance, notes that "women's 'crimes' have often had a sexual definition and have been rooted in the patriarchal double standard. Therefore, the nature of women's imprisonment reflects the position of women in society." The second part of Chapter 5 examines issues such as solitary confinement, supplies, meals, religion, jobs, education, training, and hobbies, for the Wisconsin women.

Chapter 6, "The Many Faces of Women's Health," provides a detailed discussion of both traditional and contemporary health issues (both physical and mental) facing female inmates in U.S. prisons. As illustrated by Barbara Owen (1998:8), along with "economic marginalization," ". . . histories of abuse and self-destructive choices speed women along a pathway to imprisonment." The second part of Chapter 6 includes the findings, such as HIV, AIDS, cancer, depression, medication, and pregnancy, for Wisconsin's incarcerated adult female offenders.

Chapter 7, "Living Under the Same Roof: Female Offenders and Correctional Officers," begins by exploring the historical relationships between adult female inmates and correctional officers. As documented by some investigators, the experiences of female inmates while incarcerated, and, by extension, after their release, are impacted by how they interact with staff, how they are viewed by staff, and how they perceive correctional staff. For example, at times, female inmates are treated with disdain, not realizing that the typical female prisoner is not a violent offender and thus will soon be released back into the community. Some of these women, though, will return to prison, a place they might perceive as a hostile environment. Chapter 7 then concludes by documenting the findings, which include respect, communication, and negative experiences, for Wisconsin's adult inmate population.

Chapter 8, "Critical Issues: Twenty-First Century Challenges," examines the critical issues that historically have influenced the prison experience, as well as the more contemporary issues facing women in prison. This Chapter documents that not only is the woman experience different from the male experience, but the prison experience is not constant. For instance, the traditional U.S. prisoner (i.e., African American or Caucasian) is now being joined by other racial and ethnic individuals, particularly Latinas. With these demographic changes, though, also come additional concerns–e.g., language barriers, racial/ethnic divides, hatred or distrust among inmates, and the like. The second part of Chapter 8 reports the findings, language barriers, visitors, racial/ethnic divisions, violence, gangs, and hatred among inmates, of the Wisconsin experience.

Chapter 9, "Life After Prison," provides a discussion of life after prison for the typical adult female offender. The second part of Chapter 9 reports findings, job training and life plans for after release, of the Wisconsin prisoners. Then, it will be argued that the most crucial gap to the establishment of social control remains to be bridged: from prison to the community. Otherwise, with limited resources, little hope, and a hostile community, women offenders are likely to return to prison. A discussion of twenty-first century challenges is outlined. The Chapter concludes with recommendations for the creation and implementation of a more rational, humane, and just penal system, while ensuring public safety.

Chapter 10, concludes the book by tying the various topics together, providing a comprehensive frame of reference and a context for future analyses. First, the modern logic of imprisonment will be discussed, followed by the "evolution of female criminals." Then, threats, fear of crime, and scapegoats in the context of criminalization and incarceration will be analyzed, followed by a discussion on the global nature of imprisonment and a detailed analysis of the militarism of corrections. The Chapter ends with a reference to key critical issues to consider in future research, discussion, and criminal justice policy.

In the Epilogue, Sara Nieling and Martin Guevara Urbina provide qualitative anecdotal data from the Wisconsin study, to include advice and recommendations from the inmates themselves. The author also argues that the "human side of female prisoners" should be underscored in academic literature and public discussions. Finally, the author concludes with recommendations for policymakers, who wish to make the punishment process; that is, life before prison, life during prison, and life after prison, more objective, humane, and just.

Chapter 2

CHARACTERISTICS OF AMERICAN PRISONERS: A TWENTY-FIRST CENTURY PROFILE

The first part of this chapter provides a detailed profile of the typical adult female offender in U.S. prisons in the twenty-first century, and addresses the following issues: (1) the prison boom, (2) why the inmate population is significantly up, (3) a continuum of legal sanctions, (4) who goes to prison, (5) the cost of incarceration, and (6) public option towards mass imprisonment. The second part of this chapter reports the demographic characteristics of the Wisconsin experience.

THE PRISON BOOM: A MODERN IDEA

America's first prison was built by the Quakers at the end of the eighteenth century as an alternative to corporal and capital punishment, with the objective of rehabilitation through hard work, religious study, and penitence (McNeely and Pope, 1981; Newman, 1995; Walker, 1980). Two hundred years later, the U.S. is facing an unprecedented binge in prison construction, to the point that it now has the highest number of people under the control of the criminal justice system among "first-world countries." Yet, the U.S. has the highest homicide crime rates and one of the highest violent crime rates in the industrialized world (Ruddell, 2004).

Starting in the mid 1970s, the U.S. legal system responded to the public's fear of crime, which is largely propagate by the media, by incarcerating more offenders and placing more people under surveillance for longer periods of time. According to government reports, the state and federal prison population, which stood at 129,453 in 1930, reached 329,821 in 1980, and it almost tripled to 883,656 by 1992. By the end of 1996, 1,182,169 women and men were incarcerated in federal and state prisons (Bureau of Justice Statistics, 1991, 1999a, 2001a; Ruddell, 2004). At the end of 2005, nearly 2.2 million adults were incarcerated in state and federal prisons or jails, an equivalent of one in every 136 residents. Overall, 2,320,359 people were incarcerated at the end of 2005: 1,446,269 in state and federal prisons (excluding state and federal prisoners in local jails); 15,735 in territorial prisons; 747,529 in local jails; 10,104 in facilities operated by the Bureau of Immigration and Customs Enforcement; 2,322 in military facilities; 1,745 in jails in Indian country (midyear 2004); and 96,655 in juvenile facilities (as of 2003). Further, at the end of 2005, there were 4,162,536 adult men and women on probation and 784,408 people on parole. Including people in jails, prisons, probation, and parole, approximately 7 million people (1 in every 32 adults or about 3.2 percent of the adult population) were under correctional control at the end of 2005 (Harrison and Beck, 2006).

From 1930 to 1950 an average of 2.5 women's prisons were built in the U.S., each decade rose to 7 in the 1960s. In the 1970s, though, the number increased to 17 and 34 in the 1980s (Applebome, 1992; Epperson, Hannum, and Datwyler, 1982). Today, women are incarcerated in 98 prisons for women and 93 coed facilities. Overall, women constituted about 7 percent (107,518) of all prisoners held in state or federal correctional facilities at the end of 2005. California, which has the largest prison population in the country, now has the most female prisoners in the nation, as well as the world's largest women's prison (Harrison and Beck, 2006; Schweber, 1984; Smykla, 1980).[2]

The prison boom has also led to three other issues: (1) it has created a demand for additional needs, like bilingual documents and interpreters; (2) it has created overcrowding; and (3) it has led to constitutional challenges. In 1996, for instance, the prison boom created the need for 1,075 new prison beds nationwide each week. Overcrowded facilities have become the norm in many states to the point that 39 states, the District of Columbia, the U.S. Virgin Islands, and Puerto Rico were under court orders to correct overcrowding and/or unconstitutional conditions at the beginning of 1995 (Immarigeon and Chesney-Lind, 1992; Steptoe, 1986; Strasser & Hickey, 1989). At the end of 2005, state prisons were operating between 1 percent under and 14 percent over official capacity, and the federal prison system was 34 percent over its capacity (Harrison & Beck, 2006). In early 2007, states like California housed 174,000 inmates in facilities designed for approximately 100,000, which prompted a federal judge to request that prison overcrowding be reduced by June 2007 in California's 33 state prisons (Thompson, 2007). A fact that Governor Arnold Schwarzenegger himself acknowledged: "we have 172,000 prisoners in facilities designed to hold about 100,000" (Tanner, 2007:1).

In addition to building additional facilities, most states have responded by stretching the capacity of existing prisons. In many prisons throughout the country, prisoners are double-bunked in small cells designed for one person, or they are forced to sleep on mattresses in unheated prison gyms, hallways, day rooms, or basements. Some prisoners also sleep in makeshift trailers, tents, or converted ferries. In fact, space that was devoted to work, study, or recreational programs is now being converted into dormitories to solve the overcrowding problem. Overcrowding contributes to the spread of disease, including tuberculosis and other communicable diseases (see Chapter 6).

Given the recent interest of some judges in the rights of inmates, states are trying to avoid lawsuit by implementing alternative strategies, such as early release programs, jails, probation, parole, and intermediate punishments (see Festervan, 2003). The early release approach seeks to encourage good behavior by reducing prison time, and it is designed to free space for new prisoners. However, recent truth in sentencing mandates are pressuring states to keep violent inmates incarcerated for at least 85 percent of their maximum sentences. States that do not comply with these new federal initiatives are not eligible for federal funds. Some states are forcing offenders with prison sentences to remain in county jails (Connolly, 1983; Salholz, 1990; Wirtzfeld, 1985), which in most states are designed for offenders awaiting trial and those serving sentences of a year or less. While not highly favored by some policymakers, intermediate punishments (also known as alternative sanctions or community corrections) are becoming a vital option for nonviolent offenders in some communities. Lastly, probation and parole caseloads are not only increasing rapidly, but these two correctional approaches are becoming America's newest form of imprisonment, in that we can incarcerate offenders in their own home cheaply, from a distance, and, given our latest technology, effectively.

This practice, however, has not led to a significant decrease in crime rates. In fact, states that incarcerate the most offenders continue to have the highest crime rates and those that incarcerate the least have the lowest crime rates. With few exceptions, offenders who are behind bars cannot commit additional crimes while in prison, but longer prison sentences are not always a successful deterrent to criminal behavior. In Delaware, for example, mandatory minimum sentences for drug offenses were implemented in 1989, but despite a 45 percent increase in felony drug offenders in prison, no reduction in drug activity has been achieved in Delaware (O'Connell, 1995). From 1993 to 2005, though, there was a reduction in violent and property crime rates (Catalano, 2006).[3]

REASONS FOR A HIGH PRISON POPULATION

Philosophically, there are five reasons as to why the inmate population is high, and continues to increase. First, even though the average prison sentence of two years served by inmates has remained constant since 1923, many of us believe that correctional institutions have a "revolving door," in which inmates serve far shorter sentences than before. Second, the high inmate population is attributed to the perception that incarcerating more offenders and keeping more offenders under surveillance for longer periods of time will significantly reduce crime rates. Third, we believe that rehabilitation does not work, and thus inmates need to be incarcerated for longer periods of time. Fourth, political pressure for quick fixes has led to an increase in incarceration industry. Fifth, the public's fear of crime has also contributed to the influx of new prisoners.

The mentality, "lock them up and throw away the key," of Americans in combination with large increases in law enforcement, mandatory sentencing laws, and longer sentences led to larger inmate populations across the country (see Chapters 4 and 10). Practically, the following 12 factors further explain high prison populations.

Crime Rates

In part, the increase in prison populations is attributed to changes in interpretation and reporting, and not necessarily to higher crime rates (Free, 2001; Urbina, 2007). For instance, snapshots of crime can be misleading because crime rates generally do not decrease or increase steadily. Therefore, government reports are sometimes contradictory, and depending on statistical approaches and reporting techniques, the crime, and the time selected, it is possible to have varied conclusions about the impact of existing policies. Indeed, when analyzed graphically, historical changes in crime rates for certain offenses and the increase in prison rates reveal that there is no clear relationship between incarceration and crime rates (see Currie, 1985).

Scholars continue to explore the reasons for the drop in crime rates, citing issues like more aggressive police, community-based programs, gun control legislation, control of the drug trade, and more criminals in prisons and jails; the media continues to shape public perception and public policy (Dyer, 2000; Farrington, 1992). For example, even though crime remains essentially constant, television coverage of crime on the evening news has increased significantly in some jurisdictions (Potter and Kappeler, 1998). To this end, some policymakers argue that they are simply responding to the public's fear of crime, a position that is not always supported by public opinion surveys (Beckett, 1997; Beckett and Sasson, 2003). When individuals are informed about alternatives, citizens often opt for various penalties for nonviolent crimes, suggesting that we take a closer look at alternatives to prison (Immarigeon, 1987), like Proposition 36 in California to divert drug offenders from prison.

Mandatory Sentencing Laws

The typical conversation, whether it is taking place in a coffee shop, bus station, or executive office, about the nature of crime tends to conclude with one policy implication: high crime rates are a direct result of indeterminate crime control policies. Not surprisingly, some policymakers have argued that the only way to increase public safety is by putting an end to the "revolving door" of corrections. Under pressure by the media, local politicians, and the "voting class," state legislators support strict mandatory sentencing laws to include a wide array of offenses, such as drug crimes, crimes committed with a gun, and sexual offenses. Mandatory sentencing laws, which require prison sentences for certain offenses and specify a minimum number of years the offender must serve before release, have had a large impact on inmate populations throughout the country (Kleck, 1991).

Three Strikes and You're Out Laws

States have also implemented laws requiring lengthy mandatory sentences, including laws to lock up repeat offenders for life without parole. First, the notion was that even though drug laws were being modified or implemented, offenders were either not receiving lengthy sentences or they were not serving their entire sentence. Second, given some highly publicized violent crimes or what Walker (2005) reference as "celebrated cases," especially during election years, some policymakers began to suggest that the only vital solution to reduce recidivism was to implement lengthy prison sentences.

Hence, since 1993, the federal government and over 20 states have implemented some form of the popular "three strikes and you're out" law. California's "three strikes" policy is even harsher in that it provides for doubling of sentences on a second felony conviction. The state of Georgia implemented a "two strikes" law. Evidently, these new laws have an amplification effect. For example, Jerry Williams was convicted in 1995 of a third strike for the armed robbery of a slice of pizza from some children. Since Williams had two prior robbery convictions, he was sentenced to 25 years to life under California's new law (Slater, 1995), the sentence was upheld on appeal by the U.S. Supreme Court in 2003.

Longer Prison Sentences

In addition to the various issues mentioned above, the rehabilitation concept has significantly altered how inmate populations are managed. Historically, rehabilitation was viewed as a central objective in corrections (Feinman, 1983). However, after the publication of Martinson's 1974 study, which gave audience to the popular phrase "nothing works," rehabilitation in some jurisdictions was meaningful only in theory, and social control policies–i.e., long prison sentences–became the practical reality (see Harm, 1992).

Again, even though the average prison sentence served nationwide has remained fairly constant at about two years since 1923, the length of time served by inmates in the federal system and in some states has been increasing, as an effect of the various laws, especially drug legislation. To this end, to ensure that accused individuals, if convicted, serve lengthy sentences, some states have adopted sentence enhancement laws. For example, these laws typically require that a fixed number of additional years be given to individuals who commit a crime while in possession of a weapon or other aggravating factors, like involvement in a gang.

An Aging Prison Population

If the implications of the punitive movement were not apparent at the beginning, some of them have become more obvious in recent years. The combination of social control policies such as truth in sentencing, determinate sentences, sentence enhancement laws, and parole restrictions, has altered the revolving door mechanism, creating an aging population, which in turn contributes to the prison boom. In fact, during the last 25 years, older prisoners are becoming one of the fastest growing groups within the prison population (see Chapters 6 and 8). One issue that advocates of long prison sentences often fail to knowledge is the fact that with longer sentences comes "old age," and thus reducing their abilities to survive the streets once released. Further, people tend to be less involved in crime as they get older (Aday, 2003). Consequently, the correctional system must provide things such as long-term health care and other accommodations. For women, the situation has been worse in that they are not only being prosecuted for their involvement in crimes, but they are receiving harsh penalties, at times, harsher then men because of the notion that they are now violating women's traditional roles (Kruttschnitt, Gartner, and Miller, 2000; Simon and Landis, 1991; see Chapter 10).

Anti-Drug Efforts

Perhaps no other offense has received more attention than drugs in the last three decades. Starting with the passage of the Racketeer Influenced and Corrupt Organizations Act (RICO) in 1970 by

Congress, whose primary objective was to prosecute criminal organizations by adopting mandatory fines and lengthy sentences, state and federal agencies have taken an aggressive and punitive approach against those who are involved with drugs in the U.S. or abroad (Urbina and Kreitzer, 2004). However, drug statutes, like RICO and those that were implemented in the early and mid-1980s, especially after the introduction of crack cocaine into poor neighborhoods, have a net-widening effect. People who traditionally received immunity from prosecution, particularly women, such as girlfriends, wives, mothers, and their relatives, are now being caught in the net of the new laws. Therefore, the war on drugs has led to a huge increase in both state (20%) and federal (56%) prison systems (Currie, 1985; Walker, 2005). According to a recent report, drug offenders account for approximately 2 million of the 7 million people under the control of the criminal justice system at the end of 2005 (Harrison and Beck, 2006).

Sex Offenders

With the emergence of the feminist movement in the 1960s and 1970s (Cain, 1990; Daly and Maher, 1998; Fox, 1984; Howe, 1994), the legal system's response to sex crimes became a major political issue (Brownmiller, 1975; Gelsthorpe and Morris, 1990). In the last few years, 16 states have implemented "sexually violent predator" laws and civil commitment laws for sex offenders. Further, due in part to the perceived dangerousness of sex offenders, existing laws have been modified to facilitate the prosecution of sex offenders. In fact, all states now have statutes requiring public notification when sex offenders are paroled into the community (Presser and Gunnison, 1999; Welchans, 2005). To this end, the rape-murder in New Jersey of Megan Kanka by a released sex offender created a media propagated image of a serious crime wave that forced policymakers to alter existing laws to reduce fear of crime and increase public safety (Potter and Kappeler, 1998). Yet, some critics suggest that while sex crimes are a serious concern, the action taken is not always the most appropriate and that additional research is needed to fully capture the essence of this particular behavior (Greenwood, 1997; Stalans, 2003). And indeed, the increased prosecution and conviction of this offender population, as well as longer and more severe sentences, have contributed to the prison boom.

The Mentally Ill or Mentally Handicapped

Correctional facilities, especially jails, have become a warehouse for individuals who are being released from facilities for the mentally ill, mostly for minor offenses (*New Statesman*, 1985; Salholz, 1990). According to E. Fuller Torrey (1988), in 1988 there were 100,000 people in jails who needed treatment for serious mental illness. In fact, figures show that in the early 1990s there were approximately 33 percent more mentally ill people in jails than in mental hospitals (Steadman and Cocozza, 1993). Among the incarcerated population, approximately 5 percent (50,000) are mentally handicapped (i.e., mentally retarded or developmentally disabled), and a much higher number of those on probation are also mentally handicapped (Maden, Swinton, and Gunn, 1994; Petersilia, 1997). As far as state prisons, a California study showed that 8 percent of the prison population had one of four major mental disorders, and an additional 17 percent had less severe but serious mental disorders (Specter, 1994). A study by the U.S. Department of Justice estimates that 283,800 mentally ill people were incarcerated in prison or jail at midyear 1998, and about 16 percent (547,800) of people on probation suffered from a mental condition (Ditton, 1999). Other studies report that approximately 300,000 inmates in jails and prisons nationwide suffer from major depression, manic depression, or schizophrenia. Additionally, approximately 550,000 individuals on probation have a mental condition or have spent a night in a mental hospital at some point in their lives (Butterfield, 2003; *Human Rights News*, 2003). At midyear 2005, more than half of all jail and prison inmates had a mental health problem, including 479,900 in local jails, 705,600 in state prisons, and 78,800 in federal prisons. A common health problem among violent offenders, female inmates had a higher rate of mental health problems than male inmates, and Caucasian offenders had higher rate of metal problems than African American and Latina/o inmates in 2005 (James and Glaze, 2006).

Notice that today we use the phrase "mental illness" to explain behavior we do not understand, even if the action is not a neurological problem; that is, a "disease of the brain" (Szasz, 1963:12, 1987; Tittle, 1972). Even worse, "our need to explain some criminal behavior as mental illness can easily lead us to overgeneralize and ascribe mental illness to all criminals" (Clear, Cole, and Reisig, 2006:144).

Tough Parole Policies

Even though strict parole policies are a result of a series of reported issues, there are three that probably caused the greatest impact. First, the media has highly publicized various violent crimes, creating the impression that violent crime is out of control. Second, the notion that recidivism rates are high has received great attention, creating an image that prisoners are being released early only to commit additional crimes. To this end, recidivism for women (and men) is approximately 67.5 percent re-arrest within three years after being release (Langan and Levin, 2002). Third, since rehabilitation efforts have not been extremely obvious, the argument for social control has become a politically favored position over rehabilitation and release (Beckett, 1997).

Throughout the country parole boards have modified their release criteria, resulting in an increase in inmate population. In fact, by 1995, 11 states had abolished parole altogether. Prisoners who would have been released on parole in the past are now serving longer prison sentences, and many of those who are being released are returning to prison for violating parole conditions, mostly for technical violations.

Truth in Sentencing

As with parole policies, ideas (real and imagined) of violence, recidivism, and rehabilitation have re-shaped sentencing laws. Truth in sentencing has become a politically appealing mechanism to slow the revolving door correctional leak, which resulted from overcrowding as well as other structural changes. Ideologically, the voting class needs to believe that their elected (or appointed) politicians are doing something significant to reduce crime rates by increasing the certainty of the penalties. While state prisoners continue to serve an average of two years, federal prisoners are serving longer terms after the passage of the Sentencing Reform Act of 1984. The modern idea of truth in sentencing normally requires that the prisoner serves a minimum of 85 percent of their original sentence. This is a significant increase from the average 48 percent of a sentence that violent offenders served in 1992.

Sentencing Guidelines

Given the various changes of existing policies as well as the adoption of numerous complex laws, states and the federal government were forced to implement sentencing guidelines to avoid chaos, confusion, subjectivity, arbitrariness, and ensure uniformity. While sentencing guidelines have been advocated as a logical and efficient prosecutorial tool, they have not yet proven to be the "god" of prosecution. With the exception of atypical cases, sentencing guidelines, designed to provide clear and uniform standards for punishment, have reduced judicial discretion in legal proceedings. Though, U.S. Supreme Court decisions such as *U.S. vs. Booker* (2004) and *U.S. vs. Fanfan* (2004) have given judges discretion to depart from sentencing guidelines. However, cases do not only differ with regards to legal and extra-legal factors, but there is often great variation in the history and ideology behind each case (Snow, 1981; Urbina and Kreitzer, 2004). Consequently, groups of offenders, like women, who traditionally did not end up in prison are now behind bars.

Immigration Laws

From the time the first settlers set foot on present day United States, immigration has been a hotly debated issue at times, leading to racist policies, political rhetoric and manipulation, struggle, and harsh penal sanctions (Bosworth, 2007; Calavita, 2007; Gutierrez, 1997; Welch, 2007). Immigration law, historically shaped by various social, racial, ethnic, political, and economic forces, has been used to control population rates and identity. For example, during harsh economic cycles or when the supply of labor exceeds the demand, immigration laws are used to control the labor population, at times by placing them under the control of the criminal justice system. Further, either because their country of origin refuses to take them back, or because Immigration authorities refuse to deport one (or few) at a time, hundreds of undocumented foreigners are being housed in ICE detention centers for no crime other than entering the country without proper documentation (see Bosworth, 2007; Calavita, 2007; Welch, 2007).

A CONTINUUM OF LEGAL SANCTIONS

Historically, but more so in the last 35 years, we have seen the evolution of various laws as well as sentencing options. First, beginning in 1970 with the passage of the RICO law to the passage of anti-terrorism legislation after the September 11, 2001 attacks, we have seen changes not only in the nature of law, but also in how we perceive and treat lawbreakers. One response, for example, to the perceived dangerousness, potential threat, and fear of crime, has been the modification and implementation of punitive, and polemic laws, such as laws controlling drugs, guns, drinking, sentence enhancement, juvenile waivers, and age limits—a trend that is not likely to end given international efforts to modify and implement social control policies.

Second, even though there is a wide range of sentencing options that is being used to punish those who break the law, the most politically popular option is corrections. Other options, like probation, intensive supervision probation, restitution and fines, community service, substance abuse treatment, day reporting, house arrest and electronic monitoring, halfway house, boot camp, and jails, are also being used across the country. These options are widening the net, yet these punishments are not highly favored by the punitive mentality of the American society, particularly elected officials during election years (Festervan, 2003; Kassebaum, 1999; Petersilia, 1998; Tonry, 2004).

WHO GOES TO PRISON

With one significant exception, the profile of the typical American prisoner has not changed during the last two hundred years. The typical prisoner continues to be male, young, poorly educated, unemployed, indigent, and either African American or Latino (Tonry, 1995). Further, offenders tend to have a criminal history record as well as family members who have been in prison (James and Glaze, 2006). To this end, the number of prisoners increased by 3.8 million inmates between 1974 and 2001, and by the end of 2001, more than 5.6 million adults had previously been incarcerated or were incarcerated. In regards to gender, race, and ethnicity, prevalence rates at the end of 2001 were lower for women (vis-à-vis their male counterparts), with

1.7 percent of African American women, 0.7 percent of Latinas, and 0.3 percent of Caucasian women having been incarcerated (Bonczar, 2003). At the end of 2005, 1,525,924 adults were in state or federal adult correctional facilities, with a rate of 491 sentenced inmates per 100,000 U.S. residents (or about 1 in every 136 U.S. residents, with about 1 in every 108 men and 1 in every 1,538 women). Of all inmates in state or federal facilities; 1,418,408 were men and 107,518 were women. At year-end 2005, African Americans represented an estimated 39.5 percent, Caucasians 34.6 percent, and Latinos/as 20.2 percent of those sentenced to more than one year. More specifically, an estimated 3,145 African American men and 156 African American women per 100,000 African American residents were under the jurisdiction of state or federal facilities, compared to 471 Caucasian men and 45 Caucasian women per 100,000 Caucasian residents (Harrison and Beck, 2006). The data also show that in the late 1990s, the rate of Latinas and Latinos incarcerated in state correctional facilities was not only on the rise but that there is great variation among the different ethnic groups (Knepper, 1989; Martinez, 2004). At the end of 2005, an estimated 1,244 Latinos and 76 Latinas per 100,000 Latina/o residents were in state or federal facilities (Harrison and Beck, 2006). Of the ethnic groups incarcerated, some estimates indicate that 63.8 percent were Mexican, 21.1 percent were Puerto Rican (or other Caribbean), 6.1 percent were Central or South American, 5.4 percent were Spanish, and 3.6 percent were Cuban (Martinez, 2004; see also Petersilia, 2006). In Wisconsin, the state which will be used to establish a baseline for future analysis, African Americans made up less than 6 percent of Wisconsin's population in 2000, but constituted almost half (46.8%) of the 20,929 adults in state prisons. Latinas/os constituted 6.6 percent and Native Americans constituted 2.6 percent of the prison population (*Milwaukee Journal Sentinel,* 2000b). In short, at year-end 2005, African American men (547,200 outnumbered Caucasian men (459,700) and Latinos (279,000) among inmates sentenced to more than one year. African American women were more than twice as likely as Latinas and over three times more likely than Caucasian women to have been in state or federal facilities at the end of 2005 (Harrison and Beck, 2006).

In addition to the 747,529 people in jail and 1,446,269 people in prison at the end of 2005, there were 4,162,536 people on probation and 784,408 people on parole for a total of 7,056,000 adults under correctional supervision. At the end of 2005, 1,858 people were on probation per 100,000 adult residents, the equivalent of one in every 54 adults. Women constituted 23 percent (956,200) and men constituted 77 percent of adults on probation at year-end 2005. More than half (55% or 2,290,500) of all probationers were Caucasian, almost a third (30% or 1,239,600) were African American, and an eighth (13% or 539,700) were Latinas/os. As for type of offense, felonies accounted for 50 percent, misdemeanors for 49 percent, and other infractions accounted for 1 percent. The largest percentage of probationers were convicted of a drug law violation (28%), followed by DWI (15%), and larceny/theft (12%). Further, 350 were on parole per 100,000 adults residents (1 in every 286 adults) at the end of 2005 (Glaze and Bonczar, 2006). Women made up about 12 percent (93,000), and men constituted about 88 percent of parolees at the end of 2005. In terms of race and ethnicity, 41 percent were Caucasian, 40 percent were African American, and 12% were Latina/o. The largest percentage of paroles had been convicted on a drug offense (37%), followed by a property offense (25%) and a violent offense (25%). Last, statistics also indicate that the typical offender continues to be young and uneducated (Glaze and Bonczar, 2006). For instance, one New York study found that, on average, Caucasian inmates read at about the tenth-grade level, African American inmates at the eighth-grade level, and Latinos at the sixth-grade level (cited in Macionis, 2007).

The profile of women in prison is similar to the historical profile of male prisoners, yet this group faces more challenges in that, for example, most are mothers, single, heads of households, and have various medical, psychological, and substance abuse problems (*Corrections Digest*, 1982; Ginsburg, 1980; Goetting and Howsen, 1983). The data also suggest that among all female prisoners, the ones most impacted are African American women (Bresler and Lewis, 1983; French, 1983; Hill and Crawford, 1990). Considering that Latinas and Latinos outnumber African Americans for the first time in history, the Latina prisoner profile is likely to resemble the African American profile in the coming years (Langston, 2003).

While the perception is that offenders are committing violent crimes (see Farrington, 1992), the Bureau of Justice Statistics (2004a, 2004b, 2005) reports that the majority of prison admissions are for nonviolent offenses. Hence, the majority of cases, including felony cases, are disposed by plea bargaining and never go to trial. Normally, approximately 5 percent of cases go to trial (Durose and Langan, 2005).

THE COST OF PRISON

The reality of cost is a poorly understood concept because of the perception that high cost of incarceration is a direct result of prison amenities, and thus eliminating the "country club" environment will make prisons more affordable. Realistically, the majority of resources are being devoted to construction, operation, and other hidden costs. According to the Bureau of Justice Statistics, spending on corrections has been rising, ranging from $2.3 billion in 1971 to almost $62 billion in 2004; these figures include construction, operation, maintenance, and related costs.[4] More specifically, in the mid-1990s when prison construction was expanding rapidly, the cost of construction without financing charges averaged $28,194 per minimum security bed, $58,509 per medium security bed, and $80,004 per maximum security bed. One must also note that approximately 50 percent of prison costs are for payroll (Hughes, 2006). Debt interest to finance prison construction comes close to tripling the original costs. Because issues like financing and debt service cost are seldom equated into construction figures, the total cost of imprisonment is higher than most people think.[5] In addition, there are ongoing operational costs, such as food (see Chapter 5), clothing (see Chapter 5), and health care (see Chapter 6), but most substantial for correctional staff, maintenance, utilities, and insurance, averaging about $20,000 a year per bed. Further, considering the aging population and critical issues such as communicable diseases (see Chapter 6), the cost of prisons are likely to increase significantly in the coming years. For example, the average annual expense of medical care and maintenance for prisoners over 60 was estimated to be about $69,000, three times the norm, in the early-1990s (Zimbardo, 1994). Logically, as the prison population continues to age, the cost of imprisonment will continue to increase. Case in point: In 1990, Wisconsin spent about 3.1 percent of the state budget for corrections, but by 2000 it was about 7.3 percent (approximately $1 billion) of the total state budget (*Milwaukee Journal Sentinel*, 2002).

In terms of operating costs, the entire criminal justice system employed almost 2.4 million people nationwide in March 2003, constituting approximately 2 percent of the nation's employed labor force. In March 2003, total payroll expenditures for the justice system accounted for about $9 billion (59%), corrections allocating 50 percent of its budget to payroll expenditure (Hughes, 2006). To this end, in the mid-1990s, employee salaries and maintenance absorb approximately 80 percent of all correctional costs. Another thing that is seldom mentioned is the fact that many correctional costs are paid by state agencies and not the department of corrections. For example, children whose mothers are in prison are often placed in foster care, adding an additional expense to taxpayers. Last, construction and operation of prisons also means diverting money that could be allocated to other significant social issues that target the prevention of criminal behavior. Ironically, between 1987 and 1993, state spending increases for prisons bypassed higher education by 41 percent nationwide (Walters, 1995).

In short, as of March 2003, the criminal system employed nearly 2.4 million administrators, psychologists, counselors, social workers, officers, and support staff (Hughes, 2006). The federal government, the 50 states, and public and private organizations administered corrections in 2004 at an average annual cost of almost $62 billion. On February 2007, a report by the Pew Charitable Trusts projected that the U.S. will be faced with an estimated cost of $27.5 billion to manage the growing prison population in the next five years to avoid further correctional overcrowding crises (Tanner, 2007). Even though recent investigations reveal conflicting results on the cost-effectiveness of prisons, we are witnessing a "corrections-industrial complex" that is expanding on the billions of dollars from public funds to private contractors for design, construction, equipment, and to provide service such as food service or medical care. Politicians continue to lobby to build job-producing prisons in their districts.

BELIEFS ABOUT CRIME AND PUNISHMENT

Arguably, the mentality of the public can be described in one phrase: "lock-em-up." However, this concept is more a reflection of manipulating politicians and the media than what society actually favors (see Faith, 1993b). That is, studies show that the public still views rehabilitation as a primary objective of corrections. In fact, even though the media suggests that we are facing a crime-wave, most citizens report that they "feel safe" in their communities. And indeed, the public tends to prefer community-based sanctions instead of prison for offenders who do not represent a threat to public's safety (Carlen, 1990; Chesney-Lind and Pasko, 2004).

THE WISCONSIN EXPERIENCE

To provide a comprehensive analysis of what appears to be the "new faces" in corrections–female offenders–I surveyed all incarcerated women in the state of Wisconsin. Based on prior research, female prisoners experience all the issues that male inmates face, in addition to those which are unique to women. The goal, then, was not to obtain a selected sample, but to include every adult inmate who wished to participate to develop a more descriptive profile of the experiences of adult women before, during, and after incarceration. Particularly, I focused on issues such as their demographic characteristics, employment and educational background; past histories of juvenile and other criminal behavior; substance abuse and treatment histories; experience with physical, sexual, and emotional abuse; as well as details of the women's incarceration.[6]

Demographic Statistics of Female Prisoners in Wisconsin

As Table 1 shows, even though the mean for the 456 participating female prisoners was 34.4 years of age, the age ranged from 18 to 66 years, suggesting that age will become a significant issue in the coming years. The race and ethnicity figures for African Americans and Caucasians, who constitute most of the inmate population, are consistent with prior investigations. However, the figures for Native Americans and Puerto Ricans, two groups who have received little attention in academic literature, are higher than expected, especially since both groups constitute a small fraction of the general population. Given the importance of education in a technological society, it is unfortunate, yet not surprising, that most (66.0%) participants had a high school education or less. Last, considering the practical implications of nontraditional relationships, only eighty-three (or 18.2%) participants were married at the time of the arrest, the rest were either single, divorced, or in some other relationship. As noted in Table 1, the consequences of prison are not only devastating to offenders, but to those left behind as well, in that, logically, divorce rates seem to increase once someone has been imprisoned.

Given these findings, the U.S. prison system must ensure that current correctional policies are considering the changing demographic characteristics of female prisoners; in addition to historical factors, like the influence of low levels of education. Similarly, the correctional system must modify existing programs and, when necessary, implement new programs to address changes in the demographic characteristics of the prison population, like increases in the gender, elderly, or populations. For example, increases in the ethnic population correspond to increases in language barriers, and thus a higher demand for interpretation and translation, and the hiring of bilingual staff (Diaz-Cotto, 1996; Urbina, 2004a).

In terms of prison research, researchers have been investigating the influence of factors such as race, education, and marital status for several years. However, with changes in these factors, future empirical investigations need to test the influence of ethnicity (ethnic effects), paying particular attention to the largest ethnic groups, like Cubans, Mexicans, and Puerto Ricans, while continuing to test for the influence of race (race effects). In short, with significant changes in prison demographics, the analysis needs to move beyond the traditional dichotomous approach (African American versus Caucasian) to include Native Americans, Latinas, and other racial and ethnic groups (Urbina, 2007).

Table 1
DEMOGRAPHIC INFORMATION OF ADULT WOMEN IN PRISON
IN WISCONSIN (N=456)

	Mean	Frequency	Percent
Age*	34.4		
Race			
African American		216	47.7
Asian		1	0.2
Caucasian		158	34.6
Native American		36	7.9
Multiracial		1	0.2
Other Race		7	1.5

Continued on next page

Table 1 (cont.)

	Mean	Frequency	Percent
Ethnicity			
Cuban		2	0.4
Mexican		9	2.0
Puerto Rican		14	3.1
Other Latina		9	2.0
Education			
No formal education		4	0.9
Some grade school		7	1.5
Completed grade school (8th grade)		19	4.2
Some high school (9th to 12th grade)		134	29.4
Completed high school or GED		137	30.0
Some college		117	25.7
Completed college (Not including graduate)		29	6.4
Other form of education	30.7		
Marital status at time of arrest			
Single		210	46.1
Married		83	18.2
Divorced		50	11.0
Widowed		12	2.6
Engaged		26	5.7
Separated		20	4.4
Long-term partner		15	3.3
Living with partner		26	5.7
Other relationship		11	2.4
Marital status now			
Single		216	47.4
Married		51	11.2
Divorced		67	14.7
Widowed		14	3.1
Engaged		41	9.0
Separated		24	5.3
Long-term partner		26	5.7
Other relationship		6	1.3

*Age range: 18 to 66

Table 2
EMPLOYMENT INFORMATION OF ADULT WOMEN IN
PRISON IN WISCONSIN (N=456)

	Frequency	*Percent*
Work status at time of arrest		
Working	289	63.4
Not working	166	36.4
Income prior to incarceration*		
0	47	10.3
1 to 5,000	83	18.2
5,001 to 9,999	50	11.0
10,000 to 14,999	43	9.4
15,000 to 19,999	36	7.9
20,000 to 29,999	47	10.3
30,000 or more	74	16.2
Don't know	69	15.1
Type of occupation		
Self employed	31	6.8
Working a legitimate job	175	38.4
Working an illegitimate job	29	6.4
Other job	11	2.4
Working more than one job	36	7.9
Second source of income		
Yes	301	66.0
No	150	32.9
Source of second income		
Crime	138	30.3
Prostitution	9	2.0
Public assistance	22	4.8
Child support	19	4.2
Other income	64	14.0
More than one source	47	10.3
Reasons for not working		
Child care responsibilities	14	3.1
Unable to find a job	20	4.4
No job training or skills	5	1.1
Substance abuse problems	37	8.1
Made more money from crime	23	5.0
Supported by relatives	17	3.7
No specific reason	2	0.4
Other reason	29	6.4
Multiple reasons	97	21.3

* Median: $15,000 to $19,999

Based on Table 2, employment histories of female prisoners in Wisconsin are not very positive or promising. Even though most (289 or 63.4%) women were working at the time of their arrest, the majority (56.8%) had *total* earnings under $20,000, placing them below the official poverty level of $19,307. Twenty-nine (6.4%) women reported having an illegitimate job, but most reported some form of legal job; with 175 (38.4%) women working a legitimate job, 6.8 percent being self employed, and 7.9 percent working more than one job. Not surprisingly, 301 (66.0%) women reported having a second source of either legitimate or illegitimate income. While crimes, such as shoplifting, selling drugs, and dealing stolen goods, represent the leading source of second income in this inmate population, prostitution, often used to attack the "immorality" of women, constitutes only 2.0 percent. Of course, because of the stigma, its possible that women might have underreported their involvement in prostitution. Considering the popular notion that the typical prisoner is supported by the state, only 22 women reported having public assistance and only 19 reported receiving child support, a realistic figure since many fathers are either in prison or they cannot pay child support because of a prison record, the inability to find a decent job, or savage poverty. To this end, the self reported reasons for not working prior to their incarceration are numerous, but three critical reasons—i.e., unable to find a job, substance abuse problems (see Chapter 6), and made more money from crime—suggest that the social structure needs to change if we are to alter the cycle of imprisonment.

As we have witnessed in the last few years, it has become difficult to find decent jobs even for those who hold an advanced degree—some companies are downsizing, others are leaving the country, and some employers are requiring advanced skills, especially in the area of technology. Financing multi-billion dollar wars has become a national priory, and thus job creation is not receiving serious attention at the national level; not to mention that it is cheaper to send people to prison than it is to create jobs (see Chapter 10). Still, the social structure in the community and in prison needs be modified to create additional legitimate opportunities and to prepare prisoners to work in jobs that will support a family.

Table 3
FAMILY INFORMATION OF ADULT WOMEN IN PRISON
IN WISCONSIN (N=456)

	Yes	*No*
Mother still living	363 (79.6)	89 (19.5)
Contact with mother	295 (64.7)	43 (9.4)
Father still living	283 (62.1)	168 (36.8)
Contact with father	156 (34.2)	115 (25.2)
Sisters still living	358 (78.5)	94 (20.6)
Contact with sisters	280 (61.4)	62 (13.6)
Brothers still living	383 (84.0)	68 (14.9)
Contact with brothers	269 (59.0)	94 (20.6)
Children living	349 (76.5)	104 (22.8)

	Mean	*Frequency*	*Percent*
Number of children	2.9		
0		1	0.2
1		76	16.7
2		94	20.6
3		72	15.8
4		46	10.1
5		29	6.4
6		9	2.0
7		8	1.8
8		5	1.1
9		1	0.2
25		1	0.2
Age of Children			
Under 1 year		4	0.9
Between 1 and 2		7	1.5
Between 3 and 5		23	5.0
Between 6 and 11		32	7.0
Between 12 and 15		13	2.9
Between 16 and 18		10	2.2
Over 18 years of age		67	14.7
More than 1 age category		194	42.5
Lost custody of children			
Yes		70	15.4
No		270	59.2

Continued on next page

Table 3 (cont.)

	Mean	Frequency	Percent
Caring for children while in prison			
Father of children		57	12.5
Sister of inmate		13	2.9
Foster care		15	3.3
Aunt/uncle of inmate		6	1.3
Brother of inmate		1	0.2
Mother/father of inmate		69	15.1
Cousin of inmate		3	0.7
Friend of inmate		1	0.2
Other guardian		69	15.1
More than 1 guardian		96	21.1
Seeing the children while in prison			
Weekly		47	10.3
Monthly		80	17.5
Every few months		72	15.8
Once a year		21	4.6
Never		111	24.3
Other		11	2.4
Living with children prior to arrest			
Yes		239	52.4
No		105	23.0
Children living with other people before going to prison			
Father of children		15	3.3
Sister of inmate		4	0.9
Foster care		13	2.9
Aunt/uncle of inmate		6	1.3
Mother/father of inmate		16	3.5
Friend of inmate		3	0.7
Other guardian		47	10.3
More than 1 guardian		27	5.9

Table 3 contains family information for female prisoners in Wisconsin, which reveals significant implications for policymakers. Most (79.6%) women reported that their mother was still living, but only 64.7 percent of the women reported having contact with their mothers. The reported information for their fathers is even less favorable in that 62.1 percent reported that their father was still living, and a low 34.2 percent reported having contact with that parent. For sisters and brothers, the information is not significantly different. Most (78.5%) women reported having sister(s) living, but only 61.4 percent of the women prisoners had regular contact with them. Similarly, most

(84.0%) inmates reported having brother(s) living, but only 59.0 percent of the inmates reported having contact with them.

Perhaps even more significant is the finding that most (349 or 76.5%) female prisoners were mothers, the majority having between 1 and 5 children. Of those who had children, most were dependant, with only 67 (14.7%) having children over the age of 18 and 89 (19.5%) having children 18 years of age or younger. Also, even though most (270 or 59.2%) mothers did not lose custody of their children because of their incarceration, 70 women reported having lost custody of their children because of their incarceration. Ironically, even though only 67 women reported having children over the age of 18, 105 women reported not living with their children prior to their arrest. The figures for mothers who were not living with their children before going to prison reveal the complexity of family relationships. Many dependant children, for instance, lived with more than one guardian, some with the mother or father of the inmate, a few with the father of the child, but most with some other guardian. Once in prison, the situation for both mother and child seems to get more uncertain in that there is no guarantee where the child will end up, as shown in Table 3. This is further complicated by the findings that 93 mothers reported either seeing their children irregularly: every few months or only once a year, and 111 respondents never saw their children while in prison.

These findings are significant because a supportive family relationship can provide advice, resources, and encouragement. As documented in previous studies (Gauch, 1988), a nonexistence or weak family relationship can be detrimental to the prisoner, family members, and the community (see Chapter 10). Studies have suggested that weak family relationship and chaotic social environments are influential in criminal behavior (see Chapters 4 and 10). Therefore, the development and modification of existing correctional policies must be sensitive to the importance of family ties, with the objective of enhancing community solidarity, reducing fear of crime, and increasing public safety.

CONCLUSION

Demographic information reveals that female prisoners are facing issues that go beyond those confronting male prisoners. The data also show that if education, employment, family relationships, and community solidarity, are not addressed soon, the correctional system could become more chaotic and self-destructive behavior among inmates, leading to possible lawsuits. Indeed, practical as well as legal questions need to be revisited (see Morton, 2004). For example, with less than a high school education, inability to find a job either because of prior record or drug problems, can we honestly expect a prisoner once released to find a decent job to possibly prevent recidivism (see Chapter 10)? Considering the controversial *Roe vs. Wade* (1973) U.S. Supreme Court decision, do state correctional systems have the right to provide abortion service on demand (Roth, 2004)? If a prisoner decides to give birth, should she be allowed to keep her child in prison? And if yes, for how long should mothers be allowed to keep their child while incarcerated? What can be done about the child of incarcerated mothers? How can, or even should, interaction between mother and child be maintained? Do states have the right to terminate parental rights (see Chapters 5)? In the next chapter the lives of women inmates before going to prison will be explored to provide an account that is based on a more holistic methodological approach and not simply a snapshot of the lives of female offenders.

Chapter 3

THE LIVES OF FEMALE PRISONERS BEFORE THEIR INCARCERATION

The first part of this chapter explores the lives of adult female offenders before their imprisonment. Examining the lives of incarcerated women prior to imprisonment is necessary to better understand what brought them to prison and how they cope with daily life once in prison. Barbara Owen (1998) documents that what women bring into the prison system is important for how they will adapt to prison, and how they will relate to other inmates and correctional staff. Further, the combination of institutionalized greed, structural marginalization, and destructive personal choices are factors that often result in criminal behavior and consequently imprisonment. Race is only one of the several influential issues governing the daily lives of incarcerated women. Kruttschnitt, Gartner, and Miller (2000:696), for instance, report that a "woman's economic background seemed to have a much stronger effect on how she reacted to prison than did her race. Most of the women . . . came from impoverished backgrounds." The second part of this chapter details information regarding family, alcohol and drug use, and physical, sexual, verbal, and emotional abuse, of the Wisconsin inmate population.

THE EARLY DAYS: ALWAYS RUNNING

The background of female offenders is of critical importance in how they adapt to prison and how they relate to other inmates and staff (Culbertson and Fortune, 1986; Wilson, 1968; Zingraff and Zingraff,

41

1980). As labeling theorists suggest, early experiences in life tend to shape how people perceive and act toward their peers, families, and authorities. Without having a clear understanding of the diverse experiences of female offenders before their conviction, it is difficult to fully understand their experiences in prison. Further, without a sound understanding of early life experiences, it is difficult to develop and implement programs that will best benefit women in prison.

First, as one of the most detrimental life event, abuse–ranging from verbal put-downs to beatings and violence–appears not as an isolated issue, but as a constant activity that begins early in life with most women in prison (Chandler, 1973; Gutierres and Reich, 1981; James and Glaze, 2006; Russell, 1986). One female prisoner shared the story of her childhood with a foster parent: ". . . my half sister was her real granddaughter . . . so she was treated real well. . . . I wasn't blond so I was a little house slave. I got all the beatings. [The grandmother] was wealthy but she would make me eat spoiled food. I would get sick as a dog. I was always doing something wrong" (cited Chesney-Lind and Rodriguez, 1983:52). Another inmate, half African American and half Caucasian, reports that during her childhood she kept running not only from the physical environment in which she lived but from her emotional state as well. She reports that in addition to growing up with a suicidal mother, she felt the impact of being a minority, which was exacerbated when she became "a minority of minorities: a woman prisoner" (Morris, 1987:10). Therefore, when women end up in correctional facilities, they tend to have a long history of abuse, which if not treated, could contribute to a series of health problems during old age (see Chapters 6 and 8).

Second, research reveals that millions of young women are being socialized into "victim roles" that eventually lead to self-destructive behavior. Some female inmates report the oppression and sexual violence perpetrated against them by their male relatives (Russell, 1986). One African American inmate, who was placed in foster care as an infant, was sexually abused by her foster father, and who ran away from home, reports that "I was with this foster lady who was very cruel. She was abusive. And I was no more than a maid as a child ... that was my purpose. She received welfare for foster kids . . . that was her purpose. I stayed there till I was 13, then ran away. I was tired of the physical abuse. I ran to my mother's. The man she lived with sexually abused me and I ran away again" (Arnold, 1990:155). Consequently, when women enter the prison system, they tend to face emotional confusion, psychological trauma, and a feeling of isolation and neglect.

Third, economic marginalization appears to be the norm for women offenders in the sense that they have no jobs, are employed in low paying jobs, or economically dependent on someone else, placing them in a vulnerable position (Heidensohn, 1985; Kruttschnitt, 1980–1981). This marginality is illustrated in the life of one African American inmate: "There were eight children in the family. My father had a mover's job, but we also got welfare. We moved from hotel to hotel and ended up in the projects. I needed things, so I had no choice but to steal. I've been stealing since I was ten" (Arnold, 1990:156).

Last, either as indigent women or as minorities, female offenders often face the powerful barriers of cultural isolation and intimidation by community members, and social messages. In this regard, studies show that many female offenders were victimized as young girls by an educational system that was threatening, unsupportive, culturally insensitive, alienating, and oppressive (Bergsmann, 1989a; Rodriguez, 1993). In the words of one African American inmate, "It was hard for me to get along with the teachers. Some were prejudiced, and one had the nerve to tell the whole class he didn't like black people" (Arnold, 1990:157). Based on the year 2000 census figures, of the nation's 35.3 million Latinos/as, only 11 percent have received a post-secondary education.

LIFE IN THE STREETS

Understanding female prisoners requires that we investigate the relationship between the home and the streets, which tends to serve as a middle ground for some young female offenders. In this regard, some investigators document that female victimization results in a "process of criminalization unique to women" in which "young girls faced with violence and/or sexual abuse at home . . . became criminalized by their efforts to save themselves (by running away) from the abuse. . . . Once on the streets, the position afforded these women in the criminal world indicates that, again, it was not liberation but lack of formal education and genuine employment options that forced them to continue committing crimes" (Chesney-Lind and Rodriguez, 1983:62–63; see also James and Glaze, 2006). Therefore, besides gender oppression and exploitation, class oppression extends into the streets, and it does not end at the time women become eligible (age-wise) for legal employment, becoming a significant factor in the victimization of young women whose fragile lives are jeopardized and threatened by the very socioeconomic situation in which they were originally born (Arnold, 1990).

Even though female offenders tend to share similar life experiences, research suggests that minority women often experience some of the worst injustices. A recent study showed that Latinas and African American women in prison have a long history of physical, emotional, and psychological abuse (Langston, 2003; Richie, 1996). Indeed, life in the streets for minority women is, at times, beyond chaotic, as noted by one African American female prisoner, "There was really nowhere for me to go. So, I went up on the corner, hung out, and reverted back to selling myself and doing stickups or robberies, or burglaries, whatever I needed to do. I ended up living in a shooting gallery–where dope friends go to get high, sleeping on a chair. And I'm sitting in there, and I sleep in there, and I eat in there, and I get high in there. I wasn't changing my clothes. I had long hair–I wasn't combing it. All I wanted to do was stay high. Drug addicts accept you. This was your family, you know. And I don't care what time of the night it was, if you needed one of 'em, they were there. And in my mind, I always had a place to go" (Arnold, 1990:160-161). Or, consider the turbulent life of an African American female prisoner: "I was in the street. I got arrested for shoplifting. I was picked up for vagrancy when I was almost fifteen. The judge gave my mother an option to take me home or he would have no other choice but to send me away. She says, 'Send her away, I don't want her.' So they sent me away. I went to a state home for girls" (cited in Arnold, 1994:174).

In sum, the criminalization of young females' survival strategies and mentalities is the process by which young women who are victims of abuse and violence become transformed to offenders, and eventually end up in juvenile corrections and later in prison (Bergsmann, 1989b; Chesney-Lind, 1989). Such abuse, at times, brutal and vicious in nature, normally begins early in life, escalates once the girls are out in the streets, and it worsens when they end up in prison (Gaarder and Belknap, 2002; Heidensohn, 1985). Therefore, without properly understanding the early experiences of female offenders, it seems difficult to assist women once they enter the correctional system.

THE ROAD TO PRISON

Understanding life behind bars also requires that investigators explore what we call "the survival tri-angle": the link between the home, the streets, and prison. That is, for many women, life at home during their childhood is abusive, emotionally and psychologically confusing, and violent. For instance, one early study found that about two-thirds of the 200 street female prostitutes in San Francisco had run away to escape sexual or other form of brutality in their homes (Silbert and Pines, 1981). Hence, under adverse circumstances, young girls are forced to run away and live in the street, which tend to be structurally different; yet, violent, unpredictable, and deadly. Without community ties or employment, young women are coerced into illegal behavior, as a means of survival (Balthazar and Cook, 1984). As noted by one investigator, ". . . the best available options for escape from physical and sexual violence are often survival strategies which are criminal . . . running away from home, use of drugs, and the illegal street work required to survive as a runaway" (Gilfus, 1992:63; Maden, Swinton, and Gunn, 1990, 1992).

Research has indicted a connection between physical abuse and delinquency (Cavaiola and Schiff, 1988; Chesney-Lind, 1989; Garbarino and Plantz, 1986), between childhood sexual abuse and deviance (Cavaiola and Schiff, 1988; Runtz and Briere, 1986), and drug addiction and criminality (Anglin and Hser, 1987; Chesney-Lind and Rodriguez, 1983). Further, existing research indicates that dimensions of female criminalization include structural dislocation, deviant and criminal associations, shaping and re-shaping of family relationships within the deviant world, labeling and processing as status offenders and eventually as adult criminals (James and Glaze, 2006). Once the process of young female criminalization is set in orbit, deviance becomes a norm (a way of life), which serves as a survival mechanism in a world of neglect, abuse, violence, uncertainty, and fear. Likewise, prison, like the violent streets, becomes normalized among female lawbreakers, in the sense that it provides a shelter, food, and, on occasions, a family, a community, employment, lodging, and an "escape" from the lethal and chaotic life in the streets (see Arnold, 1990; Heidensohn, 1985).

In sum, in a world of institutionalized greed (see Chapter 10), structural dislocation, and the absence of a supported family, delinquency and criminal behavior become a survival mechanism early in life for young, poor, uneducated, and unemployed women. Thus, victimization, resistance to victimization, labeling, oppression, and structural dislocation preceded early institutionalization of female offenders. Last, without a detailed understanding of the many diverse experiences of women before entering the correctional system, it is very difficult to obtain a reliable and valid analysis, and thus limits our ability to effectively intervene with these women.

DEFINING CHARACTERISTICS OF WOULD-BE PRISONERS

Historically, research on women in prison used a dichotomous approach–i.e., African American versus Caucasian (Urbina, 2003a, 2007). With the advent of the feminist movement and other historical events, researchers began to expand their analyses to include additional variables in the hope of better understanding how women do their time in correctional facilities (Howe, 1994; Pollock, 1986; Owen, 1998; see also Daly and Maher, 1998; Rice, 1990).

Indeed, as documented by various studies, gender is neither a monolithic everyday experience nor a constant identity, and thus there is significant variation and diversity in the lives of female offenders before, during, and after incarceration. For instance, some researchers emphasize women's cultural heritage and the resulting reactions to prison (Diaz-Cotto, 1996; Faith, 1993a), while others indicate that females' subjectivities (whether conscious or unconscious), as shaped and re-shaped by sexuality, ethnicity, age, and abuse, govern their experience in prison (Bosworth, 1996). More recently, Candace Kruttschnitt, Rosemary Gartner, and Amy Miller (2000) investigated race, social class, age, and histories of physical and sexual abuse as four sources of diversity to obtain a more complete picture of how women serve their time in prison. Neither Barbara Owen (1998) or Candace Kruttschnitt, Rosemary Gartner, and Amy Miller (2000) found support for race as an influential factor, but found that social class, age, and histories of abuse to shape how females serve their time in prison (see also Bondeson, 1989; Owen and Bloom, 1995a).

Still, when feasible, investigators should delineate "life before prison" as finely as possible to better capture the essence of the female prison experience in its totality. Therefore, in the next section, we will try to narrow this gap in the research literature by introducing a series of variables into the analysis. As noted before, given the various policy changes in the state of Wisconsin, this jurisdiction is a vital site for the investigation of female prisoners.

THE WISCONSIN EXPERIENCE

In this section I report findings for 456 participating Wisconsin prisoners. In order to outline the diverse experience of female offenders, a series of questions were asked regarding the nature of childhood abuse, the frequency of alcohol and drug usage before their incarceration, and the influence of alcohol and drugs on female offenders.

THE NATURE OF CHILDHOOD ABUSE

Consistent with prior studies, Table 4 shows that Wisconsin female prisoners have a long history of abuse and fear, which started at a very early age.

Table 4
THE NATURE OF CHILDHOOD ABUSED OF INCARCERATED WOMEN (N=456)

	Mean	Frequency	Percent
Physically abused as a child			
Yes		177	38.8
No		275	60.8
Age when physical abused started[1]	7.4		
People committing the physical abuse			
Mother		31	6.8
Father		29	6.4
Babysitter		2	0.4
Friends		1	0.2

Continued on next page

Table 4 (cont.)

	Mean	Frequency	Percent
Stepfather		8	1.8
Siblings (brother/sister)		6	1.3
Other abusers		27	5.9
More than one abuser		70	15.4
Emotionally abused as a child			
Yes		254	55.7
No		183	40.1
Don't know		13	2.9
Age when emotional abused started[2]	7.9		
People committing the emotional abuse			
Mother		52	11.4
Father		23	5.0
Babysitter		2	0.4
Friends		7	1.5
Stepfather		10	2.2
Siblings (brother/sister)		10	2.2
Other abusers		21	4.6
More than one abuser		125	27.4
Sexually abused as a child			
Yes		231	50.7
No		212	46.5
Don't know		8	1.8
Age when sexual abused started[3]	8.7		
People committing the sexual abuse			
Mother		1	0.2
Father		14	3.1
Babysitter		6	1.3
Friends		14	3.1
Stepfather		19	4.2
Siblings (brother/sister)		16	3.5
Other abusers		96	21.1
More than one abuser		61	13.4
In an abusive relationship with a partner			
Yes		363	79.6
No		88	19.3
Type of abuse in abusive relationship			
Physical		26	5.7
Emotional		14	3.1
Verbal		12	2.6
More than 1 form of abuse		311	68.2

Continued on next page

Table 4 (cont.)

	Mean	Frequency	Percent
Ability to leave abuser prior to incarceration			
Yes		281	61.6
No		80	17.5
Avenue for leaving the abuser			
Moved out on their own		89	19.5
Moved out with family help		39	8.6
Moved out with friends' help		11	2.4
Moved out into a domestic abuse shelter		9	2.0
Moved out and went into hiding		20	4.4
Other avenues		49	10.7
More than 1 method of leaving		69	15.1
Reasons for not being able to leave abuser			
No financial resources		11	2.4
Afraid he would harm again		13	2.9
Afraid he would harm children/family		2	0.4
No place to go		7	1.5
Wanted to work things out		27	5.9
Other reasons		14	3.1
Multiple reasons		83	18.2
(e.g., mostly resources and wanted to work things out)			

[1] Age range:0 to 19
[2] Age range:1 to 30
[3] Age range:1 to 30

Based on Table 4, 177 (38.8%) female prisoners reported having suffered physical abuse such as beatings as a child. Among those reporting physical abuse, the mean age when the abuse first began was about seven years of age. Among those committing the physical abuse, mothers and fathers were reported as committing the highest frequency of abuse, followed by stepfathers, brothers and sisters, babysitters, and friends (respectively). The severity of this particular issue is further exacerbated by the fact that 15.4 percent of inmates reported more than one abuser, which seems to extend beyond close relatives.

The figures in Table 4 also show that over half (254 or 55.7%) of respondents suffered emotional abuse, such as abusive language, name-calling, degrading phrases, and neglect, during childhood. Similar to the age when the physical abuse started, the mean age when emotional abuse first began was about 8 years of age. Among those committing the emotional abuse, mothers were reported as being the most abusive, followed by fathers, stepfathers, siblings, friends, and babysitters. However, unlike physical abuse, where about the same percentage of inmates were abused by mothers and fathers, the number of inmates emotionally abused by mothers was substantially higher than those emotionally abused by fathers. Also, like physical abuse, a substantial number (125 or 27.4%) of inmates reported being emotionally abuse by multiple individuals, and it seems that abusers extended beyond the immediate family.

In terms of as sexual abuse, about half (231 or 50.7%) of participating prisoners experienced sexual abused during their youth. Similar to the age when the physical abuse and/or emotional abuse started, the mean age when the sexual abuse first began was about nine years of age. Among those committing the sexual abuse, stepfathers were reported as being the most abusive, followed by siblings, fathers, friends, babysitters, and mothers. Also, consistent with patterns of physical and emotional abuse, a substantial number of inmates reported being abused by more than one individual.

Table 4 also shows that the majority (363 or 79.6%) of inmates reported being in an abusive relationship with a partner, prior to their incarceration. Consistent with findings of abuse by relatives and friends, inmates reported physical, emotional, and verbal abuse. Over half (311 or 68.2%) of the inmates experienced more than one form of abuse by their partner. Of those who reported being in an abusive relationship, 80 (17.5%) women reported not being able to leave their abuser. Reasons for not being able to leave the abuser are numerous, but most commonly, they wanted to work things out, followed by fear of being harmed again, no financial resources, no place to go, or fear of that their partner would harm their children and/or family. Of those who were able to leave, some went into hiding, others left for a domestic abuse shelter, some moved out with the help of the family or friends, but most moved out on their own.

These findings not only suggest a lack of emotional and financial support, but confusion, fear, anxiety, and trauma, which is capable of having long-lasting effects on a woman's life. The findings also reveal that the complexity of childhood abuse of female prisoners does not end at home, but it extends into adulthood as woman engage in domestic partner relationships. Without an understanding of the complex and sensitive nature of childhood and adult abuse, the correctional system could very likely be worsening the situation for some female prisoners in that some women might feel that they are being abused by the same system that is supposed to be helping them.

Alcohol and Drug Usage

As with abuse, the data also show that Wisconsin female prisoners have a long history of alcohol and drug use, which is further complicated by other factors (see Doege, 2006). Before outlining the nature of alcohol and drug use among female prisoners in Wisconsin, some general question were asked to obtain a global picture of the Wisconsin experience, and these results are reported in Table 5.

Table 5
ALCOHOL AND DRUG USAGE INFORMATION OF ADULT WOMEN
IN PRISON IN WISCONSIN (N=456)

	Yes	*No*	*Don't Know*
Use of illegal substance	365 (80.0)	89 (19.5)	
Use of needles to inject drugs	63 (13.8)	289 (63.4)	
Use of needles without sterilization	24 (5.3)	37 (8.1)	
Afraid of contacting HIV with no sterilization	18 (3.9)	29 (6.4)	
Currently addicted to cigarettes	109 (23.9)	314 (68.9)	29 (6.4)
Currently addicted to alcohol	64 (14.0)	372 (81.6)	15 (3.3)
Currently addicted to illegal drugs	70 (15.4)	354 (77.6)	29 (6.4)
Alcohol drinking prior to incarceration	353 (77.4)	101 (22.1)	
Viewing alcohol drinking as a problem	110 (24.1)	228 (50.0)	
	Mean	*Frequency*	*Percent*
Frequency of alcohol drinking			
Daily		97	21.3
A few times a week		95	20.8
Once a week		22	4.8
Only occasionally/socially		131	28.7
Age when first became addicted to illegal drugs*	18.6		

* Age contact range: 4 to 48

The results from Table 5 reveal that most (353 or 77.4%) inmates drank alcoholic beverages prior to their incarceration. Of those reporting drinking alcohol prior to incarceration, over 40 percent of the female prisoners reported high frequency of usage; with 21.3 percent of women drinking it daily, and 20.8 percent of inmates drinking it a few times a week. Yet, half (228) of the women did not view their drinking as a problem.

Similar to the use of alcoholic beverages, most (365 or 80%) inmates reported having used illegal drugs. While some (63) women reported using needles to inject drugs, most (289 or 63.4%) prisoners did not use needles. Of those injecting drugs, 37 inmates reported using needles without sterilization. Ironically, of those using needles without sterilization, 18 inmates reported being afraid of contracting HIV, but 29 women were not afraid of contracting HIV.

The rates for current (i.e., while in prison) addictions were low, but still significant in the sense that the typical female prisoner had been in prison for more than a few months. Of those reporting addictions, 109 women reported being addicted to cigarettes, 64 to alcohol, and 70 to illegal drugs. Last, while illegal drug addiction for some women began at a relatively young age, the mean age when women first became addicted to drugs was about 18 and a half years of age.

Considering the scope of alcohol and drug use (Table 5), the complex nature of its usage, and the consequences thereafter, the analysis was carried a step further by delineating the information into various possible combinations. Table 6 contains numerous possible combinations of ten common drugs by level of usage, and addiction before respondent's incarceration. Based on Table 6, among the least used drugs by female prisoners were heroin, amphetamines, speedballs, PCP, and prescription drugs. In retrospect, among the most used drugs by inmates were nicotine, alcohol, marijuana, and to a lesser extent, powder cocaine and crack. Indeed, as one moves down Table 6, a complicated and persistent pattern can be detected.

Alcohol Usage

First, of those who reported using alcohol, 189 (41.4%) women reported not being addicted or using it daily; 33 women not being addicted but using it daily; 44 inmates reported non-daily use but addicted; and 100 women reported being addicted and daily use of alcoholic beverages.

Table 6
NATURE OF ALCOHOL AND DRUG USAGE OF INCARCERATED WOMEN (N=456)

	Alcohol*	Nicotine	Marijuana	Heroine	Powder Cocaine	Crack	Amphetamines	Speedballs	PCP	Prescription Drugs
Did not use	87 (19.1)	131 (28.7)	168 (36.8)	375 (82.2)	273 (59.9)	264 (57.9)	376 (82.5)	401 (87.9)	412 (90.4)	302 (66.2)
Used, not addicted, not daily, no alcohol	---	17 (3.7)	51 (11.2)	15 (3.3)	44 (9.6)	21 (4.6)	15 (3.3)	14 (3.1)	9 (2.0)	33 (7.2)
Used, not addicted, not daily, with alcohol	---	12 (2.6)	76 (16.7)	17 (3.7)	42 (9.2)	22 (4.8)	21 (4.6)	13 (2.9)	17 (3.7)	25 (5.5)
Used, not addicted, daily, no alcohol	---	5 (1.1)	11 (2.4)	---	1 (0.2)	1 (0.2)	2 (0.4)	---	---	21 (4.6)
Used, not addicted, daily, with alcohol	---	25 (5.5)	20 (4.4)	1 (0.2)	---	2 (0.4)	---	---	1 (0.2)	5 (1.1)
Used, addicted, not daily, no alcohol	---	2 (0.4)	4 (0.9)	2 (0.4)	15 (3.3)	6 (1.3)	1 (0.2)	1 (0.2)	1 (0.2)	4 (0.9)
Used, addicted, not daily, with alcohol	---	7 (1.5)	20 (4.4)	3 (0.7)	20 (4.4)	20 (4.4)	10 (2.2)	5 (1.1)	4 (0.9)	5 (1.1)
Used, addicted, daily, no alcohol	---	55 (12.1)	19 (4.2)	12 (2.6)	11 (2.4)	28 (6.1)	5 (1.1)	4 (0.9)	---	14 (3.1)
Used, addicted, daily, with alcohol	---	199 (43.6)	84 (18.4)	26 (5.7)	47 (10.3)	89 (19.5)	22 (4.8)	15 (3.3)	9 (2.0)	43 (9.4)

Drug Usage: Nondaily Use, Not Addicted, No Alcohol

As outlined in Table 6, a small number of female drug users are reported in each of the nine categories. Still, the numbers are significant in that the highest frequencies, not including prescription drugs, are for marijuana, powder cocaine, and crack. For other drugs, including heroin, self reported use was low, indicating that addictions are perhaps not so severe or complicated. However, as additional rows are analyzed, it become clear that "simple" usage of a particular drug–i.e., no addiction, nondaily use, no alcohol–is not so simple.

Drug Usage: Nondaily Use, Not Addicted, With Alcohol

The third row shows a more complicated picture among female prisoners reporting not being addicted to drugs, but nondaily use of some type of drug with alcohol. That is, even though a segment of inmates reported not being addicted and nondaily use of different drugs, a substantial number of women reported using marijuana, powder cocaine, and, to a lesser extent, heroin, crack, amphetamines, and PCP with alcohol before their incarceration. Consistent with prior studies, this finding indicates that use of illegal drugs and alcohol go hand-in-hand.

Drug Usage: Daily Use, Not Addicted, No Alcohol

The fourth row in Table 6 further confirms the observation that drugs and alcohol go hand-in-hand. Specifically, drug usage substantially drops, with the exception of marijuana, or there is no drug use when no alcohol is being consumed. Logically, the few women reporting daily use without alcoholic beverages support their claim of non-addiction. Altogether these findings suggest that drug use amongst this group is a complex problem.

Drug Usage: Daily Use, Not Addicted, With Alcohol

The fifth row reveals extremely low or no drug usage in each substance category. With the exception of marijuana, where 20 inmates reported daily use with alcohol, only four women reported using some other illegal substance daily with alcohol. The low usage of daily use with alcohol could very likely be explained by the nonaddiction factor. That is, the observed correlation between alcohol and drugs tends to drop or disappear once the nonaddiction factor is included, suggesting that there is a relationship between alcohol, drugs, and addiction, as showed in rows 6 to 9.

Drug Usage: Nondaily Use, Addicted, No Alcohol

Consistent with the "alcohol-drugs correlation thesis," the frequencies for drug usage in each substance category are relatively low in the sixth row of Table 6. The highest frequency was for powder cocaine, where 15 female prisoners reported nondaily use without alcohol. These low frequencies for powder cocaine as well as other illegal substances in row 6, though, are still critical in that these female drug users reported being addicted.

Drug Usage: Nondaily Use, Addicted, With Alcohol

The findings shown in row 7 are significant because each substance category contains frequencies of "nondaily" drug users, but nonetheless addicted. As shown in row 7, the highest frequencies of addiction, even with the use of alcoholic beverages, are for potent drugs like powder cocaine and crack. Marijuana, by contrast, which is not as harsh as other drugs but a traditionally common substance among young people, is also used by these respondents. Again, these findings point to the "alcohol-drugs correlation thesis," suggesting causation: addiction.

Drug Usage: Daily Use, Addicted, No Alcohol

Row 8 in Table 6 shows that a substantial number of female prisoners were addicted to crack, heroin, or powder cocaine before their incarceration, which can partly be explained with the reported daily use even without the use of alcohol. Some inmates also reported using daily use of marijuana and being addicted, indicating that addiction is indeed a severe problem.

Drug Usage: Daily Use, Addicted, With Alcohol

Considering that the last drug combination in Table 6 carries the most critical implications, the reported findings on the bottom of Table 6 are perhaps the most significant for our discussion of life before, during, and after incarceration. As the most damaging drug usage combination, "daily use, addicted, with alcohol," each substance category contains a substantial number of female users: 199 for nicotine, 84 for marijuana, 26 for heroin, 47 for powder cocaine, 89 for crack, 22 for amphetamines, 15 for speedballs, 9 for PCP, and 43 for prescription drugs. The nature of these addictions needs to be understood, discussed, and remedied to avoid additional complications, especially with an aging female prison population. Policymakers need to recognize that even though nicotine is not an illegal substance, it can be a concern once in prison, given the potential health complications of this drug use. For this group of female offenders, their life changes drastically almost overnight in that when they show up in prison they might not get their dose of nicotine.[7]

Even more dramatic to this cohort of inmates, most will no longer have access to drugs or alcohol in prison, and thus they are only left with an addiction. (Smoking is banned in most correctional systems today.) The implications are illustrated in the following case: "Doris M. was seven months pregnant and addicted to heroin when she was sentenced to serve six months at the Santa Rita County jail for a minor probation violation. Prior to her incarceration, she sought medical assistance through a drug treatment program . . . and was in the process of beginning methadone maintenance. She was told by her doctor that she should not attempt to withdraw from drugs quickly or without medical assistance since it would most likely damage the fetus. In spite of her drug-dependent condition, Doris was forced to withdraw 'cold turkey' from heroin when she entered the jail in June of 1985. She suffered from severe vomiting, headaches, abdominal pain, diarrhea and other symptoms of traumatic withdrawal. On a number of occasions, she asked for medical help but was ignored. She was not seen by an obstetrician until almost six weeks later, and the jail staff failed to bring her to her next two appointments with the obstetrician. On August 13, 1985, when she was approximately eight and one-half months pregnant, she had severe pains in her uterus and felt no fetal movement. Three days later, she was given a Caesarean and her still-born daughter was removed" (cited in Barry, 1989:198; see also Bodine, 1981). The biggest problem in the context of drug usage, addiction and daily drug use with alcohol, is the deadliest and the most difficult to cure in that it requires immediate and long-term treatment. Yet, these women are in the greatest need of assistance in that if they are not treated prior to release and supported in the community, they will soon return to prison, costing tax payers thousands of additional dollars.

In sum, as shown in Tables 5 and 6, alcohol and drug usage is a complicated matter, carrying significant ramifications for the prisoner, correctional system, and society. For example, as reported in Table 5, using needles without sterilization and not being afraid of contacting HIV, signals a severe lack of responsibility, but also ignorance and lack of education. At a more fundamental level, given their long history of abuse and the uncertain and abusive environment in which women lived before going to prison, there is a possibility that some women have lost respect for their own body and well-being. To others, such deathly negligence could be "a way out, a form of suicide." Interestingly, one of the least abused drugs were prescription drugs (i.e., legal use of prescription drugs such as anti-depressants, stimulants such as Ritalin, or other mood modifying drugs), a critical finding considering the poor health of many female offenders. Of course, this can partly be explained by the fact that many of these women did not have health insurance, as indicated by poverty, high level of unemployment, and low paying jobs (see Chapter 2). Lastly, the reported figures in row 9 of Table 6 show that among the different combinations of drug usage, as a whole, the most common seems to be: daily use of drugs with alcohol, providing the strongest support for the "alcohol-drugs correlation thesis." Further, the reported figures in row 9 also suggest a strong connection between daily drug usage, alcohol, and addiction, which could be interpreted as an "alcohol-drugs-daily use causation thesis."

Alcohol, Drugs, and Imprisonment

As noted earlier, various empirical studies have documented a connection between alcohol or drugs and imprisonment. This section contains reported findings from institutionalized women in Wisconsin. Even though the findings in Table 7 are not, by definition, direct measures of the influence of alcohol or drugs on imprisonment, they provide insight into the complexity of the problem.

Table 7
INFLUENCE OF ALCOHOL AND DRUGS ON
INSTITUTIONALIZED WOMEN (N=456)

	Yes	*No*	*Mean*
Age of 1st contact with legal system*			20.6
Current incarceration a result of alcohol	125 (27.4)	329 (72.1)	
Current incarceration a result of drug abuse	184 (40.4)	269 (59.0)	
Current incarceration a result of drug possession	99 (21.7)	352 (77.2)	
Current incarceration a result of drug distribution	93 (20.4)	354 (77.6)	

* Age contact range: 3 to 63

For some Wisconsin female prisoners, the age of their first contact with the legal system (either as a juvenile or as an adult) was fairly young, but for other inmates it was much later in life. For this group of female offenders, the mean age for their first contact was 20.6 years of age, right around their twenty-first birthday. Close to one-third (125 or 27.4%) of female prisoners reported that their current incarceration was a result of an alcohol related offense. For drugs, we see a significant but not surprising picture. Among all the drug cases, only 93 (20.4%) female prisoners reported that their current incarceration was for distributing drugs for sale, making this the smallest group of drug offenders. A slightly higher number (99 or 21.7%) of inmates reported that their current imprisonment was due to a drug possession offense. However, 184 (40.4%) women reported that their current incarceration was a result of drug abuse, a consistent finding with Tables 5 and 6. Therefore, even though we do not know if the "possession" was with the intent of distribution or personal use, these figures indicate that most (283) women were not in prison for selling drugs, but mostly for drug abuse.

In sum, the reported figures indicate that alcohol and drugs influence legal sanctions on female offenders. As illustrated by Barbara Owen (1998:8), along with economic marginalization, ". . . histories of abuse and self-destructive choices speed women along a pathway to imprisonment." More globally speaking, the "war on drugs" seems to be having a major influence on the lives of individuals with chaotic life histories, self-reported addiction problems, and vulnerable backgrounds. Considering the influence of the media in shaping perceptions and public policy (Faith, 1993b; Farrington, 1992), the low levels of drug distribution, as reported in Table 7, do not support the severity sanctions advocated by some politicians. Once again, these findings highlight the significance of making the female experience a more explicit and better documented topic in public discussions.

CONCLUSION

Prior investigations have documented the early days of female offenders, which can be characterized as "always running." Running from home to the streets serves as an escape, which often turns into a nightmare. The turbulent trips of going back and forth between home and the streets serve to pave the way into prison. The data show that to be young, poor, unemployed, uneducated, and female creates the perfect conditions for categorization, victimization, and stigmatization on various different levels. Eloquently put, "females, as young girls, are labeled and processed as deviants—and subsequently as criminals—for refusing to accept or participate in their own victimization . . . this refusal results in structural dislocation from three primary socializing institutions (the family, education, and occupation), and leads to entry into the criminal life . . . crime becomes a rational choice in the face of dislocation from family, education, and finally work in the paid labor force, and how drugs are used to dull the pain of the reality of their lives" (Arnold, 1990: 154).

The Wisconsin study indicates that the experience of female offenders is not simple, constant, or governed by a few selected historical factors. The experiences of females before they enter prison are numerous and diverse—often surviving verbal, emotional, physical, and sexual abuse—to include factors such as fear. Many report addictions to alcohol and drugs. Even worse, sometimes women injecting drugs without sterilized needles, an avenue for contracting communicable diseases. Further, the figures show a deadly combination among alcohol and drug users: "daily use, addiction, with alcohol." Arguably, even though this is probably the most challenging group to treat, this is the group with the highest need of assistance. To this end, recently it was reported that only half of Wisconsin female prisoners who participate in drug programs are completing treatment, making release difficult and consequential in that women who do not complete treatment are at greater risk to re-offend after being released than those who complete treatment (Doege, 2006). Under these conditions, these women are not in a stable position to help others, family members, or themselves. Therefore, if not given the proper treatment while in prison, these women will not be "functional" upon release and will soon return to prison, costing taxpayers additional money to deal with a never-ending problem. As a result, public safety is threatened when we fail to help these prisoners. Finally, the drug-crime connection will continue to grow until the proper mechanisms are implemented to better understand the female experience before prison, which will assist in developing the most effective treatments for the various issues facing women when they enter prison, especially the addiction problem.

Chapter 4

INMATES' INVOLVEMENT WITH THE CRIMINAL JUSTICE SYSTEM

This chapter provides a brief overview of the history of inmates within the U.S. legal system. As noted by some scholars, female offenders were once viewed as maladjusted and misguided, and in need of treatment (Giallombardo, 1966; Street, Vinter, and Perrow, 1966), but female offenders are often viewed as threatening, danger-ous, irredeemable, unpredictable, and in need of strict social control (see Faith 1993a). Together, these changes have resulted in a rapid shift from the rehabilitative and therapeutic objectives that differentiated female prisons from men's prisons for most of the twentieth century (Strickland, 1976; Watterson, 1973, 1996; Watts, 1990). As argued here-in, one must understand the interaction of both historical and ideo-logical factors that shape and re-shape the imprisonment of women. The chapter concludes by detailing the findings about prior criminal records, offense characteristics, plea bargaining, and type of attorney, of the Wisconsin incarcerated population.

A SHIFT IN THE AMERICAN MENTALITY

Historically, female offenders have received little attention in crim-inal justice research, crime control policies, or public discussions about crime and justice (Owen, 1998; Rierden, 1997). Some investigators report that, until recently, women were deemed insignificant as a wor-thy topic of investigation (Belknap, 1996; Chesney-Lind and Shelden, 2003). Consequently, students of criminal justice, policymakers, and the public have viewed the female experience through the lens of "male-oriented correctional policies." Considering claims that such approaches were not representative of female offenders, a small, but significant, number of studies have been published in the last several years. Still, while the literature on female victims of crime has grown, empirical research on female offenders and their experiences with the criminal justice system continues to lag behind their male counterparts (Owen, 1998).

In part, this lack of attention on female issues has resulted in a distorted picture of female offenders and women in general. A common view has been that women tend to be seen as docile, submissive, mothers, caregivers, and housewives. As such, a considerable amount of crime committed by women was not viewed as dangerous, and, by extension, not aggressively prosecuted by the courts (Culbertson and Fortune, 1986). More importantly, women had not been perceived as a major social, political, or economic threat until recently.

In the last several years, though, a series of events have occurred, changing the perception of the Americans, particularly policymakers, law enforcement personal, and court officials, as to how female offenders should be treated by the criminal justice system (Farrington, 1992; Spohn, Gruhl, and Welch, 1985). In this regard, some investigators report that women's "liberation" has been a key contributing factor in how we perceive female criminality as well as the corresponding prosecutions (Adler, 1975; Bunch, Foley, and Urbina, 1983). Following the liberation thesis (Fox, 1984), some observers have noted that as the rate of women in the job market increased, so does the rate of arrests and prosecutions (Simon, 1975). As noted by Freda Adler (1977:31), "When we did not permit women to swim at the beaches, the female drowning rate was quite low. When women were not permitted to work as bank tellers or presidents, the female embezzlement rate was low." Other researchers point to specific historical factors, like the war on drugs, as a leading cause of high incarceration rates (Owen and Bloom, 1995a; see also Currie, 1985). Still others, like Nichole Rafter (1990), suggest that the "mentally shift" is inherently more vicious by indicating that the feminization of poverty since 1960 has meant that women and children now comprise 80 percent of the poor in the United States (see Gans, 1995). It is possible that very little has changed in regards to female criminality. What has changed are the reporting practices, female portrayal in the media (Dyer, 2000; Faith,

1993b), our perceptions of women, and the ways we respond to female deviance and criminal behavior.

In sum, while the reasons for female criminality are diverse (see Chapter 10), the one thing that we can be certain of is the fact that the American perceptions toward women and their roles in society has changed in ways that are detrimental to all. Today, we are experiencing a shift from what some researchers call "the old penology, which emphasized individual responsibility, diagnosis, and treatment, to a new penology concerned with the identification, classification, and management of dangerous groups" (DiIulio, 1991; Kruttschnitt, Gartner, and Miller, 2000:685), or what Feeley and Simon (1992:449) refer to as "the actuarial considerations of aggregates." Within an historical context, arrests, convictions, and the punishment of women, "as well as all other aspects of our lives, takes place against a backdrop of patriarchal relationship" (Kurshan, 1992:331). Further, "these values and practices are reinforced by academic theories that perpetuate sex role stereotypes" (Feinman, 1983:24). As noted in Chapter 3, many young girls tend to be displaced in society. As they grow older, encounters with the juvenile and criminal justice systems tends to push them even further into the periphery of society. Hence, both before going to prison and during their incarceration, female offenders are being forced to survive with little or no support.

SOMETIMES THERE IS NO OTHER OPTION

As noted in Chapter 3, some young girls are neglected and abused, which is followed by manipulation and oppression at home and in the streets. In fact, research has documented that women are often victims of triple oppression: females are victims of gender, race, and class oppression and manipulation who are structurally dislocated from the major American social institutions such as the family, school, and work (Arnold, 1990; Diaz-Cotto, 1996).

The lack of supportive family members for these young women contribute to early independence, considerable free unstructured time, and eventually dislocation. Along with an uncertain and confusing early childhood, the influence of drugs, abuse, poverty, and limited opportunity make "normal" values unlikely (Chesney-Lind and Shelden, 2003). Further, when manipulation and victimization are combined with poverty, racial and ethnic discrimination, and institutionalized greed, women have limited options for survival using legal means and thus they may feel a sense of belonging and loyalty in the world of street crime, but, oftentimes, the only world they know of (Gilfus, 1992).

Once in the streets, ". . . women tend to commit survival crimes to earn money, support a drug-dependent life, and escape brutalizing physical conditions and relationships" (Owen, 1998:11). One particular study found that abuse, especially by mothers, dysfunctional families, families with little stability and some history of criminality and/or substance abuse contributed to female delinquency. Often, mothers of female offenders lack support and resources needed to cope with their environments, and thus they are just trying to survive despite their lack of resources (Rosenbaum, 1993). In fact, some researchers point out that when women become dislocated from society, "sexual activity and motherhood are often the only bargaining chips in society available to these marginalized women . . . women on the margins are often dependent on sex role socialization that assumes a middle-class, patriarchal view of the woman's role" (Owen, 1998:12). Invariably, the lack of adequate economic and social support for women and children is a key factor in rising crime rates (Balthazar and Cook, 1984). The poverty of their lives on the street, the economic disadvantages, and lack of educational opportunities make crime a "reasonable," or sometimes the only, choice for marginalized women, with subsequent imprisonment a likely outcome (Barlow, 1999; Currie, 1985). As noted by feminist criminologists, the majority of women, who persist in criminal behavior in spite of repeated arrests and other sanctions, are motivated by the need to survive emotionally and economically in a society that emotionally and physically brutalizes women (Chesney-Lind and Pasko, 2004; Daly and Chesney-Lind, 1988; Gelsthorpe and Morris, 1990).

In sum, with little support from friends, relatives and social agencies, young women are sometimes forced into the streets, only to find out that life in the streets comes with various powerful negative influences, like limited options, guns, drugs, violence, gangs, and crime. In combination, these issues create the perfect conditions for delinquency and crime, especially prostitution and theft, as a survival mechanism. Therefore, it is important that we investigate the experiences of female offenders before they enter the correctional facility. Further, given that African American women, American Indian women, and Latinas are disproportionately incarcerated, cultural issues, which could become problematic to the correctional system once minority women are imprisoned, need to be considered. According to Juanita Diaz-Cotto (1996:2), ". . . unless one understands the experiences of Latinas . . . inside and outside the walls, one cannot fully understand the Latina(o) experience in the United States" (see also Martinez, 2004).

A SHIFT IN CRIMINAL BEHAVIOR

Is the American society experiencing a shift in female criminality? That is, are more females committing crime? Are women committing more crimes? Are females committing different crimes? Or, is it simply a change in crime-reporting practices? What role does fear of crime, largely influenced by the media, shaping public perceptions about criminality? While some investigators argue that there is definitely a shift, others are not convinced that a shift is taking place. In particular, investigators report that women offenders are not getting worse, but that the criminal justice system is becoming more punitive incarcerating women, especially for drug-related offenses (Bloom, Chesney-Lind, and Owen, 1994). Some investigators assert that the majority of female offenders are convicted for nonviolent crimes, and that they are more likely to be prosecuted and convicted of less serious property offenses (Simon and Landis, 1991). In fact, even in drug-related cases, female offenders are much more likely than men to be convicted of drug crimes with "possession" of drugs the modal offense for women, and not for distribution (Owen, 1998).

It is, however, possible that the American society is experiencing a shift in female criminality, with fear of crime and the media, especially television programs like *Cops* and *America's Most Wanted* (Kappeler and Potter, 2004; Miller, Rossi, and Simpson, 1986), playing a large role in shaping public perceptions about the nature of crime (Goode and Ben-Yehuda, 1994). Logically, it makes sense that increases in opportunities in areas traditionally "closed" to women, correspond with a higher number of females engaged in criminality. Likewise, it is reasonable to argue that increases in social ills, such as higher unemployment and poverty rates, correspond with higher crime and recidivism rates (Western, 2002). Also, given the nature of legal sanctions and "crime opportunities," it is possible that females are committing different types of crimes. For example, for female offenders, prostitution used to be a common encounter with the police. Today, the most frequent encounter with the police and the courts seems to be drug-involved: distribution, possession, and usage, as noted in Chapter 3. Of course, crime statistics are also influenced by law enforcement tactics, court response to female criminality, and reporting practices. Our ideas about crime are further distorted by the popular media with a preoccupation on violent crimes.

In sum, given the complexity of the subject matter, it would be difficult to access with precise accuracy the "evolution" of female criminality in the United States (Adler, 1975). However, it is impossible to fully understand the possible shift in female criminality and subsequent imprisonment without understanding the "roots" of female crime and deviance. For example, early teen pregnancy, especially when combined with leaving home, dropping out of school, and drug or alcohol usage, becomes part of the downward spiral for women. As noted in Chapter 3, drug use is tied to criminality, often as a result of psychological and emotional traumas caused by a world of violence, various forms of abuse, and living on the streets (Miller, 1986). For example, women who have been battered and abused for a long time may see no way out of pain, danger, and frustration but to kill the abuser (Richie, 1996). Ironically, if a woman does kill her abuser, the same criminal justice system that was unwilling to protect her is now ready to prosecute her and send her to prison (McConnell Clark Foundation, 1997; Pollock, 2002a).

DIFFERENTIAL TREATMENT

Historically, no single topic has been more problematic than the issue of differential treatment (or disparities), especially when possible variation is referenced as "discrimination" (Urbina, 2007). However, unlike male offenders, where the differential treatment debate normally revolves around racial discrimination, the gender debate tends to revolve around two controversial issues with female offenders: race and sex discrimination. Indeed, while some scholars argue that there is little empirical evidence in favor of the "nondifferential treatment thesis," others argue that the weight of the evidence lends toward the "differential treatment thesis" (see Urbina, 2007).

Sex Discrimination

Arguably the leading voice against the view of a "gendered legal system," William Wilbanks (1986:528) claims that there is sex variation in some decision points, but that, overall, the criminal justice system does not operate "uniformly in favor of females." To him, the criminal justice system operates in a gender neutral fashion. In which case, higher arrest, prosecution, conviction, and incarceration rates are simply a reflection of a wider number of females committing crimes and higher recidivism rates.

Some researchers, however, not only argue that female offenders are victims of discrimination, but that sex discrimination dates back to their birth. In fact, some investigators report that women are victims of multiple marginality or triple jeopardy largely because their gender, class, and race/ethnicity places them at the economic periphery of an unsupportive, unforgiving, and vindictive society (Bloom, 1996). Indeed, with few exceptions, studies have found support for the "sex discrimination thesis" (Mann, 1993; Bosworth and Flavin, 2007).

Race and Ethnicity Discrimination

Like sex discrimination, some critics argue that if differential treatment exists, it is largely a product of "disparities," normally an unconscious process, and not overt or subtle discrimination (Pridemore, 2000; Wilbanks, 1986). The majority of the criminal justice literature, though, suggests that race is a factor resulting in variation in the criminal justice system (Aguirre and Turner, 2006; Bershad, 1985; Free, 2001; Mann, 1993).

It is also possible that discrimination is underreported in academic studies and journalistic accounts. For instance, in a recent article in *Critical Criminology* (2007), Martin Guevara Urbina reports that few studies of discrimination have included Latinas in their analyses. Detailing the ethnic literature, the author reports that studies claiming no discrimination suffer from one or more of ten common methodological limitations. Clearly, the existing ethnic literature suggests that Chicanas suffer triple oppression because they are in a historically subordinated and marginalized ethnic group, concentrated among the poor, working class, and females. Denise Segura and Beatriz Pesquera (1998:193) document that "As Mexicans, Chicanas have been treated as 'second-class citizens' since their incorporation into the United States in 1848" (see also Acuna, 2004; Almaguer, 1994; Bosworth and Flavin, 2007).

In sum, the existing evidence supports the differential treatment thesis in regards to both sex and race/ethnicity discrimination. This fact by itself suggests that the "differential treatment thesis" be explored by the totality of events and circumstances. Further, since ethnicity research is limited to a small pool of studies, future research must investigate for possible ethnic effects, while continuing to examine race effects in the criminal justice system. Researchers should delineate the female experience with the criminal justice system before entering prison as finely as possible to better understand the essence of the female experience before, during, and after incarceration. As noted in earlier, key issues like changes in the American mentality and criminal behavior, available survival options, and differential treatment are integral for capturing a narrative that is reflective of the totality of circumstances. In the next section, a series of variables will be introduced into the analysis as we explore the female experience in Wisconsin.

THE WISCONSIN EXPERIENCE

Similar to the previous two chapters, this section reports findings for 456 female prisoners in Wisconsin. A series of specific questions were asked regarding the respondent's involvement with the criminal justice system. For instance, unless one is sensitive to the influence of legal representation, it is difficult to obtain an appreciation of "fairness and justice" in the legal system, particularly for those who end up in prison.

Before Prison Walls: Women's Involvement with the Legal System

Prior History

Table 8 outlines how Wisconsin female prisoners generally have a long and complicated history with the American legal system. Inmates were asked about prior encounters with the criminal and juvenile justice systems. Almost half (210 or 46.1%) of the entire pool of Wisconsin female prisoners reported that they were in prison for the first time, with slightly over half (242 or 53.1%) having been incarcerated before. Since some women were serving time for parole violations but still serving time for the original conviction, inmates were asked if they had "prior convictions" before the original arrest leading to the current incarceration. As shown in Table 8, over half (258 or 56.5%) of the inmates had prior convictions. Inmates were also asked for their age at the time of their first incarceration (including offenses that occurred as juveniles). Even though there was great age variation, 5 being the youngest and 63 being the oldest at the time of their first incarceration, the mean age of 24 suggests that most inmates were incarcerated at a fairly young age.

Table 8
WOMEN'S INVOLVEMENT WITH THE AMERICAN LEGAL SYSTEM (N=456)

	Mean	*Range*	*Frequency*	*Percent*
First incarceration ever				
Yes			210	46.1
No			242	53.1
Age at the time of first incarceration	24.0	5 to 63		
Age when started serving time for current incarceration	30.7	15 to 64		
Length of time in prison	31.4	.75 to 264 (months)		
Prior convictions before arrest leading to current incarceration				
Yes			258	56.5
No			189	41.4
Length of current sentence	83.3	1 to 492 (months)		

Continued on next page

Table 8 (cont.)

	Mean	Range	Frequency	Percent
Specific charges for current incarceration				
Drugs			78	17.1
Burglary			5	1.1
Robbery			18	3.9
Theft			33	7.2
Assault			22	4.8
Murder			23	5.0
Driving under the influence of alcohol			16	3.5
Domestic violence			10	2.2
Prostitution			3	0.7
Welfare fraud			3	0.7
Other behavior			109	23.9
More than 1 charge			125	27.4
Entering a guilty plea				
Yes			335	73.5
No			113	24.8
Pleading guilty to specific charges				
Drugs			73	16.0
Burglary			3	0.7
Robbery			21	4.6
Theft			31	6.8
Assault			11	2.4
Murder			11	2.4
Driving under the influence of alcohol			19	4.2
Domestic violence			4	0.9
Prostitution			4	0.9
Welfare fraud			2	0.4
Other behavior			90	19.7
More than 1 charge			70	15.4
Representation by attorney				
Yes			425	93.2
No			23	5.0
Type of attorney				
Court appointed			319	70.0
Private			94	20.6
Other type			10	2.2
Don't know			1	0.2
Request for particular facility				
Yes			61	13.4
No			381	83.6

Continued on next page

Table 8 (cont.)

	Mean	Range	Frequency	Percent
Reasons for requesting a particular facility				
Security			10	2.2
Medical conditions			2	0.4
Family			5	1.1
Traveling distance			6	1.3
Availability of resources at facility			8	1.8
Other reasons			16	3.5
More than 1 reason			12	2.6

In sum, the figures reported in Table 8 suggest not only a long criminal history, but a history that started at a very early age for many women. Given that their first incarceration takes place at a relatively young age, their prospects in the competitive job market, financial opportunities for those who wish to pursue an education and voting rights are severely hindered, especially since felons in many jurisdictions cannot vote. Logically, these issues have additional implications for female offenders. For instance, without a decent job, it becomes difficult to obtain competent legal counsel for court proceedings. Therefore, knowing their prior history is vital to understanding their current sentence and imprisonment.

The Current Sentence

Similar to the age at the time of their first incarceration, there seems to be great age variation (15 being the youngest and 64 being the oldest when these respondents started serving time for the current incarceration), with a mean age of 30.7 years, further confirming that some women were not in prison for the first time. Inmates were also asked how long they had been in prison to assess their feelings toward imprisonment (see Chapters 5 to 9). For example, someone who has been in prison for, say, three weeks, has a very different view of prison life than someone who has been in prison for 10 years in regards to basic issues like medical services (see Chapter 6), opportunities for education or rehabilitation (see Chapter 2), and controversial matters like the use of solitary confinement (see Chapter 5). The length of time in prison for the respondents ranged from three weeks to 264 months, with a mean of 31.4 months.

In trying to understand the nature of the prosecution and conviction leading to the current incarceration, inmates were asked a series of specific questions. As noted in Table 8, the length of their current sentence ranged from one to 492 months, with a mean sentence of 83.3 months. At first look, the mean sentence does not look too severe, until one sees the severity of the charges for the entire pool of participants. For instance, even though the reported charges for alleged criminal activities were wide and diverse, the most frequent reported charge was for drugs (78), followed by theft (33), both of which are nonviolent offenses. These two charges, however, were followed by charges for three violent crimes: murder (23), assault (22), and robbery (18). Driving under the influence of alcohol (16), domestic violence (10), burglary (5), prostitution (3), and welfare fraud (3) charges are also prevalent, but the frequencies are lower, especially for prostitution and welfare fraud charges. These last two charges are "unique" in that the low number of fraud charges resulting in incarceration do not support the notion that welfare mothers are manipulating the state or the notion that "prostitution, as a disease of the night, is polluting the streets" and therefore should be severely sanctioned. However, a significant number of women were not only charged for the specific offenses listed in Table 8, but for multiple changes.[8]

Given the significance of legal representation in court proceedings and the final case outcomes (Levine, 1992; Smith, 1995), four questions were asked in regards to legal counsel and pleas. To this end, the majority (425 or 93.2%) of female inmates reported having legal representation for the charge(s) that resulted in the current incarceration, with only 23 women not being assisted by an attorney. As far as type of attorney, 70 percent (319) of the women were represented by court-appointed attorneys, while 20.6 percent (94) reported being represented by a private attorney. Still, even though the vast majority of inmates had legal representation, most women reported pleading guilty to the charges that brought them to the current incarceration. For those who entered a plea, the reported findings show that the guilty pleas are consistent with the charges, like drugs, theft, robbery, and driving under the influence, leading to imprisonment, indicating that women tend to plead guilty to the original charges, consistent with figures showing that approximately 95 percent of defendants plea guilty (Durose and Langan, 2004). At one level, it could be argued that since most women plead guilty to the original charge(s), the type of attorney plays a minimal role. On another level, one could argue that even a competent attorney, court appointed or private, would encounter great difficulties convincing a judge to mitigate sentences as most of these women have a long criminal history, little education, a low-paying job or no job, poor employment histories, and labeled by society as "bad citizens." Still, we argue that competent attorneys, both private and court appointed, are vital in plea bargaining negotiations; that is, so that women will receive the best possible benefits of negotiations (Urbina, 2004a; Urbina and Kreitzer, 2004). For instance, the skills of a well-trained lawyer are vital for detailing the totality of events and circumstances and not simply the act itself and/or a few selected legal factors.

Lastly, considering that some issues, like health (see Chapter 6), are of serious concern to female offenders and the fact that not all facilities provide the same level of services, inmates were asked if they had requested a particular facility to be incarcerated and, if so, the reasons for such request. Of the 61 inmates who reported requesting a particular facility, the most common reason was security, followed by availability of resources at facility, proximity to family, and medical conditions. The fact that some females cited multiple reasons for requesting a particular prison further reveals that importance of understanding the problems women have when they enter prison, in part because these concerns can lead to additional concerns, issues, and problems.

In sum, as shown in Table 8, female offenders tend to have a long and complicated history with the American legal system, which has significant ramifications for themselves. Encounters with the juvenile and criminal justice systems at an early age, for example, hinders employment opportunities and, by extension, the ability to hire competent legal representation. Similarly, the finding that most females started serving time for their "current" incarceration as older adults has a number of possible implications. For instance, the average age when respondents started serving time for their current incarceration is about 31 years, a time when most of their children are under ten years of age, leads to a world of uncertainty and chaos for both the mother and children (see Chapter 5), subsequently contributing to a cycle of delinquency and crime. Indeed, the reported figures show that with few exceptions female behaviors are not vicious and lethal crimes, but "crimes of poverty," a reflection of a long and complicated history in combination with poverty, addiction and the forces of broader structural and ideological factors (see Chapter 10 and Epilogue). For example, the mere fact that most of these women qualified for a court-appointed lawyer demonstrates that the majority of women are in poverty or near poverty (see Chapter 2 and 10).[9] Therefore, exploring the lives of female offenders by the totality of circumstances, requires that we pay particular attention to their prior criminal history as well as the current sentence, giving us an appreciation for issues of justice and fairness as women enter prison.

CONCLUSION

Questions of crime, justice, and fairness are difficult to access without considering the historical, structural, and ideological forces that shape and reshape prison sentences. Changes in criminal behavior and the perceptions about crime, especially the voting class, are integral to understanding not only final outcomes, but issues such as differential treatment in the legal process. Likewise, understanding the current prison sentence for female offenders requires that we pay particular attention to their criminal history as well as the options available to them as they struggle for survival. For instance, as noted above, there seems to be more women engaged in crimes of poverty than there are in serious violent crimes.

Consistent with previous studies, the findings reported above suggest that the process of female criminalization is intricately tied to their subordinate position in the American society where victimization combined with social, political, and economic marginality related to ethnicity, race, class, and gender tends to neglect or blur the boundaries between female offenders and victims (Chesney-Lind and Rodriguez, 1983; Romenesko and Miller, 1989). Hence, in order to stop the revolving door of incarceration and release, require that we start giving women realistic alternatives to illegal activities as a means of economic survival, emotional stability, and safety. Since the current "legal model" is not yielding the best possible results, we must find alternative ways of investigating, analyzing, reporting, and remedying social ills and injustices. For instance, to the medical doctor, knowing the medical history of the patient is just as important, if not more, as the current illness. Similarly, we argue that in the case of female offenders, it is just as important to know their history as it is to understand their current offense, conviction, and subsequent incarceration.

Chapter 5

AN EXPLORATION OF FEMALE PRISONS AND WOMEN THEY CONTROL

The imprisonment of women in the U.S. has always been a different phenomenon than it has been for men. Women have traditionally been sent to prison for different reasons and once in prison, female inmates endure different conditions of incarceration (Butler, 1997; Damousi, 1997; Rafter, 1987). Nancy Kurshan (1992:331), for instance, reports that "women's 'crimes' have often had a sexual definition and have been rooted in the patriarchal double standard. Therefore, the nature of women's imprisonment reflects the position of women in society." This chapter will explore such phenomenon, providing a discussion of key issues in the first part of the chapter, and detailing the results, like supplies, meals, religion, jobs, education, training, and hobbies, from the Wisconsin study.

AN HISTORICAL REMINDER

Until 1870, most prisoners (women, children, and men) in Europe and in the U.S. were housed in the same prison and treated essentially the same (Foucault, 1995; Freedman, 1981; Rafter, 1992). Shortly after the Civil War (1861–1865), the House of Shelter, a reformatory for women, opened in Detroit, Michigan—becoming the model for the treatment of female offenders. Soon after the first independent female-run prison was established in Indiana in 1873, followed by the Massachusetts Reformatory-Prison for Women in 1877, and the Western House of Refuge at Albion, Michigan in 1893 (Zedner, 1995).

In 1927, the first federal prison for women was opened in Alderson, West Virginia. And, in order to reduce criminal behavior, rehabilitation programs were implemented in female's prisons facilities in the 1940s and 1950s.

However, contrary to expectations, deplorable conditions were the norm and not the exception in the newly created correctional facilities, as they did not address specific needs of female offenders (Chesney-Lind, 1991; Colley and Camp, 1992; Morris and Wilkinson, 1995). In fact, correctional programming for female offenders, which is key for reintegration into society upon release, has traditionally been based on assumptions of male criminality (Holtfreter and Morash, 2003; Morton, 1998). Nowadays, in response to "equal protection lawsuits," the notion seems to be that female prisoners be treated as their male counterparts. However, Joycelyn Pollock (1998:42) reports that "equality of sentencing has led to staggering increases of women in prison, equality in prison programming has led to more vocational programs, but [equality] has also led to more security measures [and] more formalist approaches to supervision." Altogether, Nicole Rafter (1992:17) points out that "Equal treatment usually means less adequate treatment."

Today, like male offenders, female inmates in correctional institutions tend to be young, have little education, single, separated, or divorced, and are members of minority groups (see Chapter 2). But, as it will be detailed in this chapter, female prisoners are condemned to cope with various other issues, among them, life or death situations.

FROM THE STREETS TO PRISON

Understanding who female prisoners are, their experiences in the streets, the characteristics they take to the institution, and how they physically and emotionally react to specific "disciplinary regimes is crucial to seeing the prison not as an inert institution, but as an active, contested field" (Kruttschnitt, Gartner, and Miller, 2000:685). For instance, the pre-prison experience, such as histories of drug abuse, relationships, and economic marginality (see Chapters 3 and 4), as well as institutional characteristics, such as overcrowding, impacts the ways in which females respond to prison (Larson, 1983; Larson and

Nelson, 1984; Owen, 1998; Rierden, 1997). To this end, research indicates that involvement in defiant prison subcultures such as gangs varies by ethnicity, race, age, marital status, among other personal characteristics (Alarid, 1997; Bondeson, 1989; Tittle, 1969). For example, inmates with longer prison sentences and those who serve more time tend to abide more to a collective prisoner system and have more rebellious attitudes toward the correctional system. In retrospect, in prisons with high inmate turnover, or where a large proportion of the inmate population has short sentences, collective inmate networks are less likely to develop (Genders and Player, 1990).

Thus, some researchers note that a sound understanding of U.S. prisons requires analyzing them from the inside out, and "interpreting the prison as a social space and the subcultural adaptations of different prison populations as forms of active participation in the prison process" (Howe, 1994:151; Zingraff, 1980), yet this "is a missing link" in recent investigations of female offenders (Kruttschnitt, Gartner, and Miller, 2000:685). However, "an inside-out approach" is only logical if we understand, by the totality of events and circumstances, the "root" of what took women to prison in the first place. For example, some studies suggest that the types of inmates housed within a correctional facility are as significant for a female's prison experience as her own background characteristics, which are wide and diverse (see Fox, 1984; Morton, 2004).

Even thought some women have committed heinous acts, the majority have committed nonviolent offenses and most of them have a long history of struggle. As reported by Martha Wheeler, superintendent of the Ohio Reformatory for Women (cited in Krasno, 1982:20), "The women who end up here are acting out of their inadequacies as individuals–not with criminal rings or real criminal intentions. They have two or three kids and nobody to help them, so they write [bad] checks. Most of our homicides come out of longstanding volatile situations–a person who had meaning to the woman and the situation blew up. . . . A woman who gets into trouble [but has] a supportive family [with] money will get sent to a shrink or to live with Aunt Suzie and the court approves. She can be diverted from incarceration. Incarceration is for women without resources–financial and human" (see Chapter 4).

In sum, it seems logical to argue that the gap between the streets and prison needs to be bridged to maximize the utility of a well-structured correctional policy, such as developing prison rehabilitative programs that are sensitive to women histories and current issues (Immarigeon, 1997). Otherwise, correctional policies are like cutting weeds with a lawnmower in that the weeds grow up right back. Consequently, our understanding of the problem is limited in that we have not taken the time to "dig the root" and analyze or examine these conditions. Sometimes, people do not wish to spend the time, energy, and financial resources to dip the root and instead try to "kill the weeds with some type of chemical." However, oftentimes the chemical creates even a bigger "mess." Likewise, some correctional policies worsen the problem instead of alleviating it. Therefore, subsequent chapters, we will try to delineate the female prison experience as finely as possible, with the hope that such information will yield more humane, safe, and just results.

THE MARCH TO PRISON

Arrest and confinement is a time of confusion, uncertainty, chaos, and physical as well as emotional reactions. Once in the facility, people lose their identity and become a "number," and the famous line, "you have the right to one free phone call," is only valid if person to whom the prisoner is calling is willing to accept a "collect call." Otherwise, there is no communication with the outside world. Therefore, as a life-changing event, the march to prison must be well understood.

As noted in the following examples, one's admission to prison, as portrayed by the media, is a deceiving journey in that public perception often clashes with reality (Farrington, 1992). Case in point: "We arrived here last night at five in the evening. We had traveled in jump suits and slippers in an 8-seater plane with the marshals, stopping in Ft. Worth, Texas, and then to the airport at Lexington. We were caravanned with four cars, and a van, one of the cars being the local sheriff. We drive right up the entrance of this unit. The entire prison was locked in, and there were hundreds of prisoners' faces at the windows watching this entrance. There must have been 25 police of one type or another. One woman screamed out 'Hello Susan, we know it's you.' I started jumping up and down, and screamed, 'Don't let them bury us down there.' Someone else screamed, 'We won't.' I wish and hope. They hurried us inside. Inside three doors and into the unit's own R & D [Receiving and Discharge]. Such a big deal for the two of us, it was both frightening and ridiculous at the same time" (Zwerman, 1988:31). In the words of another inmate: "When I came through the gate, I said to myself: 'This is a prison?' All the trees and flowers–I couldn't believe it. It looked like a college with the buildings, the trees, and all the flowers. But after you're here a while–and it don't take long-you know it's a prison. Yeah, that's what it is–a prison" (Heffernan, 1972: 47).

For minority inmates, particularly Latinas, the first few days in prison can be even more dramatic in that they also experience ethnic specific factors: a cultural shock, language barriers (see Chapter 8), and complex formal and informal rules (see Chapter 7). For instance, a Latina in her early fifties who had been on antidepressants since she arrived in a California prison said, "For the first three months I was here, I cried and cried and cried. I couldn't stop. I kept telling myself 'I'm not here, I'm not here.' I was here, but I couldn't accept the fact" (Kruttschnitt, Gartner, and Miller, 2000:697). Even though Latinas are a minority in prison, their numbers are increasing, suggesting that investigators pay particular attention to ethnic-specific issues.

In the business world, it's often stated that "first impressions" are the most critical in that they will shape the rest of the experience. Similarly, I argue that one's admission to prison is the first impression to the prisoners (post-conviction), governing prisoner views, expectations, and behavior. For instance, as labeling theorists would suggest, how inmates are initially treated will influence their initial perceptions, which in turn influence how they view the system, how they react to the system, and level of success (Sultan, Long, Kiefer, Schrum, Selby, and Calhoun, 1984). Hence, as in the business world, we argue that policymakers need to be more sensitive to the "march to prison."

THE PRISON EXPERIENCE

Once in prison, female prisoners find themselves in a world where two sets of agendas coexist. One agenda involves a formal set of rules, regulations, procedures, and objectives that are intended to control inmates and promote safety, and, hopefully rehabilitation. The other agenda, subtle and illusive, seeks to govern the most profound elements of the female body, the mind and the heart, at which point the system has total control of the very essence of the human soul (Berk, Messinger, Rauma, and Berecochea, 1983; Foucault, 1995).

Consequently, the female prison experience should be analyzed from three separate angles. From one angle, there are the rigid rules and regulations that inmates have to abide 24 hours a day, with the slightest infraction resulting in loss of "privileges" or severe punishment, like solitary confinement (see Chapter 5). From a second angle, there is the prejudice, differential treatment (see Chapter 4), and discrimination that female prisoners are subjected to (see Chapters 7 and 8). In this regard, Joanne Belknap (1996) argues that female prisoners are confronted with institutionalized sexism. Indeed, historically ingrained in the American society, sexism is ". . . reflected inside most women's institutions which operate with fewer resources and training programs than usually available to men's prisons" (*Corrections Digest,* 1980:7; Immarigeon, 1997; Morton, 2004; Tell, 1981). More recently, researchers such as Barbara Owen and Barbara Bloom (1995a, 1995b) have documented that the increased number of women in prison has significantly impacted the delivery of programs (see below), medical care (see Chapter 6), housing conditions, staffing (see Chapter 7), and security (see Chapter 8). From a third angle, female prisoners are subjected to the cruelest punishment: manipulation and control of the human mind and heart. To accomplish this, female prisons have utilized an effective strategic approach: "discipline, infantilize, feminize, medicalize, and domesticize" (Belknap, 1996:98). Indeed, the tendency to treat female offenders like children, the focus on "domesticating" them, and the emotional and psychological manipulation has been well documented (Diaz-Cotto, 1996; Olsen, 1995). Consequently, when the very essence of the human soul has been conquered, the inmate is emotionally and spiritually dead (see Chapter 10). "It is like stepping off the regular world . . . even the regular prison world . . . into a tomb" (Reuben and Norman, 1987:881).

Besides race discrimination, no single subject has received more attention than programs in prison and, most recently, health care (see Chapter 6). Rehabilitative and recreational programs in prisons are vital in that they are not only influential in how women will behave, react, and view the correctional system while in prison, but how they will cope with life after their discharge (see Morash and Bynum, 1995; Zaitzow, 1998; Zaplin, 1998). Therefore, as we try to understand the inner-workings of the prison system (Howe, 1994; O'Brien, 1982) and expand the knowledge base of life in prison, we need to examine the prison experience, to include programs in prison, as finely as possible.

Prison Programs

Programs in prison can be viewed as a survival mechanism for inmates, and as a key organizational element in a well-managed facility (Flanagan, Marquart, and Adams, 1998; Morton, 1998). In particular, for the inmates, most of whom are uneducated and ill-equipped for a competitive job market (see Chapter 2), well-integrated and focused programs are vital for educating inmates so that they can obtain a decent job once released. For the correctional facility, well-structured programs are essential for keeping prisoners busy (mentally and physically) to avoid disturbances, riots, and other issues that could reduce safety and increase lawsuits against the correctional system. However, the combination of various factors—e.g., lack of resources, lack of support from politicians, policymakers, the general public, and the media—has limited both amount and quality of programs in prison.

In actuality, not only are programs in prison for women limited (Weisheit, 1985), but the existing ones, which were originally developed on models based on male inmates, have not been tailored to fit the needs of female prisoners (Hunter, 1984; Immarigeon, 1997; Schupak, 1986), as in the case of mothers in prison (see below). Critical to rehabilitation objectives, the psychological needs of female inmates (Cassel and Van Vorst, 1961; Haft, 1973; Haley, 1977; James and Glaze, 2006), and the social roles of incarcerated women (Ward and Kassenbaum, 1965; Heffernan, 1972) have not always received adequate attention by the correctional system. Further, as shown in Chapter 3, the majority of women in prison have long histories of drug use, sexual and physical abuse, but few female inmates are receiving the proper treatment (Peugh and Belenko, 1999). According to a recent investigation, "the barriers to treatment expansion, development, and implementation faced by prisons include budgetary limits, lack of counselors, inadequate space and capacity, frequent inmate movement in and out of the facility, and lack of inmate interest" (Belenko, 1999:9). Other investigators report that "The female offender wants to gain economic independence by acquiring better job skills. Unfortunately, the system in which she is incarcerated very often discourages her from attaining that goal" (Carp and Schade, 1992:157).

In the context of treating women and preparing inmates for life after prison (see Chapter 9), "minor" issues such as being allowed to receive items, which are often overlooked by correctional staff, are critical for reinforcing their self-esteem, and, by extension, success (Ramsey, 1980a, 1980b; Sanford and Donovan, 1994). To this end, a recent study reports that inmates "expressed resentment about how the staff controlled what the women were allowed to have in their rooms or their access to personal hygiene items" (Kruttschnitt, Gartner, and Miller 2000:707). In the words of one California prisoner, "In the worst of my addiction, the lowest of my addiction, the lowest point I've ever reached in my addiction, I've never run out of toilet paper, or sanitary supplies, and then, yet I come to prison and I have to worry about running out of toilet paper" (Kruttschnitt, Gartner, and Miller 2000:708). In short, we argue that we need to be sensitive to female needs as well as minor issues such as communication with relatives and friends to maintain equilibrium.

Educational and Vocational Programs

In the context of high unemployment rates, companies downsizing to maximize profits, companies leaving the country because of cheaper labor and lax operating laws elsewhere, and the advances in technology, all prison programs are essential, but educational and vocational programs are of primary importance to control one of the leading causes of incarceration: "crimes of poverty" (see Chapters 4 and 10).

Beyond numbers and quality, we must come to the realization that volume and quality means little unless the skills correspond with the reality of a free market economy. In this regard, the American Correctional Association (1990) reports that few work assignments actually teach inmates marketable job skills. Even worse, female prisons not only lack the amount and quality of vocational and educational programs normally available in men's prisons to prepare women once they are released back into the community, but the existing programs tend to reflect historical stereotypes of "feminine" occupations such as housekeeping, food services, sewing, and cosmetology

(Feinman, 1983; Morash, Haarr, and Rucker, 1994), reinforcing the historical patriarchic ideology. In sum, programs in rehabilitative women's prison are actually contributing to the very same problem that they are trying to prevent, the cycle of female criminality, as well as the social control of women, "keeping women in their place." Sex-role stereotypes have resulted in limited funding and inadequate programs for female prisoners (Moyer, 1984; Sorensen, 1981) need to be acknowledged and neutralized. In addition, prison programs need to be structured in a way that will yield productive results while incarcerated and skills that will prepare them for life after their release (see Morash and Bynum, 1995; Winifred, 1996; Zaplin, 1998). Further, the innovations of some facilities, like the Colorado Women's Correctional Facility, indicate that educational challenges can be overcome by providing a complete academic education program where women are taught various kills (*Criminal Justice Newsletter*, 1983; O'Leary and Weinhouse, 1992).

Mothers in Prison

The prison experience is a life-changing event to most, if not all, offenders; yet, historically no group of prisoners has been impacted by the prison experience than mothers in prison (Barry, 1987; Bergen, 1982; Bergman, 1983; Christopher, 1987). To this tend, no single issue seems to be more important to mothers than their children (see Chapter 2). Thus, in this section, we will outline some of the leading issues and concerns facing mothers in prison.

What the Numbers Show

Historically, the reality has been that female prisoners constituted a small population (vis-à-vis their male counterparts). However, our position is that the numbers, while "small," are significant, and they continue to increase as more women end up behind bars. In 1991, there were 452,500 incarcerated parents of 936,500 minor children. In 2000, the numbers had risen to 737,400 incarcerated parents of 1,531,500 minor children. If we include the children of adults who have recently been released from prisons and jails as well as adults on parole, the number of children affected rises to 3.2 million (Travis and Waul, 2003).

In terms of gender variation, 90 percent of the incarcerated parents are fathers, but the number of incarcerated mothers has increased at a much faster rate. Between 1990 and 1997, there was a 98 percent increase in the number of incarcerated mothers, compared with a 58 percent increase in incarcerated fathers. In 1997, 65 percent of women in state prisons and 59 percent of women in federal prisons had minor children. The majority of these incarcerated women were single mothers with an average of two children (Covington, 2003). As for race and ethnicity, nearly 7 percent of African American, 3 percent of Latina/o, and 1 percent of Caucasian children have a parent in prison (Mumola, 2000).

In the federal prison system, a similar situation is taking place. For example, between October 1, 1988 and June 1, 1989, there were 73 babies born to women held in the Federal Correctional Institution in Lexington, Kentucky (Carmouche and Jones, 1989; *USA Today*, 1990). There is variation in reported figures, but its estimated that between 1997 and 1998, more than 1,300 babies were born in prison. In 2003, 284 babies were born to inmates in Texas, and more than 300 babies were born in California in 2006. The Sentencing Project estimates that approximately 2,000 babies are born in prison annually (Liptak, 2006). With the sharp increase in female prisoners, the numbers are likely to increase significantly (see Chapters 1 and 2).

Legislation

Among the various laws governing the prison experience, legislation regarding mothers and their children has received special interest in the last 40 years or so; yet, it remains elusive and uncertain. In the 1960s and 1970s states started to repeal legislation that allowed mothers to retain their children in prison (Boudouris, 1985; Holt, 1982; Reaves, 1983). However, because of the prison boom and concerns raised by feminists scholars (Daly and Maher, 1998; Chesney-Lind and Pasko, 2004) and others (see Chapter 2), some states began to modify their statutes and provide alternatives, which include prison nurseries, sentencing modifications, and community-based corrections (Deck, 1988; Norz, 1989).[10] In fact, by the early 1980s, 16 of the 50 states had implemented statutory provisions regarding pregnant inmates or women with small children (Brodie, 1982; Downing, 1989). However, legislation has been limited in scope. For instance, some states address only prenatal or post natal care for inmates' issues (Indiana), or the procedures for temporary release of inmates to give birth in local hospitals (Idaho, Maryland, Massachusetts, Minnesota, Pennsylvania), or provisions for determining custody after the birth of an infant to an inmate (Florida, Main, Maryland, North Carolina, West Virginia). Montana addresses only the procedure for the controversial termination of parental rights. Death penalty states (see Chapter 8) generally provide provisions for a delay in the execution if the inmate is pregnant.

Considering the multitude of issues surrounding child birth only five states specifically address the issues created by childbirth. California, New Jersey, and New York specify that children under two years of age may be kept with their mothers in prison if the inmate gives birth while incarcerated or the infant is under two at the time of her incarceration (Carrieri, 1990). Connecticut allows mothers to keep their infants for up to 60 days after the birth of child. Illinois allows mothers to keep their babies until the child is one year old, if the Department of Corrections determines that there are special reasons why the infant should stay with the mother. In fact, the Women's Correctional Institution at Bedford Hills in New York, where women are moved to the nursery for the last few months of the pregnancy, is an exception.[11] At Bedford Hills, mothers give birth at a nearby hospital and return to live in the nursery wing, caring for their babies up to a year, and older children are allowed to visit (see Creighton, 1988). In most states, babies born in prison are placed with a family member or a social agency/state foster care within three weeks of birth, at times, within 48 hours of birth (*USA Today*, 1990). More recently, though, programs like Washington State's Residential Parenting Program are being more sensitive to the needs of both mother and child (see Fearn and Parker, 2004).

Given the vagueness of existing laws and the upwards trend of women in prison, policymakers must act accordingly to ensure that the issues of both pregnant women and mothers in prison are remedied to reduce and, perhaps, avoid brutalization, violations of human rights, lawsuits, and ultimately the cycle of crime and deviance.

Parental Rights

Having dialogued with mothers who have spent time in prison, the issue of parental rights tends to surface above the rest at three different stages of the legal process: arrest, conviction, and upon admission to prison. In particular, female prisoners are confronted with the possibility of having their parental rights terminated by the state (Carron, 1984; Henriques, 1996; *Juvenile and Family Law Digest*, 1981), a traumatic situation for most mothers. However, to this day, the central question remains controversial and unanswered, what to do with the child when parental rights are terminated. While some argue that the state is in the best position to care for the child, others argue that it is the family (or even friends) of the inmate who are in the best position to care of the child. A close analysis, however, suggests that both alternatives carry negative consequences. In the following case, a newborn was taken by the state: "she had no one who could care for the child. The terrifying reality is that the child is now in the hands of total strangers and in a culture altogether alien to hers, for she is of Hispanic origin" (Kiser, 1991:60). In another case, one female prisoner stated: "Seeing that it was better for him [husband] to have them than the state I signed the papers and all my rights to my children away. My feelings about this are now of horror that I let myself be conned like that. I often cry and am currently undergoing therapy and trying to regain my sanity. I now realize it would have been better for the state to have them" (Kiser, 1991:59). In some cases, the situation is even more devastating: "[The birth mother] has shared with me the frustration, guilt and anger she feels knowing that her child has been separated from not only herself but from her father and oldest sister. The foster mother is neither objective nor supportive about anything, especially when it concerns the relationships between the prisoner and the child. In the past year, the child has visited on [only] two separate occasions. . . . It is no secret that the foster mother plans on keeping the daughter" (cited in Kiser, 1991:60).

Given the complexity of the matter, the termination of parental rights should be decided on a case-by-case basis, taking into consideration that the majority of women are being convicted for nonviolent crimes (Simon and Landis, 1991), and that most inmates are released at some point. In the case of termination (Ash and Guyer, 1982; Genty, 1989; Schoenbauer, 1986), it would be difficult to quantify which approach is more suited for children of incarcerated women. Children of incarcerated mothers should not be regarded as a "case or number," but simply as children in need of understanding, care, and love. The love of a mother for her children cannot be "incarcerated" (Bergman, 1983). In the words of one Illinois inmate: "What can I do while I'm here to help me get back the love and trust of my family" (Kiser, 1991:63; see also Dodge, 1999)? Otherwise, we are actually setting up the ground for future generations of prisoners.

Programs for Mothers in Prison

Like educational and vocational programs, programs to address the psychological and physical needs of mothers in prison and their children are being modified and expanded to address additional demands (Fearn and Parker, 2004, 2005; Schupak, 1986). Because of the importance of proper socialization and social interaction, about 90 percent of states make "parenting classes" available to female prisoners and nearly 75 percent provide "special visiting areas" for parents. Unfortunately, few programs "get beyond the assumption that all that is needed is retraining in parenting skills, or that women's needs are limited to the parenting area" (Logan, 1992; Morash and Schram, 2002: 99; Pollock, 2002b). As noted above, prison programs should not only correspond with the increased number of mothers in prison, but they should be based on a sound and holistic approach to ensure that women are able to function independently once released from prison.

Visiting Mothers in Prison

Because of limited resources, location of prisons for women, and facility rules and regulations, visiting mothers in prison has been a major challenge to the correctional system, incarcerated mothers, and those who wish to visit their mothers. Of particular significance are the nature of visits and transportation. In some states, children may meet with their mothers at almost any time, for extended periods, and in play areas where physical contact is allowed to reinforce the social bond. However, few prisons allow overnight visits (28%) or have nurseries (7%), which help nurture the bond between mother and child (Pollock, 2002b).

In regards to transportation (because this population has limited resources to), some states actually transport children to visit their mothers. However, transportation, especially for mothers who are incarcerated out-of-state, is a major gap that needs to be bridged. The difficulties of visiting a prison were illustrated by one observer, "The burden of providing for her children leaves these extended members in a financial bind. After clothing, feeding, and sending the children to school, there is little motivation or money to plan a trip down to Dwight, which is 80 miles from Chicago. Most importantly these family members do not own a car and outsiders are unreliable" (Kiser, 1991:60–61). New York's Bedford Hills Correctional Facility, which created the nation's first nursery program and the Dwight Correctional Center in Illinois, that arranges weekend retreats similar to camping trips for mothers and their children are the exceptions (Applebome, 1992; Sametz, 1980).[12] The more common situation is in places like Wisconsin where women with infants see their children only during limited visiting times.

More fundamentally, a lack of visitation tends to create emotional crises for both the mother and child. Case in point: "At times, I couldn't understand why my family would tell me they were coming on a certain day and then had to cancel because of other obligations. I would feel very hurt and even unwanted or forgotten. I would go to my room and cry in 'privacy'" (Kiser, 1991:60; Roberts, 1989). Some visits can be emotional: "When Mary comes here to Dwight to see me every two weeks it is an OK visit until time to go home, then she cries and sometimes has to be dragged away from me. My [adult] son gets very depressed and cries also at times. My older daughters cry at times. . ." (Kiser, 1991:61). During the holidays, the situation can be more depressing, ". . . [Family visits on] the holidays, Mother's Day and my birthday are the hardest. There have been times when the officers would have to pull us apart, put my family out of the institution, and talk to me to ease my hurt and crying so I could get myself together to return to my cottage" (Kiser, 1991:62).

In short, mothers in prison have great difficulties maintaining contact with their children in that they might be incarcerated 100 or more miles away from home (Abdul-Alim, 2000; Datesman and Cales, 1983). Transportation to and from the prison is difficult, visits are rare, short and confusing for children, and phone calls are uncertain (see Kolman, 1983) and expensive. During the visits, children are asked to conform to facility rules and regulations governing adult visits such as no physical contact. Even worse, the difficulties and uncertainty led to emotional turmoil, like stress and depression (see Chapter 6), creating a barrier to future success.

Pregnant Women in Prison

In the last few years the correctional system has begun to address issues raised by pregnant female offenders by keeping some in county jails (*Corrections Digest*, 1988a; Moss, 1988), placing them in a particular facility, or unit within the prison, while trying to provide the proper diet, exercise, and medical care (see Chapter 6). Even though some correctional budgets are among the highest in the states, the prison experience for pregnant women in correctional facilities continues to be cruel, inhumane, and unjustified (Stefan, 1989; Wooldredge and Masters, 1993).

As illustrated in the following cases, pregnancy creates problems that need to be addressed. "Louwanna Y. was pregnant and serving a one-year sentence at the Kern County Jail in Bakersfield, California on a charge of welfare fraud. When she was incarcerated, she was approximately five months pregnant. Although she was a low-security prisoner, she was confined, twenty-four hours a day for several months, in grossly overcrowded cells. She was forced to sleep on the floor for almost two weeks after she arrived at the jail. She was exposed to several contagious diseases, including tuberculosis and measles, head lice and crabs. She was never seen by an obstetrician during the course of her pregnancy. When she went into labor on May 11, 1987, she reported her condition to the guards on duty, but was told that she would have to wait because there was no medical staff available at the time. Three hours later, she gave birth on a thin mat outside of the door of the clinic in the jail" (cited in Barry, 1989:189; see also Holt, 1982; Norz, 1989). This is not an isolated incident. A few years ago, Jane Kennedy reported that ". . . usually whenever they took women to the local hospitals they chained their wrists and put manacles on their ankles. I did hear of women having babies while chained to their beds" (DeClue, 1981:36). More recently, a 1998 Illinois case reveals the cruelty of childbirth in prison: "My feet were still shackled together, and I couldn't get my legs apart. The doctor called for the officer.

. . . No one else could unlock the shackles, and my baby was coming. . . . Finally the officer came and unlocked the shackles from my ankles. My baby was born then" (Amnesty International, 1999). In 2005, the *Miami Herald*, reported the conditions pregnant women face: "A former inmate is suing over the death of her baby, born over a cell toilet even though she complained of labor pains for nearly 12 hours. The mother was leaking amniotic fluid, running a fever, had complained for nearly 12 hours about labor pains, and had asked repeatedly to be taken to a hospital before the March 5th birth." Despite complaints and occasional lawsuits, shackling prisoners in prison in labor continues to be common. Only California and Illinois have laws forbidding shackling during labor. In 2000, Illinois enacted the first law forbidding restraints during labor. Similarly, 23 state corrections departments and the Federal Bureau of Prisons have policies that allow restraints during labor. Five state corrections departments, including the District of Columbia, prohibit restraints during labor. The remaining states do not have laws or formal policing governing labor practices in prison. Washington State forbids the use of shackling during labor as a matter of departmental policy rather than law. After the story of Merica Erato, who delivered her baby with chains around her ankles in Fond du Lac, Wisconsin in May 2005, was published in a newspaper in January 2006, the state of Wisconsin noted that it would stop the use of inmate restricts during labor, delivery, and recovery (Liptak, 2006). According to one researcher, ". . . the heart of the problem is that the pregnant prisoner finds herself in a condition that cries out for solicitous care, while held in an institution which by nature is rift with possibilities for abuse via the capricious exercise of authority" (McHugh, 1980:238). William F. Schulz, executive director of Amnesty International U.S.A., describes this draconian practice as: "Its almost as stupid as shackling someone in a coma" (Liptak, 2006).

The Impact of Mothers' Incarceration on Others

The impact of separation, which often begins way before women offenders enter a correctional facility, creates a difficult situation for their children not only because of insensitive correctional policy but law enforcement policy as well. For example, the following case is a typical arrest situation in the ghetto and barrio (Rodriguez, 1993): "At the time of her arrest Jane was handcuffed and pushed by officers as her children (including a 3-year-old) watched and cried for their mother. They wanted to come but were not allowed. Instead they were left in the care of a neighbor" (Kiser, 1991:58). Further, when women are incarcerated, their children are not the only innocent victims of separation, other individuals suffer as well (Kiser, 1991). The incarceration of women drastically impacts on the lives of their family, friends, and the community as a whole (Koban, 1983; Henriques, 1996). The author has seen the devastating impact on other individuals, which in turn creates even a bigger emotional impact on the arrestee. For those who have husbands or partners, the situation could be even more critical in that separation could result in a divorce. Only a few state prisons have established overnight family visits for husbands, parents, or other immediate family members (Neto and Bainer, 1983). Thus, the context in which separation takes place and the issues resulting from separation need to be reconsidered by policymakers to create a "smooth" transition and reduce negative consequences.

Thoughts for the Future

Having mothers in prison creates a complex and consequential situation for everyone involved in corrections. Particularly, lack of parental programs, especially programs that are sensitive to cultural, race, and ethnicity issues, creates a significant gap (Browne, 1989). For example, because of limited financial assistance from friends and relatives, visitation is often irregular. However, without constant healthy contact, complete separation may be damaging to the mother-child relationship as well as the child's future growth and development (Baunach, 1985; Deck, 1988). For African American women and Latinas, who makeup the majority of the prison population, the situation can be even more devastating due to factors such as cultural and language barriers for Latinas and poverty for African Americans (Bresler and Lewis, 1983; Langston, 2003). Therefore, it is time that the correctional system seriously considers other options, paying particular attention to gender, culture, race, ethnicity, geography, and economics.

For instance, Australia, Bolivia, Colombia, Denmark, Ecuador, Great Britain, Japan, Mexico, Sweden, Venezuela, and West Germany allow women to keep their babies and preschool children with them in prison. Even though most of these countries restrict the eligible age to infants under three years of age (Boudouris, 1985), the 3-year time period allows some women to be released, enables other mothers to make proper child care arrangements, allows some relatives and/or friends to make plans, evaluate the best possible options, and make decisions regarding the children of the incarcerated mother (Phillips and Bloom, 1998). In the United States, this proposition might appear "illogical." Realistically, though, for some children, prison life is safer than the streets, where children experience violence, poverty, and death everyday (Rodriguez, 1993). In fact, U.S. states that have experimented have not witnessed catastrophic consequences, such as hostage takings. More fundamentally, the notion that "its *their* children" must change.

Privacy in Prison

Over time, the issue of privacy in corrections has changed significantly. Originally, there was little privacy for female offenders in that punishment was public (Foucault, 1995). With the birth of the prison system, though, also came secrecy, which has served as a cover-up for injustices behind bars (Newman, 1995). Later, as a result of reform efforts, the correctional system began to restructure facilities, redefine daily operations, and make efforts to demystify prisons by partially informing and showing the mechanics of the system to the public. The privacy issue, however, was redefined with the advent of technology, particularly the camera, and the arguments of lethal inmates, sick inmates, or suicidal inmates. Consistent with previous research, much of which was done during the 1980s, a recent study reports lack of privacy in female prisons (Kruttschnitt, Gartner, and Miller, 2000).

Solitary Confinement

Solitary confinement was introduced into the prison system in 1829 by the Quakers under that argument that total isolation would led to self-reflection, penitence, and rehabilitation (Foucault, 1995). As one of the most controversial correctional issues, long-term solitary confinement is viewed as one of the most effective mechanisms of social control within the correctional system. Yet, in *Cages of Steel* (1992), control units like solitary confinement are characterized as instruments of manipulation, subornation, domination, and torture. To others, this same mechanism ". . . represents the penultimate synthesis of technology and space in the service of social control and dehumanization. . ." (Shaylor, 1998:387). Ironically, "The cult of silence preserved by the masculinist guard culture protects guards from anything but the lightest disciplinary sanctions" (Shaylor, 1998:391).

The Who and Why of Solitary Confinement

Solitary confinement is primarily intended for inmates who do not abide to institutional rules or who present a threat to the institution. In practice, the majority of inmates who are sent to solitary confinement do not represent a serious threat to the institution. Prisoners are sent to solitary confinement for minor rule infractions and for issues that have little to do with the safety of the prison.

In particular, since a primary historical function of the prison has been to punish females who do not conform to a model of femininity that has been shaped and reshaped as Caucasian, passive, moral, heterosexual, and maternal, solitary confinement has been reserved for those who are viewed as different, outsiders, and nonconformists. A California study, for instance, showed that most of the women in solitary confinement were African American and Mexican (Shaylor, 1998). African American women, Latinas, and Native American women have not fit America's patriarchal notions about femininity because historical race and ethnic prejudice and discrimination have served as barriers to such norms (Aguirre and Turner, 2006; Leonard, Pope, and Feyerherm, 1995). For instance, viewing "white femininity as *the model,*" African American women are perceived as loud and aggressive, Latinas as belligerent, sexually aggressive, or undocumented immigrants unwilling to speak English, and Native American women are perceived as backward, savages, and primitive (Diaz-Cotto, 1996; Olsen, 1995). Besides minority women, others who are placed in solitary confinement are mentally ill women (see Chapters 2 and 6), suicidal inmates, gang members (see Chapter 8), political prisoners (see Chapter 8), lesbians (see Chapter 8), and people with communicable diseases (see Chapters 2 and 6). Sometimes females are sent to solitary confinement for seeking justice. For instance, refusing to have an abortion after being raped by a correctional officer and threatening to retaliate, a woman was sent to a control unit (Shaylor, 1998).

Similarly, in 2002, a mentally ill Wisconsin prisoner was impregnated by a guard, and she was then sent to solitary confinement as punishment for nearly one year (Twohey, 2004). In February 2004, 21-year old Christina Maves was placed in handcuffs and leg irons after resisting to be placed in solitary confinement during an investigation of her relationship with a veteran captain (Twohey, 2004). The ultimate objective in this treatment is to produce "docile bodies," at which point the female prisoner becomes "self-controlled" (Foucault, 1995; Hannah-Moffat, 1995).

Living in Solitary Confinement

For female prisoners, the solitary confinement process is brutal, excessive, and humiliating, especially in comparison to their male counterparts. First, female prisoners are often denied basic necessities, including food and personal hygiene supplies such as toothpaste. Second, every time female prisoners leave their cell to attend court, take a shower, see a legal advisor, they are handcuffed and strip searched (see Chapter 8). As reported by one 21-year-old African American, "they don't do this because of 'safety and security of the institution,' they do it for humiliation. . . . They are just tryin' to break us down" (cited in Shaylor, 1998:391). Third, considering that the medicalization model is regularly used on female prisoners, inmates are given psychotropic medications, but few receive psychiatric treatment (see Chapter 6). Heavily drugged, some women can barely speak or move, some inmates hallucinate, others yell constantly, others engage in crying spells, and still others experience paranoid delusions and hallucinations. Drugged (or not drugged), some females react to their anger and frustrations by harming themselves, including self-mutilation and suicide attempts (see Liebling, 1995). At times, female prisoners are covered in urine and feces. Such acts represent stages of psychological and emotional breakdowns that have been observed in political prisoners (see Chapter 8) and prisoners of war (Frankl, 1992; Wiesel, 1982). In the words of one California female prisoner, "It's like living in a black hole" (cited in Shaylor, 1998:386). Lastly, beside the physical brutality, there is the emotional and psychological destruction of the human body. Correctional officers call the prisoners "dogs, niggers, bitches, whores, and black bitches" (Rafter, 1987; Shaylor, 1998). One California female prisoner reported, "They treat us like animals.

No, you wouldn't treat an animal the way they do us here. I am sure they don't treat their dogs the way they treat us" (Shaylor, 1998:396). Of course, the "subhuman" characterization has a powerful connection to slavery—where slaves were dehumanized so that they could be easily controlled and managed as chattel by slave owners (Messerschmidt, 2007; Williams, 1991; Young and Spencer, 2007).

Implications of Solitary Confinement

Based on previous investigations, it appears that the nature of the process and the length of time in solitary confinement have a negative effect on all prisoners. However, logically, solitary confinement has a more devastating effect on prisoners who suffer from stress or depression (see Chapter 6), inmates who have personally experienced emotional trauma, and mentally ill prisoners, many of whom were sent to solitary confinement because they were acting out as a result of their illness (see Chapters 2 and 6). Consequently, because many female prisoners have experienced some form of physical, emotional, or sexual abuse (see Chapters 2 and 3), solitary confinement, particularly cell extractions (see Chapter 7), for many women is traumatic, often leading some women to re-experience previous traumatic situations. In the words of one inmate, "It is about humiliation and total loss of dignity, and I don't care what they call it. I call it rape" (cited in Shaylor, 1998:392).

The Right to Live

Even though the prison system is designed to punish those who break the laws, all inmates have the right to live, especially since most inmates have entered prison for nonviolent crimes, at times, simply as scapegoats (see Chapter 10). Practically, though, the history of corrections has been brutal, violent, vicious, and inhumane (Davidson, 1974; Fogel, 1979; Foucault, 1995; Goffman, 1961; O'Halloran, 1984). According to criminal justice historian Samuel Walker (1980:244), "the Constitution did not follow the prisoner into prison and, upon conviction, the offender was the 'slave' of the state." In *Ruffin vs. Commonwealth* (1871), the Court ruled that the prisoner was the "slave of the state." In 1951, for instance, 31 inmates in the Louisiana prison at

Angola slashed their Achilles tendons to protest inhumane conditions. In the 1960s, at the peak of the civil rights movement (1955 to 1965), inmates at the Cummins and Tucker prison farms in Arkansas were "subjected to constant 'peril and degradation'; inmates were forced to sell their own blood to obtain food, medical care, and protection from personal attack" (Walker, 1980:244–245). In fact, in the late 1960s, Warden Tom Murton discovered the graves of murdered inmates in Arkansas. However, it was not until the 1970s and 1980s that the courts declared correctional systems, like Arkansas, Alabama, and Texas prison systems had violated constitutional protections of cruel and unusual punishment.

Despite years of reform, the combination of physical brutality, emotional torment, and negligence for human rights still reappears in different forms. Indeed, researchers have documented excessive and arbitrary enforcement of minor regulations by correctional officers and excessive reliance on lockups as punishment. Case in point: "I was locked up for six weeks in a room with nothing to do. [The] only time I could leave was to take a shower. They would bring me my meals. The reason I was locked up was 'cause I was always fighting, fighting for my rights . . . but I am more humble now. . . . I have learned you have no rights in here" (cited in Chesney-Lind and Rodriguez, 1983:61). Of course this is not an isolated case. For example, the Women's High Security Unit at Lexington, Kentucky was closed in 1988 as a result of an international human rights campaign. For years, the prison kept female inmates in isolation in deplorable conditions, staff implemented sleep deprivation practices, conducted unjustified strip searches (see Chapter 7), and denied privacy, allowed correctional officers to watch showers and engage in sexual abuse (Albisa, 1989; Human Rights Watch Project, 1996).

Beyond the fear of physical brutality, female inmates are experiencing anxiety, stress, and depression, which is becoming a "nightmare," particularly for those who cannot afford the medications (see Chapter 6). In the words of one female inmate, "Some days I can feel the depression as a tangible presence in here—in the lethargy of women half my age, in the hours of TV watching, in the lines of women walking down every night to get their 'mental med.'. . . There are days when I don't want to walk out of my cell, to be hit by it, fearful that it will take me under its sway" (Clark, 1995:318). Sometimes, medications in prison are not so much about "helping inmates, but controlling inmates." "When I got sentenced, I completely lost it. I broke down. They sent me to the hospital and put me on thorazine. When I got to Bedford, they kept me on thorazine. I was like a zombie. They wanted to keep me on it, to keep me like that. I told them I wanted to get off of it, that it was destroying me, and they threatened to write me a charge sheet if I stopped taking my medication. So I stopped on my own" (Clark, 1995:319).

As a new form of social control, it has been argued that medication in prison is being utilized to "legally" manipulate, coerce, and punish inmates (Forer, 1982). Yet, parenting, family, and social issues are not being properly understood and addressed to effectively treat other concerns, such as substance abuse (see Chapter 3), which is connected to other critical factors, such as the spread of communicable diseases (see Chapter 6). Consequently, when a conscious inmate sees the conditions in which the inmate population is being forced to *exist*, she develops resentment towards the prison system and society in general. In the words of one California prisoner, ". . . it's like hell . . . it's a nightmare. . . . I would put my life on the line before I would step foot in here again. That's how bitter I have become" (Kruttschnitt, Gartner, and Miller 2000:709).

Taken together, some people characterize women prisons as college campuses, yet "looks are deceiving. The reality is much more subtle, and more frightening than . . . imagined. . . . A prison can effectively strip a resident of her initiative, turn her into an automaton. . ." (Krasno, 1982:18). In a sense, "the brutality that leaves no bruises is often the worst" (Krasno, 1982:18; Foucault, 1995). Former antiwar activist Jane Kennedy reports that prison ". . . negates the dignity of human beings, it cuts out the human core. It eats away at one's self-respect" (DeClue, 1981:33). Reflecting on her prison experience, Kennedy adds, "It's not just the monotony and differences from everyday life, the same three pairs of pants, five tops, two pairs of shoes, and four pairs of socks. The same underwear, with holes that keep growing larger and elastic that keeps getting looser. The dehumanization is the thing. . ." (DeClue, 1981:35; Foucault, 1995). In Kennedy's experience, "Prison . . . was almost like death" (DeClue, 1981:35).

Prison as a Teaching Experience

In the context of the prison population as a whole—which tends to be poor, uneducated, unemployed (see Chapter 2), and plagued with illness (see Chapter 6), addicted to alcohol and drugs (see Chapter 3), and marginalized into some of the worst areas of society (see Chapters 3 and 4)–the prison experience serves as a powerful lesson for some female offenders.

Some inmates, for instance, believe that the prison experience actually serves as a deterrent to future criminal behavior, which in reality has little to do with the weak connection between recidivism and an institution's disciplinary mechanism (Martinson, 1974; McGuire, 1995). Still, we argue that such perception might be of utility to the inmates' development, particularly self-esteem and motivation during and after incarceration (Ramsey, 1980a, 1980b; Sultan, Long, Kiefer, Schrum, Selby, and Calhoun, 1984). To this end, some prisoners do take advantage of the various programs available to them to improve self development, self-esteem, and to better their relationship and ties with their family, friends, and the community. One inmate pointed out, "My connection to my son has been key to my survival; the sense of myself as a mother was key to my sanity" (Clark, 1995:322).

From a survival standpoint, Barbara Own's (1998:40) California (Central California Women's Facility, CCWF) study shows that ". . . for many women, prison is a better and safer place than their disrupted and disruptive lives on the street . . . women within the criminal justice system are also women on the social, racial, and economic margins of conventional society." First, as noted in Chapter 3, life in the streets for female offenders tends to be chaotic and destructive. For example, before being incarcerated, one inmate reported that "I was in a prison within myself. The drugs controlled my life" (Clark, 1995:309). Even worse, drugs tend to correlate with criminal behavior (see Anglin and Hser, 1987; Chapter 4). When discussing what she had to do to survive the streets and support a drug habit, one African American inmate said: "I started using drugs–heroin, cocaine. Not only was I selling my body to support the habit, I was doing robberies, burglaries, whatever I had to do. Within a six-month period, I was back in jail, and it didn't faze me because I was secure there. I had a home, had a roof over my head, had three hot meals. I had clean clothing. I didn't have to sell my body for a chicken dinner" (Arnold, 1990:160). Hence, given the violent and uncertain conditions of the streets, some women adopt and actually benefit from the prison experience. In this regard, a 32-year-old California prisoner who lived in the streets since she was fourteen reported, ". . . after doing so much time, I'm used to it. . . . I don't even think about the streets any more.

It doesn't even bother me being here" (Kruttschnitt, Gartner, and Miller, 2000:698). A Latina prisoner in California reported, "I like it here . . . I've had a good experience here" (Kruttschnitt, Gartner, and Miller, 2000:699).

Isolated and marginalized by mainstream America, it should not come as a surprise that for many women who are in and out of prison frequently that other inmates become their friends, "pseudo-family" (see Chapter 8), as they cope with life in prison (Romenesko and Miller, 1989). To a 62-year-old California prisoner, she would be missing "the security of [prison] . . . and the friendships and camaraderie. . . . Prison is a place, I would say, that if it's used in the right way, if your mind and head is right, then it could help you a whole lot" (Kruttschnitt, Gartner, and Miller, 2000:698). Another inmate, a woman in her mid-40s serving time in a California prison, said: "I've lost years of my life with other people [on the outside], but I've also made compensations. I've made friends here, friends that I will have for the rest of my life. I mean, we've been on hell and back" (Kruttschnitt, Gartner, and Miller 2000:705). To some inmates, the prison experience seems to have a more profound impact. One inmate reported, "I was able to retrieve some of what I had lost when I entered prison: my humanity" (Clark, 1995:325). Referring to prison as "the concrete womb," Kathryn Burkhart (1973:59) states that "Jail has just become a bigger part of the world—an extension of the life and the 'family'; a reinforcement of *natural* self-destruction learned during formative childhood years from models who never asked *why*? either. Abuse for many people is a way of life. It's the world."

In sum, for many female inmates, prison serves as a safe place, away from the various problems, issues, and pressures women face on the streets from the time they are born, such as weapons and violence, drugs, inadequate housing, poverty, and fear. In prison some inmates receive care, attention, resources, the social bond that they never received on the streets. In combination, it is probable that these elements give women hope during their time in prison and after release (see Chapter 9). Unfortunately, by nature we tend to focus on the "bad," giving little, if any, recognition to the good. Thus, we argue that the "positive aspects" need to be studied with care and objectivity. If certain elements of the prison system have changed for the better, it is likely that they can be improved even more, and ultimately, expanded to create a more safe, humane, just, and beneficial prison experience.

THE WISCONSIN EXPERIENCE

As in the previous three chapters, this section reports findings from 456 female prisoners in Wisconsin. Trying to help us understand the female prison experience as finely as possible, a series of specific questions were asked regarding their incarceration. In particular, in addition to understanding the everyday events and activities behind bars, one must be sensitive to the inmates' perceptions and emotions.

The Nature of the Correctional System

Prior Incarceration(s)

For the purpose of comparison and to better understand their current incarceration, inmates were inquired about prior institutionalizations. Consistent with prior investigations (see Chapter 4), Table 9 shows that over half (255 or 55.9%) of the inmates had been incarcerated in another prison, indicating that a high percentage of women have been in and out of prison. For those who had been incarcerated in another prison, their average stay was 8.7 months, ranging from .75 months to 96 months. Further, given the importance of visitation and difficulties of traveling, 93 (20.4%) inmates were previously incarcerated within 100 miles from their hometown, but 72 (15.5%) women were incarcerated more than 100 miles away from their hometown and 58 (12.7%) inmates had been incarcerated outside the state of Wisconsin.

Considering that the American correctional model tends to focus on isolation, especially in comparison to some other countries, we asked inmates about their feelings towards their confinement, which are significant not only in the rehabilitation process (Feinman, 1983), but also how they serve their sentence. Of those who had been incarcerated in another prison, 125 women reported that the facility housed only women, while 127 inmates said that the facility housed both women and men. In facilities housing both men and women, most (153) inmates reported that there was no interaction between female prisoners and male prisoners, but 31 women reported that there was some form of interaction, such as visitation, meals, or work. In regards to their feelings about being institutionalized in a facility that housed both men and women, 10 inmates reported that they did not like their experience, but the majority either liked it (29) or were not bothered (93) by the interaction.

Table 9
ENTERING WISCONSIN'S CORRECTIONAL INSTITUTIONS (N=456)

	Mean	*Range*	*Frequency*	*Percent*
Incarcerated in another prison				
Yes			255	55.9
No			197	43.2
Length of time in other facility	8.7	.75 to 96 (months)		
Location of other facility				
Within 100 miles from hometown			93	20.4
More than 100 miles from hometown			72	15.5
Outside the state of Wisconsin			58	12.7
Population of other facility				
Housed only women			125	27.4
Both women and men			127	27.9
Interaction in facility housing men and women				
Yes			31	6.8
No			153	33.6
Conditions for interaction				
Visitation			11	2.4
Meals			7	1.5
Work			7	1.5
Other reasons			13	2.9
Feelings about facility that housed both males and females				
It does not bother me			93	20.4
I do not like it			10	2.2
I like it			29	6.4
I don't know			9	2.0
Feelings about facility that houses only women				
It did not bother me			239	52.4
I did not like it			140	30.7
I liked it			29	6.4
I don't know			38	8.3
Comparison of other prison(s) with current facility				
About the same			39	8.6

Continued on next page

Table 9 (cont.)

	Mean	Range	Frequency	Percent
A little better			54	11.8
Much better			96	21.1
A little worse			19	4.2
Much worse			43	9.4
Don't know			7	1.5
Required to wake up in the morning				
Yes			356	78.1
No			89	19.5
Required to bed at a certain time				
Yes			229	50.2
No			210	46.1

Current Incarceration

Because of claims of overcrowded prisons (see Chapter 2), we inquired about the number of women that were assigned to a room/cell and the number of beds in a room/cell. Because of one facility with two pods of 80 inmates each, where inmates are housed in a large dormitory setting, the range and the mean are skewed when all inmates are included. However, not including these units, one to four women were often housed in a single room/cell. All women, however, (including those in the pods) reported having their own beds. As policymakers push for harsher laws that increase the number of women in prison, overcrowding is an issue that must be avoided in that it sets the foundation for other issues, like illness (see Chapter 6).

Additionally, considering the significance of "time" in a strict disciplinary prison regime (see Foucault, 1995), inmates were asked about wake up and bed times. As eloquently illustrated by Michel Foucault (1995), the concept of time is focal to the prison system. For example, a minor infraction can result in loss of "privileges" and even solitary confinement (see Chapter 5). The majority (356 or 78.1%) of inmates reported being required to wake up at a certain time in the morning, and 89 (19.5%) women reported otherwise. As far as being required to be in bed at a certain time, about half (229 or 50.2%) said yes and 210 (46.1%) inmates said no, suggesting some flexibility in the prison regime.

Last, in regards to their feelings about being "currently" incarcerated in a facility that houses only women, 29 inmates preferred these arrangements, but the majority reported not liking it (140) or not being bothered (239). Because not all facilities are the "same," and because of actual requests by inmates (or their attorneys) to be imprisoned in a particular facility, women were asked to compare other prison(s) where they had served time prior to this imprisonment. Thirty-nine inmates characterized facilities about the same. However, substantially more (150) inmates reported that their previous prison(s) were "better" than their current facility, with only 62 inmates characterizing their current prison as a "better facility."

In sum, policymakers must not only analyze the operations of a particular facility, but also variation among facilities as well as attitudes and perceptions of the inmate population. For instance, if inmates are reporting that their current prison is worse than the one they experienced previously, this indicates a possible problem in correctional reform. Of course, such views are partially shaped by the simple fact that they are no longer serving time in their previous prison, and they wish to see improvements in their current facility, even if the facility is not in actuality worse. Still, if claims of variation are legitimate, it is possible that prison conditions can be improved to ensure uniformity in the correctional system.

Solitary Confinement

Since the role of solitary confinement is to instill fear, control troublesome inmates, and punish those who do not abide by correctional rules and regulations, inmates were asked a series of questions regarding solitary confinement in Wisconsin. First, inmates were asked if they knew whether the facility had solitary confinement. Interestingly, most (417 or 91.4%) inmates reported knowing that the facility had solitary confinement cells, and only 34 (7.4%) inmates reported not knowing. Of the 456 respondents, 195 reported having spent time in solitary confinement in the facility where they were currently incarcerated. The number of times placed in solitary confinement ranged from none to 40 occasions, with a mean of 1.5 times for the total sample. The number of hours spent in solitary confinement was varied, ranging from 0 to 480 hours, with a mean of 133.1 hours for the total sample of inmates. Inmates reported the following infractions/violations resulting in solitary confinement: fighting (23), unwilling to obey orders (23), drug passion or use (3), making too much noise (7), other unspecified reasons (76), and multiple reasons (53). Given the psychological and physical brutality of solitary confinement, inmates were also asked if the experience had affected them in any way. Thirty inmates reported not being affected by the experience. However, 161 inmates reported being affected by solitary confinement, with 62 experiencing an emotional impact, three having a physical impact, and ninety-six women experiencing both a physical and emotional impact.

Table 10
SOLITARY CONFINEMENT IN WISCONSIN'S CORRECTIONAL
INSTITUTIONS (N=456)

	Mean	Range	Frequency	Percent
Solitary confinement in facility				
Yes			417	91.4
Don't know			34	7.4
Number of times in solitary confinement	1.5	0 to 40		
Total time spent in solitary confinement	133.1	0 to 480 (hours)		
Reasons for solitary confinement				
Fighting			23	5.0
Unwilling to obey orders			23	5.0
Drugs			3	0.7
Making too much noise			7	1.5
Other reasons			76	16.7
Multiple reasons			53	11.6
Impact of solitary confinement				
No affect whatsoever			30	6.6
Yes, emotional			62	13.6
Yes, physical			3	0.7
Yes, both emotional and physical			96	21.1

In sum, given the historical brutality and negative psychological consequences of solitary confinement (see Churchill and Vander Wall, 1992; Walker, 1980), policymakers need to carefully analyze the "reasons" for solitary confinement. Solitary confinement may be overused to control a troublesome, yet not necessarily violent population. Indeed, a close examination of costs and benefits of solitary confinement might reveal that the consequences outweigh the benefits in some cases. To this end, solitary confinement must be analyzed within the context of the prison industry (see Chapter 10), the political economy of the prison boom (sees Chapter 2 and 8). Before resorting to solitary confinement, correctional staff should explore other options, like placing the inmate in a single cell, or losing privileges. Above all, solitary confinement should be reserved for those who in actuality threaten the safety and operation of the institution.

Items in Prison

One issue that has received great attention, particularly by the media, is the notion that prisoners have access to unlimited possessions. Items in prison, though, are integral not only to the everyday functions of the prison system but motivations, attitudes, perceptions, and behaviors–governing how women serve their time in prison (Schupak, 1986; Sultan, Long, Kiefer, Schrum, Selby, and Calhoun, 1984). As shown in Table 11, items were viewed as valuable by most of the 456 female prisoners who participated in the study.

Prisoners were asked how satisfied they were with items such as sheets, blankets, pillows, and clothes that Wisconsin provides. Of those who responded, 115 (25.2%) reported being satisfied, but most (312 or 68.4%) inmates were dissatisfied. The majority (412 or 90.4%) of the women reported that more items should be allowed in prison. Interestingly, almost all (245 or 93.2%) of the inmates reported being allowed to buy items from the commissary store. Yet, 132 (28.9%) women reported that they seldom bought items, and 288 (63.2%) women reported buying items often. Surprisingly, 276 (60.5%) female prisoners reported not being allowed to receive packages from friends or relatives. Considering the significance of small gifts, the fact that most women have children, and the limited items allowed in prison, only 170 (37.3%) women reported being allowed to receive items. Inmates were asked how they felt about not being able to receive packages. Of those responding, 16 claimed not to be bothered, 64 reported being sad, 134 were mad or angry, and 52 inmates reported experiencing multiple feelings.

Table 11
ITEMS IN WISCONSIN'S CORRECTIONAL INSTITUTIONS (N=456)

	Frequency	*Percent*
Satisfaction with state items		
Very satisfied	22	4.8
Somewhat satisfied	93	20.4
Not sure	19	4.2
Somewhat dissatisfied	135	29.6
Very dissatisfied	177	38.8
Allowing more items in facility		
Yes	412	90.4
No	27	5.9
Being allowed to buy items from store		
Yes	425	93.2
No	10	2.2
There is no store	11	2.4
Buying items from store		
Often	288	63.2
Seldom	132	28.9
Never	6	1.3
Being allowed to receive packages		
Yes	170	37.3
No	276	60.5
Feelings about not receiving packages		
Does not bother me	16	3.5
Sad	64	14.0
Mad	26	5.7
Angry	108	23.7
Other feelings	14	3.1
Multiple feelings	52	11.4

In the context of punishment, limiting some items seems logical. However, in the context of prison management, rehabilitation, and justice, personal possessions play a critical role in that "minor" things alter views, emotions, attitudes, and behaviors of most prisoners. For instance, minor privileges, such as having access to a pencil and paper, which can be difficult to obtain are extremely significant to a mother who is trying to write her children a letter, or simply express her emotions. Therefore, we argue that policymakers need to balance the benefits and consequences of limiting possessions in prison vis-à-vis correctional goals, such as rehabilitation and punishment.

Prison Dining

Another area that has received great controversy is dining in prison, as the public often believes that inmates not only eat three hot meals a day, but that they eat quality food. Since meals tend to be a sensitive issue due to cultural, racial, and ethnic diversity in prison, female prisoners were asked a series of question regarding meals in the Wisconsin prison system.

As shown in Table 12, of those responding, 263 (57.7%) women reported eating three meals per day on average, but 135 (29.6%) reported eating two meals per day and 40 (8.8%) reported eating only one meal per day on average. In particular, almost half (220 or 48.2%) of the participants reported not eating breakfast, considered by some physicians as the most important meal, 71 (15.6%) reported missing lunch, and 88 (19.3%) inmates did not eat dinner. Reasons for missing meals include: health problems (10), poor food quality (143), to stay thin (30), not enough time (15), security (1), multiple reasons (137), and other reasons (76). Last, while the majority (416 or 91.2%) of women reported eating meals in the main dining room, 32 women reported not eating their meals in the main dining room for various reasons, such as security (6), disciplinary problems (6), dislike for other inmates (3), dislike by other inmates (1), or other unspecified reasons (24).

Table 12
DINING IN WISCONSIN'S CORRECTIONAL INSTITUTIONS (N=456)

	Frequency	*Percent*
Meals per day		
One	40	8.8
Two	135	29.6
Three	263	57.7
Four or more	4	0.9
Eating breakfast		
Yes	220	48.2
No	213	46.7
Eating lunch		
Yes	365	80.0
No	711	5.6
Eating dinner		
Yes	339	74.3
No	88	19.3

Continued on next page

Table 12 (cont.)

	Frequency	Percent
Reasons for missing meals		
Health problems	10	2.2
Poor food quality	143	31.4
To stay thin	30	6.6
Not enough time	15	3.3
Security	1	0.2
Other reasons	76	16.7
Multiple reasons	137	30.0
Eating meals in main dining room		
Yes	416	91.2
No	32	7.0
Reasons for not eating in mean dining room		
Security	6	1.3
Disciplinary problems	6	1.3
Do not like other inmates	3	0.7
Disliked by other inmates	1	0.2
Other reasons	24	5.3

The reported findings indicate that dining in prison barely meets minimal standards: the nutritional quality is low and the quantity is small. Considering the high cost of incarceration (see Chapter 2), feeding women just enough to stay alive might seem logical, especially for those who advocate severe punishment. However, a poor diet leads to more severe problems, health issues, which are more expensive than food (see Chapters 2 and 6).

Religion in Prison

Historically a controversial issue, religious practice in prison has received great criticism (normally under operational, safety, or constitutional demands) as the prison population has become more diverse in the last few decades (see Chapter 2). In order to better understand this issue the prisoners were asked a series of questions regarding religion in Wisconsin prisons.

Table 13
RELIGIOUS PRACTICES IN WISCONSIN'S CORRECTIONAL
INSTITUTIONS (N=456)

	Frequency	Percent
Religious affiliation		
Yes	399	87.5
No	48	10.5
Name of religion		
Catholic	75	16.4
Baptist	130	28.5
Protestant	114	25.0
Other religion	83	18.2
Allowed to practice religion in prison		
Yes	368	80.7
No	45	9.9
Practicing religion regularly		
Yes	246	53.9
No	155	34.0
Feelings for not being able to practice religion		
It does not bother me	27	5.9
Sad	37	8.1
Mad	14	3.1
Angry	59	12.9
Other feelings	4	0.9
Multiple feelings	29	6.4

The findings in Table 13 indicate that religion is indeed fundamental to the majority of female prisoners in Wisconsin, and probably elsewhere as well. That is, the majority (399 or 87.5%) of women reported having a religious affiliation: Catholic (75), Baptist (130), Protestant (114), or some other religion (83). Of those with a religious affiliation, the majority (368 or 80.7%) reported being allowed to practice their beliefs while incarcerated, but 45 inmates reported that their practices were denied. Slightly over half (246 or 53.9%) of the inmates reported practicing their religion regularly while in prison. Last, a significant number of inmates reported how they feel for not being allowed to practice their religion, or how they would feel if they were not allowed to practice their religion if incarcerated: not bothered (27), sad (37), mad (14), angry (59), other unspecified feelings (4), and multiple feelings (29).

Considering the significance and implications of religion, religious practice in prison must be analyzed with caution and sensitivity to reduce possible harmful ramifications, while preserving institutional safety. Particularly, as the two most reported feelings, anger and sadness could lead to negative consequences. For example, sadness could lead to stress, depression, and ultimately suicide, the eighth cause of death in the United States (see Murray and Lopez, 1997; World Health Organization, 2006). Though, the suicide rate in jails dropped from 129 per 100,000 inmates in 1983 to 47 per 100,000 in 2002. Suicide had been the leading cause of deaths in jail in 1983, but the death rate for illnesses and natural causes was higher in 2002 (69 per 100,000). Suicides in state prisons, which have been much lower than in jails, also dropped from 34 per 100,000 to 14 per 100,000 state prisoners in 2002. Still, in 2002, the rate of suicide in the resident population (11 per 100,000) was lower than in state prisons (14 per 100,000) and lower than in jails (47 per 100,000 inmates). Indeed, suicides accounted for 314 deaths in jails and 168 deaths in prisons (Mumola, 2005). Anger could lead to hostility, disturbance, riots, and homicides (see Mumola, 2005). Lastly, as the Latina (particularly Mexican and Puerto Rican), Native American, and Hmong populations increase in Wisconsin, religion will become a more important concern.

Employment in Prison

Dating back to the beginning of the prison system, the issue of inmate employment has been for political, economic, brutality, legal, or constitutional challenges by advocates or opponents of prison industries (Arnold, 1990; Hunter, 1986; Walker, 1980). In the last few years, though, the "nature and utility" of employment is being redefined once again due to various political, economic, and social changes-this time, taking a different approach. For example, society expects prisoners to be employed by the prison system to reduce cost and so that they learn marketable job skills to avoid further recidivism and dependency. Therefore, participating female inmates were asked a series of questions regarding employment in Wisconsin prisons, which are reported in Table 14.

Table 14
EMPLOYMENT IN WISCONSIN'S CORRECTIONAL INSTITUTIONS (N=456)

	Yes	*No*
Employed in facility	254 (55.7)	187 (41.0)
Payment for employment	197 (43.2)	83 (18.2)
Job satisfaction	154 (33.8)	109 (23.9)
Reduction of sentence for job	10 (2.2)	319 (70.0)
Doing prison job upon release*	71 (15.6)	146 (32.0)

* Don't know: 47 (10.3%)

Of the 456 respondents, slightly over half (254 or 55.7%) reported being employed while incarcerated, and 187 (41.0%) reported having no job in prison. Of those who had a job, 197 (43.2%) women received payment, and 83 (18.2%) reported not being paid for their job. Also, considering the influence of attitudes on motivation and productivity, inmates were inquired about job satisfaction. While 154 (33.8%) women reported being satisfied with their job, 109 (23.9%) inmates reported not being satisfied with their prison job. Only ten women reported having their sentence reduced for having a job. Last, women were asked if their current job was a kind of job that they would like to do upon release. As expected, only 71 women were willing to pursue a similar job once released from prison.

Because incentives are minimal and adequate employment opportunities are low, the issue of employment in prison must receive serious consideration. Specifically, modifications in existing laws, like "truth in sentencing," have reduced the number of incentives, such as early release for "good time," credits for inmates. And, due to technological advances, the majority of prison jobs are of little utility for inmates upon release. Therefore, policymakers and correctional administrators must ensure that there is ample opportunity for inmates who wish to work, while avoiding exploitation (see Chapter 10). Further, the correctional system must provide incentives to increase motivation and productivity. Finally, future employment in prison must be analyzed within the context of three critical factors: (1) the difficulty of obtaining a decent job upon release; (2) the high cost of incarceration and lack of alternatives (see Chapter 2), and (3) the political economy of the prison system (see Chapters 8 and 10).

Educational and Vocational Training in Prison

More than employment, educational and vocational training in prison is not only important to the goals of the American correctional system, but, more than ever, the prison population upon release as well as society in general. As suggested by some investigators, we need to realistically evaluate the nature of education and expectations of the educational opportunities in prison. Table 15 contains the results for the 456 Wisconsin prisoners.

Table 15
SCHOOL IN WISCONSIN'S CORRECTIONAL INSTITUTIONS (N=456)

	Yes	*No*
Receiving vocational training	201 (44.1)	246 (53.9)
Sentence reduction due to vocational training	5 (1.1)	182 (39.9)
Utility of vocational training upon release*	121 (26.5)	22 (4.8)
Going to school in prison	202 (44.3)	248 (54.4)
Sentence reduction due to school	7 (1.5)	170 (37.3)
Working on a degree	160 (35.1)	38 (8.3)
	Frequency	*Percent*
Type of degree		
GED	48	10.5
High school diploma	61	13.4
College degree	43	9.4
Other degree	37	8.1

* Don't know: 42 (9.2%)

Of those who responded, over half (246 or 53.9%) reported not receiving vocational training while incarcerated, and 201 (44.1%) women reported receiving some type of training in prison. Consistent with other findings, only five inmates reported a "sentence reduction" due to their vocational training. However, 121 women reported that their vocational training would be of utility in obtaining a job upon release from prison. As for education, 202 (44.3%) women reported going to school (i.e., attending classes) while incarcerated, and 248 (54.4%) reported not going to school. Of those who reported going to school, 160 females claimed to be working on a degree: GED (48), high school diploma (61), college (43), and other type of degree/certificate (37). Similar to employment and vocational training, very few (seven) women reported having their sentence reduced because of their participation in prison education.

The findings show that a significant number of women in prison are receiving some type of vocational training or a formal school education. Realistically, though, we need to be sensitive to both the nature of schooling in prison and correctional expectations. Why? Because the educational factor in and of itself is central to the survival or disappearance of the prison system (see Chapter 10 and Epilogue). Currently, we are in a time when most skilled jobs require formal education, some of them no less than a bachelor's degree. In states like California, the state government is spending more money on corrections than education, creating a *vicious cycle and an inverse effect*. That is, if people are not getting the best education in the "free world," it becomes difficult to compete in a competitive job market, increasing the possibility of ending up in prison. As noted earlier, many of these women are incarcerated for "crimes of poverty." Once in prison, one is less likely to receive a quality education, further reducing their chances of employment and survival once released. If the state is not providing a quality education to its "law-abiding citizens," certainly it is not to its "bad citizens." And indeed, once released, the uneducated and unskilled prisoner is confronted with the forces of poverty, a prison record, the stigma of being a felon, and a judgmental and unforgiving society (see Chapter 10). Shortly after, many women end up in prison again—and the cycle begins anew.

Recreation in Prison

Recreation in prison is surrounded by two critical notions (Williams, 1981). First, there is the notion that prisons are intended to punished and not for recreation and entertainment. Second, there is the notion that prisons are already too costly to be adding recreational equipment. Thus, inmates were asked about their involvement in such activities while incarcerated in Wisconsin.

Table 16
RECREATION IN WISCONSIN'S CORRECTIONAL INSTITUTIONS (N=456)

	Yes	No
Opportunity to participate in sports	209 (45.8)	239 (52.4)
Sports participation1	26 (27.6)	114 (25.0)
Opportunity to enjoy hobbies	252 (55.3)	194 (42.5)
Private time	163 (35.7)	275 (60.3)

As shown in Table 16, of the 456 participating female prisoners, less than half (209 or 45.8%) reported having the opportunity to participate in recreational activities, like sports, in prison. Yet, only 126 reported actually participating in sports. Similarly, slightly over half (252 or 55.3) of the inmates reported having the opportunity to enjoy their own hobbies while incarcerated. Last, slightly over one-third (163 or 35.7%) of the women reported having private time for themselves.

Arguably, theory and reality often clash. Notably, recreation in prison is significant because it promotes the constructive use of idle time. Further, as other issues, recreation in prison is not only significant in the context of how women do their time, but the organization and management of the facility as well. As overcrowding increase, opportunities in recreation decrease.

CONCLUSION

Criminal justice historian Samuel Walker (1980) documents that there has never been a "golden age" in the history of the American criminal justice system. More critically, David Fogel's *We are the Living Proof* (1979:265) characterizes the American correctional system as having a "150-year history of failure." Logically, as we entered the twenty-first century, we would expect to find a "rehabilitated prison population" and a "rehabilitated prison system." Consistent with previous studies, however, the twenty-first century Wisconsin prison experience indicates that significant gaps remain to be bridged in female prisons. Further, the findings reported by Wisconsin female prisoners indicate that minor issues such as possession or opportunities for recreation can also be extremely demoralizing and disheartening, impacting how women do their time in prison as well as the operation and management of the facility. Thus, as the prison population gets larger and more diverse, significant improvements must be made to avoid the continuation of a vicious cycle of imprisonment (Burden, 1983).

Of course, the findings from the Wisconsin prison experience suggest that important strides have been accomplished. And indeed, effective ideas, like nursery programs, need to be retained, expanded, and improved. However, the design and operation of women's prisons needs to be seriously considered in the future to facilitate other needed improvements (Maxey, 1986; Rock, 1996). Further, the correctional system must implement programs that will stop the cycle of imprisonment. In particular, the prison system must provide gender-specific and intense treatment to reduce recidivism and drug use (Peugh and Belenko, 1999). Otherwise, the majority of female inmates will serve their time only to be released to resume their lives of addiction and crime and eventually a return to prison, influencing future generations of drugs, addiction, and crime (see Chapters 9, 10, and Epilogue). To this end, policymakers must continue questioning inmates' capacity and willingness to reform, but also the effectiveness of correctional policies, the social and economic environment women face upon release, and societal reactions to a marginalized population. Finally, *all* correctional changes need to correspond with social, technological, political, and economic changes in society at large to avoid total detachment of these two populations.

Chapter 6

THE MANY FACES OF WOMEN'S HEALTH

The first part of this chapter provides a discussion of both traditional and contemporary health issues (both physical and mental) facing female prisoners in U.S. correctional facilities, who make up about 6 percent of the adult prison population. The central objective is to determine if correctional facilities are operating in accordance with 8th Amendment Constitutional rights, which mandate that correctional facilities provide medical care to all inmates.[13] In particular, institutional change has been left to the legislature and executive branches, and the courts intervene only if constitutional rights are being violated.[14] The second part of this chapter will include the findings related to our inquiry about communicable diseases, cancer, depression, medication, pregnancy, and various other medical issues facing women prisoners in Wisconsin.

THE GLOBAL NATURE OF WOMEN'S HEALTH

A sound examination of the nature of health care in female prisons requires an exploration of three intertwining factors. First, health care needs to be analyzed as a whole, not restricting the analyses to a particular time frame, geographical area, specific illness, or ethnic/racial group to avoid misunderstanding. For instance, even though heart problems were portrayed as a "disease of middle-aged men," recent studies indicate that heart attacks are the number-one cause of death for women. And indeed, the five leading causes of death among women in the United States are heart problems, cancer, stroke, accidents, and severe obstructive lung problems. More recently, other deathly ills are spreading widely. For instance, women, particularly African Americans and Latinas, constitute the fastest growing group of people with AIDS in the United States (Langston, 2003). Further, twice as many women as men are diagnosed with diabetes, a disease affecting millions of Americans, particularly minority women. Other illnesses, while less deadly, not only impact women's health but their ability to work. For example, arthritis, the most common chronic illness among older women, causes pain, restricted activity, and disability. According to a recent report by the Bureau of Justice Statistics, between 2001 and 2004, there were 12,129 deaths in state prisons, to include 11,645 men, 482 women, 5,898 Caucasians, 4,714 African Americans, and 1,285 Latinas/os. Ten of the leading causes of state prisoner deaths between 2001 and 2004 include: heart diseases (27.3%), cancer (23.3%), liver diseases (10.1%), AIDS (7.2%), suicide (6.1%), respiratory diseases (4.1%), cerebrovascular diseases (3.2%), septicemia (2.2%), influenza/pneumonia (1.9%), digestive diseases (1.7%), kidney diseases (1.6%), and homicide (1.6%). Almost nine in ten (89%) of such deaths in state prisons from 2001 to 2004 were attributed to medical conditions, with heart diseases and cancer causing half of the deaths. When combined with liver diseases and AIDS, two-thirds of all inmate deaths in prison were caused by these four medical conditions (Mumola, 2007).

Second, for female offenders, the situation is even more complicated in that most women offenders have experienced various social, political, and economic difficulties throughout their entire lives. As noted in Chapters 2, 3, and 4, the typical female offender has a long history of drug, alcohol, physical, emotional, and sexual abuse. These factors, particularly substance abuse, either directly or indirectly, contribute to delinquency and crime (Blount, Danner, Vega, and Silverman, 1991), further exacerbating the chaotic environment in which they live. Given the social conditions in which they live, women offenders tend not to have regular medical examinations: they do not have medical insurance, ignorance about their own health issues, cultural difference, lack of minority physicians (particularly female doctors) in some areas, and fear (McDonald, 1995). Consequently, besides alcohol and drug abuse (see Chapter 3), female offenders suffer from a wide range of health issues–such as sexually transmitted diseases, AIDS, pregnancy-related and gynecological problems, obesity, hypertension, diabetes, epilepsy, respiratory illnesses, reproductive disorders, pancreatitis, dental problems, neurological disorders, and mental illness before they even enter a correctional facility (James and Glaze, 2006; Resnick and Shaw, 1980; Young, 1999). Two-thirds of illness-related deaths in prison from 2001 to 2004 resulted from pre-existing conditions, including 94 percent of AIDS-related deaths (Mumola, 2007). Upon entering prison, some of these health issues, like neurological disorders, which are often caused by alcohol addiction, head injury or trauma, and communicable diseases, like hepatitis, tuberculosis, pneumonia, and influenza, present a major challenge to correctional systems (Geballe and Stone, 1988; Waring and Smith, 1991).

Third, once in prison, female inmates with health issues become an absolute dilemma in that there is no clear mechanism for dealing with the situation. To begin with, in addition to being poor, uneducated, drug or alcohol addicted, and in poor health, female prisoners have a long history of neglect, abuse, incest, and violence (Gilfus, 1992; James and Glaze, 2006). Arguably, this historical characterization has manifested itself into a "silent voice" in that health care for female prisoners has traditionally received limited attention in academic research, public discussions, and correctional policies (Newton, 1980; Ingram-Fogel, 1991; Schupak, 1986). In fact, until recently, little attention was given to health problems and health care needs of incarcerated women. Still, what is available, including staff, to female prisoners is sometimes limited vis-à-vis their male counterparts (Fearn and Parker, 2005; Ingram-Fogel, 1991). In part, this medical gap is attributed to an imbalance in correctional policies and services. That is, at the same time that some correctional systems are making significant improvements in certain areas, they are leaving some significant areas virtually unattended. For example, at the same time that states like Wisconsin are bringing back inmates housed out-of-state to make family contact more accessible, additional space is not being made and thus leading to more severe problems.[15] In particular, crowded conditions in Wisconsin and elsewhere have become a breeding ground for illness, like drug-resistant and highly contagious tuberculosis and AIDS.[16] Further, without proper living conditions, life-threatening infections like pneumocystis pneumonia are likely to increase.

In sum, to develop an effective women's health care model in prison, researchers and policymakers must analyze the medical history of inmates by the totality of events. Otherwise, "medical gaps" are created, often resulting in more severe problems. In particular, in addition to gender difference, investigators and policymakers need to be sensitive to cultural differences in the delivery of medical services. Lastly, without proper health care, rehabilitation will have a minimal impact (Feinman, 1983).

Medical Services

A close analysis of medical services in prison reveals that there are three significant gaps: the gender gap, the race/ethnicity gap, and the need gap. These gaps are unlikely to disappear without the intervention of serious, honest, and sound reform efforts. In fact, if not properly addressed, it is very possible that these gaps will worsen the health care situation in the American correctional system and might lead to other problems.

The Gender Gap

For several years, feminist scholars (Chesney-Lind and Pasko, 2004; Gelsthorpe and Morris, 1990), have tried to document the gender gap in the American society, including the lives of people in prison. Still, after more than 40 years of continuous efforts, the "gender gap" not only remains to be bridged, but it is possible that it will get even wider due to a combination of ever changing factors (see below, Chapters 7 and 8).

First, even though the female prison population is much smaller than the male prison population, female prisons provide fewer services as a whole, including medical care. Second, female prisons sometimes lack specific medical services, especially since, compared with male prisoners, female prisoners have a higher incidence of drug abuse, asthma, diabetes, and heart-related problems, and women also have gynecological needs (Bershad, 1985; Yang, 1990). Further, drug addiction, mental illness, HIV/AIDS, and tuberculosis, affect female prisoners more than they impact male inmates. For instance, government statistics show that a higher percentage of female than male state prison inmates (2.9% versus 1.9%) test positive for HIV. Statistics also show that nearly 24 percent of females in state prisons are considered mentally ill, and 60 percent use drugs during the month before entering prison (Bureau of Justice Statistics, 1999b, 2004c). Additionally, a higher number of female than male inmates report medical problems since their admission to prison (Bureau of Justice Statistics, 2001b, 2001c). Third, for women who are pregnant (see Chapter 5), diet and prenatal care is particularly important for the development of the child and the health of the mother. Likewise, some inmates have dietary concerns because of their chronic health problems. Yet, specific dietary needs are not always properly addressed. For example, people with diabetes are provided only standard prison food, which is often high in fat, sugar and carbohydrates (Forer, 1982; Wooldredge and Masters, 1993).

The Race/Ethnicity Gap

Traditionally, the medical approach in prison has been more global than specific in scope–with little attention to the influence of historical and environmental factors, race, ethnicity, or culture. When race is considered, it usually takes a dichotomous approach–i.e., African American versus Caucasian, excluding other racial and ethnic groups or lumping them together–creating a "race/ethnicity gap" in medical research and service delivery in prison.

First, in regards to actual service, studies show that African American prisoners with health issues, like heart problems, were less likely to receive immediate treatment than their Caucasian counterparts (Gamble, 1997). Second, difference in perception of medical care plays a role as to who obtain prisons' medical services. One study shows, for example, that minority prisoners (i.e., African American, Latinas, Native Americans, and Alaskan Natives), who view the quality of medical care less favorably than Caucasian women, received fewer health services overall (Young, 1999). Third, service delivery is also governed by ethnic and racial barriers. African America women, who make up most of the prison population, report greater health care dissatisfaction, and Latinas, especially if they are undocumented, continue to confront barriers, like longer waiting periods and language, to access medical care (Johansen, 2005; Williams and Torrens, 2001). Native American prisoners often report that prison officials do not understand their culture (Young, 1999).

The Need Gap

Even though there are numerous barriers influencing the development and implementation of a sound health care system in prison, no single barrier seems to be more challenging to advocates of health care reform than claims of limited resources. Realistically, though, prison officials, like the U.S. government, normally find resources for issues they deem "important" (Urbina, 2003b). And indeed, the healthcare system itself is a prime example of a "double standard" that the correctional system customarily operates under.

At the same time that policymakers are citing limited or no financial resources for medical service in prison, they are managing to finance medications which are being used as a social control mechanism. Hence, some of the medication that is being used in prison is not to prevent or alleviate health issues, but to prevent and control disturbance and resistance. In fact, as a form of social control, medication in prison has taken a life of its own in that it is being widely prescribed by physicians. According to one researcher, ". . . as a substitute for physical restraint . . . the administration of drugs in prisons in widespread, pervasive" (Forer, 1982:563), even though unneeded medications have deleterious side effects. Interestingly, few claims are being made against the "prevalence of medication as a social control mechanism."

In sum, understanding these gaps and their implications is vital for creating a more inclusive health care model in the American correctional system. First, as the rates of women in prison significantly increase (see Chapters 1 and 2), investigators and policymakers must pay particular attention to the dynamics of the gender gap, especially since women offenders are often viewed as violent criminals (see Chapter 4). Globally speaking, eliminating the gender gap will not solve the problem because health care in male prisons continues to lag behind the actual need, and women tend to suffer from additional and more chronic health issues. Further, when the medication that is being used as a social control mechanism is taken out of the "medical equation," the amount of medication that is being used to actually alleviate health issues is significantly reduced. Second, as the prison population becomes more racially and ethnically diverse (see Chapter 2), investigators and policymakers must be sensitive to race, ethnicity, and cultural factors that result in variation in health care delivery and use.

Third, the double standard in health care delivery must be carefully explored and scrutinized so that the general public has a better understanding of the functionality of a system that is being paid for by their tax dollars. Last, female offenders tend to lack knowledge about their own health problems (Epp, 1996). However, a functional health care system requires that inmates be educated about their own health problems so that they can assist in the amount and quality of medical service delivery.

TYPE OF OFFENDERS IN THE HEALTH CARE SYSTEM

A functional and inclusive healthcare model in prison requires that the holistic nature of women's health be equated, and that significant gaps in medical service delivery be addressed in a timely and proper manner. In addition, we argue that the "classification of inmates" be utilized as a defining mechanism for the investigation of illnesses, prevention, and treatment. Currently, the classification of inmates is being utilized primarily for issues such as security and housing. The classification of prisoners, which typically includes: the situational offender, the career criminal, the sex offender, the substance abuser, the mentally ill, the mentally handicapped offender, the offender with HIV/AIDS, the elderly offender, and the long-term offender, can be of great utility in identifying general and specific care issues in prison. In this context, we extended this list to be more inclusive and to obtain a more detailed picture of the "many faces of women's health."

Situational Offenders

Based on personal observations, "situational offenders" do not seems to present a major health care challenge to the correctional system in that they tend to be one-time offenders serving a short sentence for a nonviolent crime. Arguably, because these individuals seem to be the least marginalized before entering prison, they tend to have a lower frequency of health care problems and thus less likely to request medical service while incarcerated. Logically, from a legal and medical standpoint, this observation is likely to remain constant in the future.

Career Offenders

Opposite to situational offenders, "career offenders" present a major health care concern to the prison system in that they are in and out of the prison system. While not necessarily violent female criminals, recidivism results in long criminal records, leading to issues like a stigma and lack of social support when they are in the streets and complications when they are incarcerated, especially during the later stages of their criminal career. For instance, when they are in the streets, many cannot find a decent legitimate job because of their criminal record, preventing them from having health insurance or resources for medical care. Once in prison, these individuals are likely to suffer from various untreated illnesses, which the correctional system must deal with at one point or another. However, because some health problems require long-term treatment, it is difficult to properly treat offenders who are in and out of prison. Also, for sick offenders who are in and out of prison, it is difficult for the correctional system to keep an accurate and updated medical history record, further complicating the delivery of service.

As a population, the health care situation for both inmates and institution is likely to get worse. First, the combination of media propagated images of career criminals and a fearful society, which has led to legislation like truth in sentencing and three-strikes, will result in a larger population of career offenders behind bars. Second, as this population gets older, they will suffer from additional and more severe care problems (see Aday, 2003). Third, given the mentality of the American society (see Chapter 3), the gender, race/ethnicity, and need gaps are likely to remain unchanged.

Depressed Prisoners

Since the early 1960s depression has increased sharply in the United States, making anti-depressants a highly prescribed medication.[17] Estimates vary, but studies suggest that 5 to 17 percent of people in the U.S. will experience a major depressive disorder at some point in their lifetime. Recent studies estimate that depression affects almost 20 million people in the United States. Depression, however, varies by sex, class, and age. Women are almost twice as likely as men to experience a depressive episode in their lives. Among those most likely to experience depression are women in poverty, particularly poor single mothers of young children (see Bland, 1997; Murray and Lopez, 1997; World Health Organization, 2006). In the context of the correctional system, approximately 23 percent of state prisoners and 30 percent of jail inmates reported major depression at midyear 2005 (James and Glaze, 2006).

Considering the profile of the typical female offender (see Chapter 2), depression has major implications for female offenders in that depression tends to lead to drug use and addiction, which are linked to crime, HIV, and suicide. To this end, studies show that low self-esteem and poor self-concept are major problems among female prisoners (Fletcher, Shaver, and Moon, 1993; Hannum, Borgen, and Anderson, 1978). Further, women, perhaps more than men, are likely to mutilate their own bodies, have suicidal thoughts, attempt suicide, and commit suicide (Liebling, 1994, 1995). And indeed, the rates of suicide are higher in jails and prisons than the general population (Hayes, 1995; Mumola, 2005).

With few signs that stress and depression rates are likely to decrease, limited resources, and questionable depression treatment in prison, we predict that depression will become a much bigger problem facing inmates in the coming years. Because of the high cost of treatment (counseling and anti-depressants), it is unlikely that depression will be a high priority for policymakers.

Mentally Ill or Handicapped Prisoners

The American public links mental illness, criminal behavior, and insanity defense because of a few highly publicized trials, such as that of John Hinckley, the would-be assassin of former President Ronald Reagan (Fletcher, 1988; Low, Jeffries, and Bonnie, 1986). The common notion in society is normally one of two things: that these individuals claimed mental illness as an "easy" way of escaping harsh punishment or that they are indeed sick people who need to be separated from the rest of society.[18] Beyond highly publicized trials and crime stories in popular television shows, mentally ill offenders are neglected in the streets or "forgotten" behind prison walls or jails (Roberts, 1989; see Chapter 2).[19] Not surprisingly, the incarceration rate of mentally ill people is higher than that of the general population (Ditton, 1999; James and Glaze, 2006).[20] To this end, the conscious decision to use the label "sick" or the terms psychopath or sociopath implies mental illness, making the individual appear less capable and worthy and thus makes it easier to justify harsh punishments. In fact, even educated people tend to call these individuals "emotionally ill" even when there is no reliable or valid evidence of such illness (Szasz, 1987).

While in prison, mentally ill offenders are often the subject of demoralizing jokes and exploited as sexual objects or scapegoats, a critical situation for women who tend to suffer from low self-esteem and depression (Sanford and Donovan, 1994). As with other illnesses, mental illness varies by gender and race, with women reporting a higher rate of mental illness than men and Caucasian female prisoners reporting higher rates (29%) than African American (20%) and Latina (22%) prisoners (Ditton, 1999; see also James and Glaze, 2006). Though, as with Caucasian inmates, mental health problems for African American women and Latinas results from depression which is normally linked to histories of neglect, abuse, and addiction (Langston, 2003; Moulden, 2000). Last, even though women are more likely than men to report treatment, only six in 10 mentally ill women received treatment while incarcerated (Ditton, 1999). In 2004, 19.3% of all state prison inmates had received mental health treatment (James and Glaze, 2006).

As a result of factors like negative stigma, lack of understanding, and low priorities, the problem of "mental illness" in prison is not being properly addressed. First, prison officials are normally not prepared to deal with the mentally ill. Second, the availability and type of treatment varies, but the two most common types involve therapy/counseling or dispensing medications. Normally, though, the tendency is to overmedicate prisoners, often as a form of social control. Third, although some inmates benefit from the medication they receive while incarcerated, others suffer, as the stress of imprisonment worsens their depression and intensifies delusions–leading to mental breakdowns, and, at times, suicide.

In sum, in some cases offenders might indeed be mentally ill. But, in other occasions the combination of childhood abuse, drug addiction, and trauma might be leading to a situation where individuals appear to be mentally ill; yet, suffering from some other illness. With claims of limited resources, mental illness as a low priority, and an increase in the prison population, most of which is minority with a long history of abuse, addiction, and poverty, we predict that mental illness will become a much bigger problem in the future. Logically, policymakers must implement a health care model following the legal and medical definition of mental illness, while being sensitive to other related factors. Additionally, since few prisons provide 24-hour mental health care in specialized housing, states should strive to create mental health units in every facility and, when possible, putting one prison aside to house only the mentally ill. Finally, considering that it is economically cheaper to keep mentally ill people in jail or prison (rather than long-term care), policymakers must avoid prisons from becoming a dumping ground for mentally ill people.

Substance Abusing Prisoners

The typical female offender has a long history of addiction (see Chapter 3). However, even though the prison system has been taking steps to address the treatment needs of female drug offenders, the existing programs are few and limited, in part because they continue to be male-oriented (Kruttschnitt, Gartner, and Miller 2000; Ramsey, 1980a, 1980b). Consequently, drug offenders continue to suffer from multiple health problems, presenting a serious challenge to the prison system as prison rates continue to sharply increase.

In particular, substance users, especially cocaine and methamphetamine users, are at higher risk of weight loss, dehydration, digestive disorders, skin problems, dental problems, gynecological and venereal infections, tuberculosis, hepatitis B, hypertension, seizures, respiratory arrest, and cardiac failure (Daley and Przybycin, 1989). Addicted prisoners typically come from families with high incidences of alcohol or drug dependence, mental illness, violence, and suicide. As children, female prisoners were often exposed to poverty, neglect, trauma, and various other types of abuse at home, foster care, or the streets—like incest, rape, and prostitution (see Chapters 3 and 4). For minority prisoners, particularly African Americans, who constitute the largest racial group in prison, the situation is more devastating because of a series of historical factors, like low levels of education, high unemployment rates, and fear. According to Mary Lou Ramsey (1980a:360), "The black female drug offender suffers from a triple oppression; she is black, female, and most often poor."

Further, in addition to the various health problems mentioned above, drug usage for some female offenders results in other detrimental situations. Particularly, women who share needles for drug use (or who have sex with HIV infected individuals) are at risk of getting infected with HIV and thus passing on the virus to their newborn infants (Wells and Jackson, 1992). Also, female drug users, have been socialized to be dependent (Ramsey, 1980a, 1980b; Owen, 1998), leading to self destruction when no one is willing to assist. For instance, studies show that African American and Caucasian female drug users have very poor self-images of themselves (Prendergast, Wellisch, and Falkin, 1995; Waring and Smith, 1991), resulting in depression, isolation, and even suicide–further worsening the problem for both the inmate and the correctional system.

In sum, considering the drastic increase in the female prison population and no signs of lower levels of drug usage, substance abuse offenders will become an even bigger concern to the correctional system in the coming years. Also, given the interactions with other medical health issues such as communicable diseases, policymakers must carefully institute a health care model that maximizes benefits and minimizes negative consequences (Franklin, Fearn, and Franklin, 2005). In this venture, drug treatment must be gender and culture sensitive, not rely on sexual or historical stereotypes, nor humiliation tactics, and it must be approached as a never constant phenomenon. Further, to effectively remedy drug use, drug-related illness, and drug-related crime, the correctional system must move towards a system-oriented approach to service delivery–linking criminal justice agencies, drug treatment programs, social services agencies, and the community (Prendergast, Wellisch, and Falkin, 1995).

Sex Offenders

As a population, "sex offenders" are becoming a "nightmare" for the American correctional system. First, until recently, sex offenders received little attention in academic studies, public discussions, policy decisions, and treatment (Melby, 2006).[21] As a result, the sex offender population continues to be poorly understood, making it difficult to develop and implement adequate rehabilitative programs in prison. Second, policymakers are focusing primarily on making sure sex offenders receive harsh sanctions, with little attention to proper treatment. Third, the media has portrayed the typical sex offender as violent, vicious, and dangerous, which has contributed or justified harsh sanctions, negative perceptions, and lack of treatment. Fourth, the general public has taken a very punitive stance towards sex offenders, often reacting with phrases like "not in my community," when it comes to finding housing for released sex offenders. As a result, sex offenders continue to be a serious concern to the correctional system even after they are released from prison. Therefore, treatment for sex offenders who suffer from physical, emotional, and/or neurological problems requires medication, counseling, and educational programs. Further, treatment for sex offenders does not end when they are released from prison, but continues for those who are paroled. However, obtaining funding for such an expensive treatment is complicated because of limited resources, priorities, and resistance from policymakers and the general public.

Given the current legislation, treatment, portrayal, and perception towards sex offenders, it is probable that sex offenders will become the biggest challenge to the correctional system in regards to safety, housing, and health care. Perhaps more than any other group of offenders, a well-grounded health care program for sex offenders requires the inclusion of all relevant issues, events, and circumstances. For example, legislative changes must be sensitive to gender and culture variation. And, of course, sex offenders must be examined in the context that women in America are socialized differently in regards to social interactions, like touching, hugging, and kissing. The point being that the correctional system should not use treatment models that have been developed for male offenders, most of which are questionable in the first place.

Prisoners with HIV/AIDS

The Severity of the Problem

As one of the most critical health care issues currently facing inmates and the prison system, Human Immunodeficiency Virus (HIV) and its full-blown symptomatic stage, Acquired Immune Deficiency Syndrome (AIDS), has had a major impact on American corrections that extends beyond health care to include things like housing, safety, release, as well as legal and moral obligations (Franklin, Fearn, and Franklin, 2005; Harlow, 1993). Further, studies show that "the women's immediate emotional reactions to their HIV diagnoses included varying combinations of devastation, shock, indignation, and hysteria. The most common enduring consequence was depression . . . suppression of the diagnosis, shame, and thoughts of suicide" (Hansen, 2005:17).

To place the current situation into perspective, consider the statistics of the entire prison population, male and female. By the late 1980s, AIDS was the leading cause of death among prisoners in states like New York, New Jersey, and Pennsylvania. In addition, prisoners with AIDS in the state of New York lived only half as long as AIDS positive individuals who reside in the community (Cade and Elvin, 1988; *Corrections Digest*, 1985a), a disparity that seems to be attributed to inadequate medical care to prisoners. Julia Cade and Jan Elvin (1988) further document that by the 1980s, the typical New York female AIDS inmate mortality was African American, or Latina, single, with a long history of intravenous drug use (see Chapter 3). More recent figures show that inmates with HIV in New York constitute one-third of all HIV-positive inmates in the country. Ironically, more than one in five (21.5%) inmates in New York State prisons is known to be HIV-positive. Consequently, AIDS is the cause of death of nearly one-third of inmates who die in New York State prisons (Ace Program of the Bedford Hills Correctional Facility, 1998; Langston, 2003). As we move into the twenty-first Century, the situation does not seem to be getting better. According to the Bureau of Justice Statistics (2004c), the rate of AIDS in correctional facilities is now much higher than in the total U.S. population. Though, the Bureau of Justice Statistics recently reported that while the death rate from all other illness increased by 82 percent between 1991 and 2004, the death rate for AIDS dropped by 84 percent (Mumola, 2007). As for gender variation, rates of HIV are higher among female inmates (2.9%) than male inmates (1.9%). In terms of race and ethnicity, investigations show that HIV and AIDS disproportionately affect African American women and Latinas (Langston, 2003).

In actuality, the situation is probably much worse as these numbers underestimate the problem because many HIV infected offenders in prison (or on parole) are undiagnosed. For instance, only 18 states test all new inmates for HIV. Other states conduct tests only if an inmate is in a high-risk group, if there is evidence suggesting that the inmate is HIV-positive, or if the prisoner recently assaulted another inmate or staff member. The state of Wisconsin, our focus of investigation, only tests upon request or after a medical referral. Evidently, these statistics suggest the importance of proper investigations, policies, and treatment to better understand the scope of the problem.

The Causes of HIV/AIDS

The origin of the HIV, a lentivirus, epidemic remains a mystery, but the primary causes of HIV are well documented within the medical community. However, as with various other medical problems, knowledge about HIV and AIDS in the correctional system remains limited and vague. AIDS is a communicable disease that occurs when the HIV virus breaks down the human immune defenses, at which point the body becomes unable to resist or fight infections. The virus is transmitted by means of contaminated blood or semen, particularly by sharing needles used for intravenous drugs and by sexual activities. Maternal transmission also accounts for 85 percent of pediatric cases, with a significant race and ethnicity variation–i.e., 77 percent of children with AIDS are African American or Latina/o.

In the context of women in prison, HIV is largely attributed to three related factors: (1) high risk behavior such as intravenous drug use, (2) needle sharing, and (3) unprotected sex. However, the process in which HIV is transmitted is extremely complex. First, childhood sexual abuse, which is common among female offenders (see Chapter 3), is link to HIV/AIDS risk-taking behavior among female prisoners (Mullings, Marquart, and Hartley, 2003). Second, there is a strong link between drugs and HIV, which begins early in life for most female offenders. As shown in Chapter 3, most women who enter prison are drug or alcohol users in withdrawal stages in need of detoxification. Consequently, sharing contaminated drug paraphernalia, like dirty needles, accounts for some HIV infection cases. When these factors interact, the results are more severe. For instance, among drug-dependent females, cocaine-addicted women, who are likely to have a higher number of sexual partners, and thus have a higher risk of being infected with the HIV virus. Likewise, females whose sex partners are IV drug-users, and women who support their drug habits by prostitution have a higher risk of being infected with HIV (Waring and Smith, 1991). In fact, studies show that 95 percent of HIV among female prisoners is attributed to IV drug use (Hammett, 1988). Third, in addition to childhood abuse, drugs and alcohol usage, malnutrition also weakens the immune system, making women even more susceptible to the HIV virus.

The causes of HIV among female offenders must be understood within the context of the drug crisis in America, poverty (which often results in behavior like prostitution), and a lack of education, which results in risky behavior such as unprotected sex and dirty needle sharing. Likewise, an effective prevention and treatment HIV/AIDS program requires an all inclusive approach, which includes an understanding of childhood abuse, to avoid medical gaps and ensure continuity (Franklin, Fearn, and Franklin, 2005; Viadro and Earp, 1991).

Housing for HIV/AIDS Prisoners

Because of the severity of the problem and the complex nature in which HIV is transmitted, housing for inmates with HIV or AIDS has become a major concern (Ace Program of the Bedford Hills Correctional Facility, 1998). Typically, depending on the number of infected inmates and availability of resources, prison officials have selected (usually on a case-by-case basis) various housing options, such as keeping inmates in the general population, single cells, housed together in double cells, or confined to hospital or a infirmary. Whatever option is taken, however, raises safety, moral, and legal questions. For example, should AIDS-positive inmates be released from prison so that they can spend their last few days out in the streets, based on compassionate release policies? Or, should they be kept in prison to avoid "dumping" them in the streets? Given the current mentality of the American society (see Chapter 4), prisons are likely to become a "dumping ground" for people infected with HIV or AIDS.

Implications of HIV and AIDS

Because of the nature of HIV/AIDS, investigation, prevention, and treatment of this illness is very difficult. First, even though HIV/AIDS has received great attention among the general population, HIV/AIDS and related illnesses remain understudied among females in prison. For example, cervical cancer, which is known to occur at higher rates among women with AIDS, has received little attention by health care investigations, and Karposi's sarcoma, a standard by the Centers for Disease Control criterion for the diagnosis of AIDS, rarely affects women (Hooper, 2000; Waring and Smith, 1991). In regards to treatment, even though prison officials may prescribe FDA-approved AIDS drugs, like AZT, aerosolized pentamidine, dapson, and bacterium, some prisoners are not receiving the most frequently used AIDS drug–AZT (Waring and Smith, 1991). Second, the long incubation period of HIV, the time between the infection and the appearance of outward symptoms, makes early prevention very difficult. Consequently, carriers of HIV may engage in unsafe drug use and/or sex without knowing that they are infecting other people. Third, drug addicts with HIV, especially women, who continue to use drugs get sicker faster and die sooner than people who stop using drugs (Waring and Smith, 1991; Wells and Jackson, 1992). Considering that most female prisoners have multiple children (see Chapter 2), women in terminal stages of AIDS do not have the opportunity to provide for their children.

In sum, the HIV/AIDS epidemic is severe, difficult to investigate, prevent, treat, and expensive to confront. In fact, women in prison with drug addiction and HIV/AIDS are the most underserved group in the entire prison population (Rierden, 1997; Waring and Smith, 1991; Zaitzow, 2001). With the increase in prison rates, mostly minority women, significant medical gaps in investigation, policy, and treatment, we predict that HIV and AIDS will become a bigger problem in the future. As the AIDS epidemic continues to grow, prison administrators must develop policies covering such matters as ways to prevent disease transmission, proper housing for those infected, and effective medical care for inmates already infected. Further, administrators must rationally approach disease prevention. For instance, should condoms and hypodermic needles be provided to inmates? Should each state require screening? A key way to prevent AIDS transmission is knowledge about the virus (Franklin, Fearn, and Franklin, 2005; Zaitzow, 2001). If possible, all correctional facilities should implement HIV/AIDS prevention programs, with sessions in both English and Spanish. People need to know how the virus is transmitted and how to prevent transmission (Hansen, 2005; Viadro and Earp, 1991). As noted by Andi Rierden (1997), we need to deal with the AIDS virus openly.

Pregnant Prisoners

With the introduction of crack cocaine into the ghetto, prison officials are now confronting a much more complicated pregnant population, like "crack mothers" giving birth to "crack babies" and the fetal
alcohol syndrome, which occurs when pregnant women engage in
excessive drinking and thus resulting in lifelong damage to the fetus,
causing babies to have impaired cognitive functioning, similar to crack
babies (see Humphries, 1999). An investigation of eight states found
that 9 percent of female inmates give birth behind bars (*New York
Times*, 1992). Overall, about 25 percent of incarcerated women are
pregnant on admission to prison or have given birth during the previous year, needing special medical and nutritional resources for their
own health and the health of the fetus. However, pregnant women in
prison often lack adequate medical care, prenatal care, and nutrition
(McCall, Castell, and Shaw, 1985; Schupak, 1986). In one particular
institution, less than half of the inmates received prenatal care, and
only 15 percent received special diets and counseling (Wooldredge
and Masters, 1993). Combined with inappropriate work activities,
these factors result in accidents and miscarriages (Stefan, 1989). Case
in point: in one California jail, the infant mortality rate was 50 times
higher than for the entire state of California, the state with the largest
prison population (Stefan, 1989).

The issue of medical care for pregnant women, however, cannot be
properly analyzed without taking into consideration other relevant
factors. Pregnancies raise a wide spectrum of challenges for corrections, including special diets, abortion rights, access to delivery rooms
and medical personnel, and length of time that newborns can remain
with their mothers in prison (see Chapter 5). Further, even though teen
pregnancy has decreased in recent years, most pregnant women in
prison are older than 35, have histories of drug abuse, have had prior
multiple abortions, and carry sexually transmitted diseases. In addition, pregnant prisoners not only have to cope with the physical aspect
of incarceration but must endure psychological stress over whether to
have an abortion, who should care for the infant after birth, and separation from the child (see Chapter 5). Some correctional systems are
allowing infants to stay with their mothers, creating in-prison nurseries, developing special living quarters for pregnant prisoners and
new mothers, instituting counseling programs, and improving stan-

dards of medical care (*Corrections Digest*, 1989; Fearn and Parker, 2005; Wooldredge and Masters, 1993), but a gap remains between need and delivery service.

This medical gap is, in part, a result of not having post-conviction rights of pregnant prisoners well-defined (McPeters, 1984; Stefan, 1989).[22] In particular, even though women have the constitutional right to an abortion under *Roe v. Wade* (1973), the Supreme Court ruled in *Maher v. Roe* (1977) that inmates do not have a federal constitutional right to abortion funding from the federal government (*Corrections Digest*, 1985b, 1987a, 1988b; Vitale, 1980; Vukson, 1987), creating a difficult situation for inmates, most of whom are poor. As a consequence, while prisons seek abortions on behalf of inmates who have been declared "incompetent" to make their own abortion decisions, some inmates who want abortions are denied access or they have to go through a difficult, unclear, and time-consuming process (see Roth, 2004; Stefan, 1989). From a legal standpoint, sexual assault in prison has exacerbated the situation in that it has resulted in litigation over abortion for incarcerated women, particularly incompetent and mentally ill prisoners.

In sum, in the case of pregnant prisoners, it is not only essential that the prison system provide adequate health care for the mothers, but also the infants before being born and afterwards. Here too, we predict that the situation for pregnant prisoners will worsen due to the manifestation of other factors such as addictions, communicable diseases, and depression, which are difficult to cure. Thus, in addition to separate housing for pregnant women, special diets and exercises, light work assignments, allowing of maternity clothes to be worn, sufficient resources for deliveries, miscarriages, false labors, premature births, postnatal care, counseling, training, and education (Wooldredge and Masters, 1993), policymakers must equate factors that could very likely intervene in the care and treatment of pregnant prisoners.

Elderly Prisoners

In the context of the prison boom (see Chapter 2), age seems to be playing a minor role in sentencing and parole decisions. For instance, under recent legislation, like "truth in sentencing," inmates must serve out 85 percent of their sentence before being released. This prosecutorial approach, however, is already resulting in an increase in the "elderly prison population" (Aday, 2003). And, of course, as in the general population, elderly offenders tend to have a host of problems–e.g., homelessness, chaotic interpersonal relationships, poor lifestyle choices, unemployment, and poverty–and tend to suffer from multiple illnesses, requiring multiple medications (Aday, 2003; Kuhlmann and Ruddell, 2005). One recent study shows that elderly inmates present a high-risk for self-harm, victimization by other inmates, suicide, and problems that extend beyond the actual incarceration in that "the boundaries between community and jail are very permeable" (Kuhlmann and Ruddell, 2005:57). Indeed, from 2001 to 2004, mortality rates increased significantly with age (Mumola, 2007). Actually, in the case of female prisoners, the situation is more severe in that female offenders normally have a long history of medical problems, which serve as the highest source of jail and prison (Schlanger, 2003).

Under current state and federal statutes, then, the utility of the prison system for older inmates is shifting from "social control and safety" to "warehousing and treatment" of the elderly, since few crimes are committed by people over 60 years of age. With no significant signs of changes in prosecutorial practices, especially drug legislation, which carries lengthy prison sentences, we predict that health care for female offenders will become a major concern to prison officials in the very near future. Thus, without major changes in prosecutorial behavior, states must devise a health care model in prison that is broad enough in scope to capture the many health problems of female prisoners, but also specific in nature to deal with a diverse inmate population. Last, policymakers must prevent the elderly population from being forgotten behind prison walls, creating a much larger medical gap in medical service delivery as well as legal and moral issues.

Long-Term Prisoners

From a prosecutorial standpoint, many long-term prisoners are not necessarily convicted by the nature of their crimes, particularly violent crimes. Rather, their convictions seem to be more directly influenced by the impact of laws like mandatory sentencing, sentencing guidelines, and sentence enhancement laws (Urbina and Kreitzer, 2004). Consequently, the United States has experienced a sharp increase in incarceration rates, incarcerating more people than any other country in the industrialized world. In fact, there are more prisoners serving long prison sentences in the United States than in any other Western country, with prison sentences in the U.S. ranging from 20 years to life in prison with no possibility of parole, in which case inmates will eventually die in prison (Walford, 1987).

At the present time, long-term prisoners are beginning to present a major problem in regards to medical care. Based on a recent study, death from illness increased drastically for inmates serving lengthy prison terms (Mumola, 2007). Hence, because of these three factors, the long-term prisoner population is likely to increase, and many of whom will become elderly prisoners, contributing to a possible crises with the elderly inmate population (Aday, 2003; Lord, 1995; Walford, 1987). For instance, in states with capital punishment (see Chapter 8), two sentencing options are already increasing: executions or life in prison with no parole or some type of parole provision (Urbina, 2002a). In states with no capital punishment, such as Wisconsin, life in prison with no possibility of parole or some type of parole restriction is on the rise (see Urbina and Kreitzer, 2004).

In sum, as a population, female prisoners suffer from multiple illnesses, some of which date back to the day they were born, as in the case of "crack babies" and babies suffering from the effects of the fetal alcohol syndrome. As noted above, the classification of prisoners is not only of utility in understanding the many faces of women's health, but also planning for prevention and treatment. Therefore, investigators and policymakers must understand medical problems of female offenders as finely as possible. Logically, a sound medical health care model in prison must be based on the totality of events and circumstances. As a starting point, we investigated the Wisconsin prison population.

THE WISCONSIN EXPERIENCE

Historically, Wisconsin has made national news in the area of crime, law, punishment, and justice. In the early 1980s, for instance, there was the highly publicized 1981 murder conviction of Laurie Bembenek, a former Milwaukee police officer and *Playboy* model, who later was popularized by the phrase, "Run, Bambi, Run" (Barton, 2002). In the early 1990s, Wisconsin was back on national news with the capture and prosecution of Jeffrey Dahmer (1960–1994), one of the most noto-rious serial killers in U.S. history. A Milwaukee native, Dahmer was a necrophiliac and cannibal who apparently enjoyed killing people, killing 17 men and boys (mostly African Americans) between 1978 and 1991 (Dahmer, 1994; Masters, 1993). Then, right as we entered the twenty-first century, the *Milwaukee Journal Sentinel* (2000a:1A) report-ed that "A Wisconsin prison term can equal a death sentence." The 8-month investigation, covering approximately 10 years, revealed that "Dozens of Wisconsin inmates have died under questionable circum-stances . . . in a flawed Corrections health system that keeps internal reviews of prison deaths secret" (Zahn and McBride, 2000a:1A). Among the various reported findings (McBride and Zahn, 2000:1-11; Zahn and McBride, 2000a:1A, 14A-16A; 2000b:1-6) include:

- *Ill inmates were given questionable medical care and sometimes . . . were ignored when they pleaded for help.*
- *Most prisons are without around-the-clock health care. Corrections officers receive little medical training. Only about one-third of prison officers are up-to-date on CPR.*
- *Nurses are making diagnoses that doctors should be making. Nurses some-times make critical decisions based on phone calls from officers.*
- *Medical equipment is old, in poor condition and inadequate.*
- *There are gross medication errors.*
- *Doctors and nurses . . . have had their licenses limited or suspended by the state Medical Examining Board.*
- *In the majority of cases, the Department of Corrections apparently violat-ed its own policy by not notifying police or sheriff's officials each time an inmate died.*
- *Police investigations into inmate deaths often are closed without a review for potential medical neglect or criminal negligence once a natural cause of death is established. The natural cause can range from asthma to appen-dicitis—virtually anything short of a homicide or suicide.*
- *Under state law, it is a felony to abuse, neglect, or ill-treat people confined in prison or to allow any mistreatment.[23] However, almost none of the inmate deaths reviewed by the* Journal Sentinel *was referred to the local district attorney for review, even when there was a potential question of medical neglect.*
- *All deaths are reviewed by a largely secret internal Corrections mortality review committee.*

- *Police and coroner investigations into inmate deaths often are cursory or nonexistent, and record-keeping is slipshod.*
- *No death certificate was filed [in every case], a violation of state law.*
- *Most deaths are handled: quietly and quickly.*
- *Corrections officials have refused to released the final mortality review reports on deaths of inmates and on the health care they received, even to the inmates' families.*
- *The final reports of the committee are denied to the dead inmates' families and to the public. In fact, family members generally do not even know such report exists.*
- *Pervasive lack of accountability in the deaths of Wisconsin inmates.*

In August of 2000, Wisconsin Department of Corrections Secretary John Litscher further fueled the corrections debate when he announced the return of all 347 women who were imprisoned out-of-state (Jones, 2000). According to the U.S. Bureau of Justice Statistics, Wisconsin had been the nation's leading exporter of inmates, and no other state comes close when both male and female offenders were combined. Obviously, a logical move in that the money could be spent in Wisconsin, and allow inmate mothers to be closer to their children. However, without the proper mechanisms in place, this novel move could escalate the prison crisis in the Wisconsin correctional system, particularly in the areas of housing and health care. As noted in Chapter 1, given the nature of life behind bars, as reported by the *Milwaukee Journal Sentinel,* we opted to conduct a detailed investigation of female prisoners in Wisconsin.

Parallel to previous chapters, the following section contains findings for female prisoners in Wisconsin. In an attempt to delineate the medical situation of female prisoners as finely as possible, a number of questions were asked regarding their medical health. In particular, in addition to understanding the nature of female illnesses, the implications and delivery of service must be well-documented for future planning.

The Nature of Women's Health in Prison

Considering the long and complicated medical history of the typical female offender, the respondents answered a number of questions about their physical and mental state as well as the consequences of being disabled. As shown in Table 17, slightly over one-third (165 or 36.2%) of the participating inmates reported suffering from some type of physical illness, and 125 (27.4%) women reported suffering from some form of mental illness. Of those suffering from some type of illness, 82 (18.0%) women reported being disabled: mobility impaired (4), visually impaired (3), hearing impaired (4), mentally disabled (23), physically impaired (7), multiple disabilities (23), and other disability (15).

Table 17
THE NATURE AND IMPLICATIONS OF WOMEN'S HEALTH IN
WISCONSIN'S PRISONS (N=456)

	Frequency	Percent
Physical illness		
Yes	165	36.2
No	271	59.4
Don't know	10	2.2
Mental illness		
Yes	125	27.4
No	291	63.8
Don't know	25	5.5
Disabled		
Yes	82	18.0
No	365	80.0
Type of disability		
Mobility impaired	4	0.9
Visually impaired	3	0.7
Hearing impaired	4	0.9
Mentally disabled	23	5.0
Physically impaired	7	1.5
Other disability	15	3.3
Multiple disabilities	23	5.0
Type of difficulties due to disability		
Ability to receive work assignments	9	2.0
Ability to receive education	1	0.2
Limits on the work I should be doing	9	2.0
Other limitations	9	2.0
Multiple difficulties	19	4.2
Differential treatment due to disability		
Yes	40	8.8
No	34	7.5

Continued on next page

Table 17 (cont.)

Contributors of difficulties	Frequency	Percent
Other inmates	9	2.0
Correctional officers	12	2.6
Correctional administrators	2	0.4
Other individuals	2	0.4
Multiple people	44	9.6

Implications of Disability in Prison

Types of disabilities facing inmates include: work assignments (9), education (1), work restrictions (9), multiple difficulties (19), and other limitations (9). Of the 82 women reporting disabilities, about half (40) reported experiencing differential treatment in prison because of their disability, indicating that, as a whole, differential treatment in Wisconsin female prisons might be a much bigger problem than expected. People contributing to difficulties or differential treatment include: other inmates (9), correctional officers (12), correctional administrators (2), multiple people (44) and other individuals (2).

In sum, consistent with prior investigations, a substantial number of women in prison are suffering from some type of illness. In fact, the reported figures might be underestimated in that some women are not aware of their own health problems and institutions are not testing them on a regular basis. Last, as inmates become older, illness and disability rates will increase, resulting in additional medical challenges and expenses.

Depression Among Women in Prison

As stated earlier, depression is one of the leading illnesses in American society (see Chapter 2). For female offenders, though, depression is probably much more prevalent and a more complex problem. As shown in Table 18, over half (253 or 55.5%) of the 456 participating inmates reported suffering from depression, but only 146 (32.0%) women reported that they were receiving treatment; which include: medication (102), individual counseling (4), group counseling (1), and multiple treatments (43).

Evidently, institutions seem to be relying primarily on medications, which may have significant long-term side effects when anti-depressants are not properly administered, with minimal reliance on counseling. Last, with sentencing laws resulting in long prison sentences and severe physical illness on the increase, depression among female prisoners is likely to increase as well.

Table 18
DEPRESSION AMONG INCARCERATED WOMEN IN WISCONSIN (N=456)

	Frequency	Percent
Suffering from depression		
Yes	253	55.5
No	173	37.9
Don't know	20	4.4
Depression treatment		
Yes	146	32.0
No	93	20.4
Type of treatment		
Medication	102	22.4
Individual counseling	4	0.9
Group counseling	1	0.2
Multiple treatments	43	9.4

HIV and AIDS in Prison

HIV/AIDS is not only one of the severe illness facing both inmates and correctional institutions, but also one of the most complicated problems in that it is difficult to detect, prevent, and costly to treat. In order to increase our understanding, female prisoners were asked a series of questions regarding HIV/AIDS infection and knowledge, which is vital to HIV prevention.

Based on Table 19, nine women reported being infected with HIV, and 10 inmates did not know whether they were infected or not, suggesting the possibility of infection. Similarly, five inmates reported having the AIDS virus, and 8 inmates reported not knowing whether they were AIDS positive or not, indicating possible infection and lack of knowledge.

Table 19
HIV AND AIDS IN WISCONSIN'S CORRECTIONAL SYSTEM (N=456)

	Frequency	Percent
HIV infected		
Yes	9	2.0
No	423	92.8
Don't know	10	2.2
AIDS infected		
Yes	5	1.1
No	425	93.2
Don't know	8	1.8
Origin of AIDS		
Man-made virus	41	9.0
Homosexual activity	42	9.2
Monkey infected in Africa	89	19.5
God's punishment for crime	12	2.6
Other origins	21	4.6
Don't know	110	24.1
Multiple causes	70	15.4
Exposed to HIV but not infected		
Yes	233	51.1
No	99	21.7
Don't know	95	20.8
No symptoms yet spreading HIV		
Yes	340	74.6
No	22	4.8
Don't know	74	16.2
Development of antibodies after HIV infected		
Immediately	47	10.3
Within 1 month	10	2.2
Within 3 to 6 months	123	27.0
After one year	31	6.8
Don't know	203	44.5
Transmitting HIV between women		
Yes	364	79.8
No	18	3.9
Don't know	54	11.8
HIV transmitted through oral sex		
Yes	377	82.7
No	16	3.5
Don't know	42	9.2

Continued on next page

Table 19 (cont.)

	Frequency	Percent
HIV transmitted through genital sex		
Yes	400	87.7
No	4	0.9
Don't know	31	6.8
Children getting HIV		
From their mother at birth	73	16.0
From blood transfusions	9	2.0
As punishment from God	1	0.2
Through homosexual activity	1	0.2
Other methods	1	0.2
Don't know	24	5.3
Multiple causes	322	70.6

The Origin of AIDS

Since understanding the "root" of the problem is essential to prevention and treatment, inmates were questioned about the origin of AIDS, and related issues. Interestingly, their responses reveal two significant findings: (1) they have limited knowledge about specific issues regarding HIV/AIDS, and (2) their views seem to be shaped by media propagated myths. As to the origin of AIDS, there views are diverse: man-made virus (41), homosexual activity (42), monkey infected in Africa (89), God's punishment for crime (12), multiple causes (70), some other origin (21) and "don't know" (110). Evidently, both forms of limited knowledge are detrimental not only to prevention and treatment, but also influence social interactions, possibly resulting in prejudice and discrimination against individuals in and out of prison.

Inmates were also asked if they knew how soon after becoming infected with the HIV virus do antibodies (substances having the power of destroying the growth of microorganisms) develop? Their responses include: immediately (47), within one month (10), within three to six months (123), after one year (31), and "don't know" (203). Again, a substantial number (203 or 44.5%) of females reported not knowing, suggesting a possible delay in seeking treatment. Logically, a lack of knowledge or fear of stigma will influence if and when an individual will seek treatment.

In reality, of course, AIDS remains an historical and global mystery. Arguably, there is no reliable documented case of HIV or AIDS before 1959, with the earliest known cases of AIDS taking place in central Africa (see Curtis, 1992; Hooper, 2000). In the United States, the first cases of AIDS were reported in the early 1980s.[24] Since then, scientists have debated its origin in academic theories, which range from ultra-conservative to ultra-liberal explanations, such as the hunter theory, the oral polio vaccine theory, the contaminated needle theory, the colonialism theory, and the conspiracy theory. We might never know when, where, or how AIDS actually originated. Still, we argue that AIDS is probably a result of an intertwining combination of historical and modern events, to include wars, colonial practices or genetic engineering, injections, world travel, contaminated pharmaceutical drugs, modern medical experiments, unprotected sex, lack of and misleading information, drugs, and polluted physical environments (see Boer, 2005).

The Transmission of AIDS

As reported in Table 19, inmates also have limited prevention information. Specifically, over half (233 or 51.1%) of the respondents reported that people can be exposed to HIV and not get infected, 99 inmates thought otherwise, and 95 did not know. This notion is critical in that people might be inclined to engage in unsafe sex and share contaminated needles. However, the majority (340 or 74.6%) of inmates reported that HIV-positive people showing no symptoms can spread the HIV virus, and only 22 women reported otherwise—with 74 prisoners not knowing.

Considering the claims that female offenders are likely to engage in high-risk sexual activities before entering the prison system, and the notion that lesbianism is common in female prisons (see Chapter 8), inmates were asked about specific issues. First, the majority (400 or 87.7%) of inmates reported that HIV can be transmitted through genital sex, 4 reported otherwise, and 31 women did not know. Second, most (364 or 79.8%) prisoners reported that a woman can transmit the HIV virus by having sexual contact with another woman, 18 inmates thought otherwise, and 54 did not know. Third, the majority (377 or 82.7%) of prisoners reported that HIV can be transmitted through oral sex, 16 inmates said no, and 42 women did not know. Last, considering that HIV is found among children (see Chapter 2), inmates were asked how they thought children get AIDS. Interestingly, 24 did not know, but the majority (322 or 70.6%) reported multiple causes, and 73 women noted that children get AIDS from their mothers at birth.

In summary, even though a small number of females reported being HIV/AIDS positive, the reported findings are significant as they reveal limited knowledge, which is critical for prevention. Of course, the reported figures might be underestimated because: (1) inmates might not know if they are HIV-positive, and (2) Wisconsin only tests for HIV/AIDS upon request or medical referral. Last, granted that the origin of AIDS remains in question, inmates need to be educated about historical and modern medical discoveries to reduce the possibility of transmitting the virus to other people or even their own children.

Severity of Health Problems in Prison

Understanding the severity of women's health problems in prison is not only essential for an all inclusive investigation, but also essential when measuring the demand for medical service delivery, and, possibly, the rate to which women seek medical assistance. Additionally, with limited resources and prison overcrowding on the rise, severity assessment becomes critical to proper future planning. As a first step, women were asked about what seems to be the common health problems in female prisons. Table 20 shows findings for 21 specific health issues.

Table 20
SEVERITY OF ILLNESSES WHILE INCARCERATED IN WISCONSIN (N=456)

	No Problem	Mild	Moderate	Severe	Don't Know
Asthma	285 (62.5)	47 (10.3)	57 (12.5)	21 (4.6)	10 (2.2)
Allergies	217 (47.6)	69 (15.1)	67 (14.7)	50 (11.0)	14 (3.1)
Diabetes	354 (77.6)	9 (2.0)	15 (3.3)	10 (2.2)	23 (5.0)
High blood pressure	309 (67.8)	28 (6.1)	38 (8.3)	20 (4.4)	20 (4.4)
AIDS related symptoms	393 (86.2)	1 (0.2)	---	---	14 (3.1)
Heart disease	358 (78.5)	20 (4.4)	7 (1.5)	11 (2.4)	19 (4.2)
Epilepsy/seizures	384 (84.2)	6 (1.3)	4 (0.9)	2 (0.4)	14 (3.1)
Bronchitis	339 (74.3)	22 (4.8)	25 (5.5)	13 (2.9)	14 (3.1)
Cancer	374 (82.0)	5 (1.1)	6 (1.3)	5 (1.1)	19 (4.2)
Arthritis	299 (65.6)	34 (7.5)	41 (9.0)	30 (6.6)	15 (3.3)
Migrant headaches	230 (50.4)	58 (12.7)	67 (14.7)	52 (11.4)	11 (2.4)
Sinus headaches	228 (50.0)	66 (14.5)	71 (15.6)	41 (9.0)	10 (2.2)
Vision problems	213 (46.7)	71 (15.6)	76 (16.7)	47 (10.3)	13 (2.9)
Hearing problems	317 (69.5)	32 (7.0)	34 (7.5)	19 (4.2)	12 (2.6)

Continued on next page

Table 20 (cont.)

	No Problem	Mild	Moderate	Severe	Don't Know
Dental problems	222 (48.7)	72 (15.8)	64 (14.0)	51 (11.2)	11 (2.4)
Drug/Alcohol addiction	292 (64.0)	25 (5.5)	30 (6.6)	57 (12.5)	11 (2.4)
Depression	166 (36.4)	85 (18.6)	77 (16.9)	82 (18.0)	10 (2.2)
Schizophrenia	369 (80.9)	11 (2.4)	8 (1.8)	6 (1.3)	14 (3.1)
Bulimia/Anorexia	369 (80.9)	10 (2.2)	7 (1.5)	6 (1.3)	16 (3.5)
Sexually transmitted disease	384 (84.2)	7 (1.5)	3 (0.7)	2 (0.4)	14 (3.1)
Mononucleosis	390 (85.5)	2 (0.4)	1 (0.2)	1 (0.2)	14 (3.1)

Note: Because not every participant responded to each and every question, not every row/column adds up to 456.

* Numbers in parentheses indicate percentage of total.

As outlined in Table 20, there is a wide variation in the level of health care needs (ranging from mild to severe) in Wisconsin prisons. Ranked by severity, the most severe problems (with over 40 women reporting the problem as severe) are depression (82), followed by alcohol/drug addiction (57), migrant headaches (52), dental problems (51), allergies (50), sinus headaches (41), and vision problems (47). Consistent with findings in Table 18, depression seems to be the most severe problem among incarcerated women. Also, among the most severe problems, are dental and vision conditions, which normally worsen with age.

Ranked by the number of inmates suffering from specific illnesses, the most severe problems include: depression (244), vision problems (194), dental problems (187), allergies (186), sinus headaches (178), migrant headaches (177), asthma (125), alcohol/drug addiction (112), arthritis (105), high blood pressure (86), and hearing problems (85). As the most common illness, depression affects over half of the participating inmates. Here too, vision, dental, and, to a lesser degree, hearing problems, are among the most common health care issues in Wisconsin prisons, suggesting a critical situation as the prison population ages.

Other illnesses, while less severe, include: bronchitis (60), heart disease (38), diabetes (34), schizophrenia (25), bulimia/anorexia (23), cancer (16), epilepsy/seizures (12), sexually transmitted diseases (12), mononucleosis (4), and AIDS (1). While less common, these illnesses are critical to both the inmates and prison system in that some require special treatment, like schizophrenia, and some are delicate and expensive to treat, like heart disease, cancer, and AIDS.

Three significant conclusions can be made from the findings reported above. First, depression seems to be the most common and severe problems in prison, and AIDS seems to be the least common illness, both findings being consistent with findings reported in Tables 18 and 19. Second, some of the most common or most severe health problems in prison are primarily of the "old." Third, while small, a significant and consistent number of inmates in each category reported not knowing the severity of their illnesses, suggesting the importance of education and testing in prison. With prison rates on the rise, increases in the long-term prisoner population, and an aging population, proper future planning in the area of investigation, policy, prevention, and treatment, must be made a high priority.

Frequency of Delivery Service in Prison

The severity of inmate health problems needs to be investigated in the context of access to medical care from the time women enter prison until they are released. Knowing the frequency of health care distribution allows for comparison with the demand of specific issues, such as those shown in Tables 17 through 20, and thus provides information for future investigation, policy modifications, prevention, and treatment. Table 21 contains the findings for a series of key questions about health care and delivery in female prisons.

Of the 456 respondents, over half (278 or 61.0%) of the group reported taking medication, administered by the following people: medical doctor (20), nurse (37), correctional officer (118), correctional administrator (6), other inmates (7), multiple individuals (43), and "other" individuals (42). Evidently, medication is not being delivered primarily by physicians or nurses, but correctional officers, staff members and inmates. Additionally, even though 138 women reported having "regular" access to prescribed medication, 147 inmates reported irregular access to medications, and 146 women reported not having access to prescribed medications.

Table 21
FREQUENCY OF HEALTH CARE SERVICE RECEIVED WHILE
INCARCERATED IN WISCONSIN (N=456)

	Frequency	*Percent*
Currently taking medication		
Yes	278	61.0
No	162	35.5
Administering medication		
Medical doctor	20	4.4
Nurse	37	8.1
Correctional officer	118	25.9
Correctional administrator	6	1.3
Other inmate	7	1.5
Other individual	42	9.2
Multiple individuals	43	9.4

	Regularly	*Seldom*	*Never*
Physical examinations	96 (21.1)	208 (45.6)	135 (29.6)
Dental examinations	76 (16.7)	220 (48.2)	142 (31.1)
Hearing examinations	25 (5.5)	111 (24.3)	295 (64.7)
Eye examinations	54 (11.8)	175 (38.4)	202 (44.3)
HIV screening	68 (14.9)	183 (40.1)	178 (39.0)
Gynecological examinations	106 (23.2)	167 (36.6)	157 (34.4)
PAP smears	130 (28.5)	173 (37.9)	132 (28.9)
Breast examinations	86 (18.9)	155 (34.0)	187 (41.0)
Prenatal care if pregnant	42 (9.2)	60 (13.2)	236 (51.8)
Postnatal care if recently delivered	30 (6.6)	63 (13.8)	244 (53.5)
Access to prescribed medication	138 (30.3)	147 (32.2)	146 (32.0)
Swift emergency care	38 (8.3)	141 (30.9)	235 (51.5)

Note: Because not every participant responded to each and every question, not every row/column adds up to 456.
* Numbers in parentheses indicate percentage of total.

According to these inmates, the frequency of health care delivery is inadequate as the majority of inmates do not receive medical service, such as physical, dental, hearing, vision, gynecological, and breast examinations, HIV screening, PAP smears, and prenatal and postnatal care, and many never receive services. For instance, 295 women have never received hearing examinations, a critical situation as the inmate population gets older. Similarly, only 38 inmates reported receiving "swift emergency care" when needed, a critical problem in the case of a serious illness, which could result in death. Hence, lack of swift emergency care is consistent with the findings reported by the

Milwaukee Journal as part of its eight-month investigation of the Wisconsin prison system.

In sum, health care delivery services, or what Murphy (2005:25) refers to as "symbolic medical care," do not seem to correspond with demand. Unfortunately, a lack of health care delivery service for various common illnesses, limited access to prescribed medication, and lack of emergency care not only contribute to a critical medical gap in prison, but it creates a structural problem that is difficult to resolve without overhauling the entire prison system (Murphy, 2005). Daniel Murphy (2005:27) reports that the dehumanization process, which begins early in life for some delinquent girls, allows for a "symbolic presentation of health care to go unquestioned" and thus "reducing expenditures on medical care frees more resources for human warehousing–and the cycle of inhumanity disgracefully rages on." However, it is a medical gap that can be bridged if made a priority. Otherwise, this medical gap will worsen as prison overcrowding increases, making it difficult for the prison system and inmates, particularly the elderly population and those who suffer from severe illnesses.

HEALTH CARE RECOMMENDATIONS

1. Thorough physical examination upon entering the facility.
2. Pregnancy screening at the intake to ensure proper planning (see Fearn and Parker, 2005). In regards to pregnant prisoners, prisons should focus on women who present a high risk for health problems and outcomes.
3. Prisons should focus on chronic illnesses, like AIDS and HIV detection, intervention, and counseling.[25]
4. Prison administrators (and state legislators) should lobby at the national level to obtain prescribed medication from pharmaceutical companies at low cost or no cost for leading health issues, like depression.
5. Better regulation of who provides prescribed medication to inmates, especially the elderly, mentally ill, and severely ill inmates who might not be fully aware of what they are actually taking (Korn, 1988a).
6. Continuous monitoring to detect inmates with chronic commu-

nicable diseases or disorders. As noted by some investigators, prioritizing communicable diseases in the areas of prevention and treatment can "yield broad social benefits" (Glaser and Greifinger, 1993:143; see also Fearn and Parker, 2005).

7. Regular examinations to detect health care needs. It is less costly and time-consuming to prevent an illness than to treat it. Prevention includes, continuous screening for infectious diseases, annual PAP smear, mammography, breast self-exam, prenatal care, chronic disease monitoring, regular exercise, proper nutrition, dental, hearing and mental health screening, and immediate treatment (Epp, 1996; Kort, 1987; Moulden, 2000).

8. Trauma therapy for inmates diagnosed with HIV/AIDS or some other chronic disease to reduce the possibility of other health care issues, like stress, depression, and even suicidal thoughts.

9. Need to be sensitive to specific issues facing the racial and ethnic population, which makes most of the prison population. For instance, African Americans are known to have about 10 percent more bone mass than Caucasian women. African Americans have more risks factors and higher incidents of developing obesity related illnesses such as diabetes and possibly depression. In 2006, nearly 44 percent of African Americans had some form of heart disease. Ways to reduce heart problems: balanced diet and exercise (Kort, 1987).

10. Education, to include both inmates and correctional staff, must be made a high priority in order to ensure continuity in treatment and prevention (Fearn and Parker, 2005; Macher, Kibble, Bryant, Cody, Pilcher, and Jahn, 2005).

11. Implementation of outside review to avoid the secrecy and increase responsibility for medical negligence.

CONCLUSION

Consistent with prior investigations, the findings presented above suggest that a significant medical gap exists in the delivery of health care services in a female prison system. The data also suggest a series of critical questions that remain to be properly addressed. For instance, for years investigators have asked the question: should mentally ill offenders be incarcerated? However, a more pressing question seems to be: should offenders who are suffering from chronic depression be incarcerated? Likewise, should offenders who are suffering from severe illnesses, like AIDS, be incarcerated? A sound analysis involves the assessment of both consequences and benefits of incarceration versus some other form of treatment or sanction. A close examination might reveal that there are more consequences than benefits to the incarceration of a population that does not present a serious social threat to the community.

As for offenders who "must" be incarcerated, some investigators note that the lack of proper medical care is "resulting in the development of more serious health problems that are exponentially more expensive to treat" (Acoca, 1998). Therefore, as noted by one investigator, "defuse the time bomb," proper and timely medical care needs to be provided to all female prisoners (Acoca, 1998). Notably, health care costs for Wisconsin state prisoners increased more than 500 percent between 1992 ($9.9 million) and 2003 ($61.4 million) mostly due to more expensive drugs, a growing and aging inmate population, expensive medical advances, and a prison population that tripped between 1990 and 2000 (Marley, 2004). The rising health care expenses for Wisconsin prisoners, which jumped from $1,362 to $3,378, mirror a national trend (Marley, 2004). Yet, limited resources must not be used as an excuse for not making health care reform a priority. The Michigan Department of Corrections, for example, has sought to provide female prisoners health programs that target their specific needs (Epp, 1996). Otherwise, efforts to improve the treatment of women in prison will continue to lag, especially if they are based on stereotypical sex roles or models based on male inmates. Finally, the female prison system must ensure proper monitoring of health care issues, adequate record-keeping, and outside review.

Chapter 7

LIVING UNDER THE SAME ROOF: FEMALE OFFENDERS AND CORRECTIONAL OFFICERS

This chapter explores the social interactions between adult female inmates and correctional officers. The experiences of females while incarcerated, and, by extension, after release, are impacted by how they interact with staff, how they are viewed and treated by staff, and how they perceive correctional staff. For example, it is not uncommon for female inmates to be treated with disdain, despite the fact that the typical female offender is not in prison for a violent crime and thus will soon be released back into the community. Some of these women, though, will return to prison, a place they might perceive as a hostile environment, making subsequent incarcerations more devastating for both inmates and correctional staff. The chapter concludes by documenting the interactions between prisoners and officers in Wisconsin prisons.

RELATIONSHIPS BETWEEN PRISONERS AND CORRECTIONAL STAFF

The relationship between women in prison and correctional officers must be analyzed in the context of everyday behavior, attitudes, perceptions, and historical stereotypes. In particular, there is indication that correctional officers perceive female inmates as more open to expressing their emotions, and, by extension, making it more difficult to work with than male prisoners. There is also the notion that women are more prone to "acting out" in prison in response to diverse issues, ranging from minor to serious rule infractions, "making" them institutionally different from male prisoners. As a result, some correctional officers may feel that they must treat women more leniently to avoid immediate emotional reactions, resulting from issues such as lack of control, manipulation, moodiness, and physical and psychological factors. According to Joycelyn Pollock (1984:90), officers report that "the absence of the stoic norm makes it acceptable for the women in prison to show a whole range of emotions, from love, affection, or friendship to sadness and anger toward other inmates or toward officers and administrators." However, a related notion is that institutional behavior of female offenders is not so much a matter of personal achievements than it is of self-expression (Benn and Ryder-Tchaikovsky, 1983). These issues, though, might be a reflection of historical stereotypes of female offenders and women in general. Realistically, whether the officers' perceptions derive from actual female behavior in prison or historical gender, racial, or ethnic stereotypes (Bobo and Hutchings, 1996; Oboler, 1995), the effects of their interaction with female inmates is the same. Further, there is a significant gap between what people say and what people do, especially in institutional settings that are subject to little outside review.

Prior Investigations of Female/Officer Behavior

Previous investigations report inconclusive, mixed, or contradictory results about the weight of the evidence suggests that the relationship between women in prison and correctional officers is not constant, but intimidating, depressing, unpredictable, and violent and frightening for inmates (see Kurshan, 1996).

For instance, some investigators have reported that women are frequent rule violators, most commonly for not obeying orders, creating disturbances, fighting, using vulgar language, and possession of contraband (Faily, Roundtree, and Miller, 1980; Tischler and Marquart, 1989). Other studies have reported that women tend to commit more rule infractions than men, but that men historically committed more serious rule violations (Lindquist, 1980). Yet, one study found no gender difference in regards to frequency or severity of rule infractions in prison (Tischler and Marquart, 1989). In regards to punishment for rule violations, some studies document that females are treated more leniently than men (Lindquist, 1980), but others report that discipline for women in prison is generally harsher than it is for men. One study, for instance, found that Texas female inmates are far more likely to be cited for rule violations, and to receive more severe sanctions (McClellan, 1994). In all, a number of studies document the injustice, intimidation, fear, and cruelty of women in prison in "modern" America (Belknap, 1996; Díaz-Cotto, 1996; Owen, 1998; Rierden, 1997).

Re-experiencing Earlier Traumas

As noted in Chapter 3, the pre-prison experience of female offenders influences how women react to prison life. In a classic study, Kruttschnitt, Gartner, and Miller (2000:701) report the experience of one California prisoner: ". . . after being in abuse for years, you lose your own identity, you lose your self-esteem, and then they put you here, where, you know, they're telling you what to do, when you can do it, so you don't have to think. . . . Being from an abusive background, it's like I was scratching back to all the abuse that I had lived already." Another California prisoner reports her prison experience: "And I feel sometimes that I'm still getting abuse, you know? . . . [T]here's a lot of males, mostly male c.o.s here, you know? . . . They have this attitude where you know they have full control over us, you know? . . . [W]When I lived with an abusive man, you know, full control. And these men have that same attitude. They make me feel the same way. . . . I was abused by the guy in my case. . . . I know what it's like to be brutally and physically abused. I mean I still have bite marks, you know, stuff like that. I know what it's like to be brutally and physically abused and have an officer sit there and get this close to your face, you know where they're barely an inch between the two of you, and yell at the top of his lungs" (Kruttschnitt, Gartner, and Miller, 2000:702).

With a growing prison population that is becoming extremely stressed and depressed (see Chapter 7), allowing this type of abusive or confrontational behavior to continue is likely to result in a major medical gap in the delivery of medical service in prison for female offenders in that depression is difficult to treat, expensive, and leads to more critical issues, like suicide. For women who have children, the situation gets even more devastating in that they will not be in a stable position to care for their young children upon release.

Verbal Abuse of Prisoners

Verbal abuse is one of the most powerful psychological mechanisms to humiliate, intimate, and control, and this conduct in female prisons seems to be more of a norm than the exception. Consider the following statements: "They [males] call us bitches; they refer to us as bitches, or 'f . . . ing' bitches. I mean, my environment wasn't like that before. . . . I'm not one that came from that environment. And it's just very strange, and frightening" and "There have been times when I've known that officers have been listening to phone calls, which they do have a right to do. Some of them will turn the intercom up so loud that everybody hears your conversation, you know? Personal conversation with your family, and here was an officer that made a comment about the way my son was talking" (Kruttschnitt, Gartner, and Miller, 2000:707). In the words of one California prisoner: ". . . there's a lot of officers that will call us bimbos, or bitches, whores, stuff like that. . . . They have a real bad thing about, you know, 'inmates have nothing coming.' And they don't care about our welfare. . ." (Kruttschnitt, Gartner, and Miller, 2000:706).

Even though verbal abuse from correctional staff has been documented by researchers as a constant issue in female prisons, ranging from minor derogatory words or phrases to full-blown emotional and psychological abuse, there has been a lack or none-existence of cultural, gender, and diversity training in prisons. Of course, correctional policies, if they exist, are difficult to enforce if there is no outside review, and thus what happens in prison stays in prison.

The Significance of Power in Prison

Historically, "power" has been the focal element in American prisons (Fogel, 1979; Foucault, 1995; Harris, 1988). After a series of constitutional challenges resulting from the abuse of power, correctional officials have sought to eliminate abuse of excessive power in institutional management. Based on recent studies, however, the influence of power has manifested itself in more subtle ways, such as name calling, looks of disdain, insensitivity for issues like culture, gender, and physical appearance, and negligence for female concerns, needs, and desires. Case in point: "Some of them are stuck on their badges in a way that it's a power trip for them and they just, you know, they just go with it as far as they can and push it to its limits and try to, you know, show so much power. And you know it's really like they've got the biggest ego and it's really, its really bad. Others they come in and they don't care one way or the other. And still others try to follow the program, and they're pretty decent, but for the most part, they're not . . ." (Kruttschnitt, Gartner, and Miller, 2000:707). Also, in an environment where the smallest possessions are extremely valuable, the power to control what inmates have and do not have shapes everyday social interaction. In fact, most women resent staff's ability to control what the women are allowed to have in their room, which includes personal hygiene items. To one middle-class 50-year-old woman prisoner in California, adjusting to prison was the most difficult in that "I'm not used to being treated that way. I've never been treated that way in my life, and its very hard to accept, being treated like a non-person" (Kruttschnitt, Gartner, and Miller, 2000:697).

In the context of the prison system, abuse of authority has been historically defined or viewed as an unjustified act (e.g., physical, verbal, psychological, or emotional) against the prisoner, such as brutality (O'Malley, 1999). However, power is just as significant when there is no act where there should be one, creating a state of silence, negligence, and ultimately creating an atmosphere where women are forgotten (Roberts, 1989).

Social Interactions Across Time and Space

Abuse of social interaction between female inmates and correctional officers appears constant across time and space (Harris, 1988). One investigator, for example, cites one female prisoner saying: "But the guards are scary. They make the rounds three or four times a night. And you're truly impotent. If they hurt you or beat you—it's your word against theirs and yours doesn't count. It's very frightening" (DeClue, 1981:37). Investigations of sexual misconduct by officers in women's prisons in California, Georgia, Illinois, Michigan, and New York show that male officers had raped, sexually assaulted, and abused female inmates (Jones, 1982; McCampbell and Layman, 2000; *New York*

Times, 1996). In a federal facility in Arizona, two women reported being forced to unnecessary vaginal and anal examinations by male staff (Korn, 1988b). In 2002, Jackie Noyes became pregnant while in Taycheedad Correctional Institution in Wisconsin (Twohey, 2004). The Wisconsin Department of Corrections hired consultants from the U.S. Department of Justice to investigate sexual misconduct. The July 2003 report, which contains a series of specific findings and recommendations, concluded that "Despite new laws, policies that affect inmates haven't changed" (Twohey, 2004:A1). Corrections Secretary Matt Frank confirmed that despite reform efforts, the problem persists and that it will take time to remedy sexual misconduct in prison (Twohey, 2004).

These negative or abuse social interactions in institutional settings contribute to confusing, conflicting, hostile, untrusting, and violent relationships between correctional staff and female prisoners. Logically, negative relationships influence medical treatment, inmate labor productivity, and ultimately harm institutional management. And, depending on the nature of the relationships, there are also legal implications, possibly resulting in criminal prosecution or civil litigation (Alpert, 1982; Barry, 1991; Schlanger, 2003).

In sum, virtually all of the female prisoners typically complain about correctional staff, and the majority of women ". . . pointed out example after example of what they saw as arbitrary restrictions, inhumane treatment, and abuse from staff . . . " who are actively hostile towards incarcerated women (Kruttschnitt, Gartner, and Miller, 2000:705-706; Rafter, 1987). Still, investigators report that some staff did their jobs well while others did not. For instance, one 32-year-old California prisoner said that "Staff is most excellent" (Kruttschnitt, Gartner, and Miller, 2000:706). Under such contradictory conditions, female prisoners typically respond to abuse by correctional staff by either avoiding interaction or by trying to be as respectful as possible at all times to stay out of trouble, keep a clean record, and cope with the lack of privacy.

RELATIONSHIPS AMONG FEMALE PRISONERS

Considering that much of the correctional literature is based on experiences of the "male prison model," one must be sensitive to gender variation. Historically, relationships in male prisons have been governed by a multitude of racial, ethnic, political, economic, geographical, and social factors. And, even though, male prisons have been viewed as socially fractured, male inmates have relied on solidarity for self protection or to direct attacks against the institution. Female relationships in institutional settings, though, not only differ significantly from male institutions, but they continue to change. A close look suggests the social relationships are shaped and re-shaped by historical and ideological factors, most notably "power."

Social Solidarity and Power

Social relationships in female prisons must be analyzed within the context of power differentials in that the nature and level of solidarity, and, by extension, trust with other inmates is governed by how women react to loss of power (Larson and Nelson, 1984), isolation, intimidation, fear, and negligence. In an environment where "power" becomes almost nonexistent for inmates, contributing to extreme isolation, intimidation, negligence, and fear, the choices for daily life are limited, critical, and consequential.

Contrary to the male experience, relationships among female prisoners seem to be shaped and re-shaped more for social solidarity and survival than it is for racial, ethnic, political, economic, or geographical difficulties (Diaz-Cotto, 1996). One study reports that whereas men tend to direct attacks on correctional staff, female prisoners tend to attack one another physically to protect themselves, friends, or property (Tischler and Marquart, 1989). However, even though studies continue to report that female prisoners tend to be close and friendly among themselves, often forming pseudo-families in which they adapt to various "survival and social" roles (Owen, 1998; see also Giallombardo, 1966; Heffernan, 1972; Leger, 1987; Moyer, 1978; Ward and Kassebaum, 1965), recent studies report that personal relationships may be less stable and less familial than in the past, indicating that there is certain variation within the female prison experience. In fact, some studies report higher levels of mistrust among women and greater economic manipulation than previously thought (Greer, 2000). Another recent study found that most women normally limit their relationships with other inmates to one or two (Kruttschnitt, Gartner, and Miller, 2000). A common reason, as noted by one

California prisoner: "As far as having anyone you can trust, inmate or staff, very, very rarely can you trust anyone" (Kruttschnitt, Gartner, and Miller, 2000:704).

Last, social relationships in female prison are also influenced by external factors, like addictions (see Chapter 6), family relationship (see Chapter 2), and life before prison (see Chapter 4). Andi Rierden (1997:18), for example, documents a case in which a female prisoner in Connecticut reported disliking young inmates who: "come in off the streets looking like zombies, bone thin and strung out on crack cocaine. 'You can tell them by the abscesses on their bodies from shooting liquid dope cut with meat tenderizer. Before long these inmates fatten up on the prison's starchy food and the junk they order from commissary, smuggle in their drugs, and sleep around with women, even though they likely have a boyfriend or husband on the outside. Once released, they'll return to the streets, get arrested and then return to the Farm [prison]. Once settled in they'll unite with the old flames and 'just chill.'" To this end, other studies report that changes in the characteristics of the inmate population coincided with changes in the level of institutional conflict and the nature of the inmate culture (Fox, 1982, 1984).

Taken together, a close analysis indicates that social relationships among women in prison are not constant, but governed by both historical and ideological factors, and an ever-changing correctional system that is growing larger and more diverse. Historically, women have to cope with a system that remains insensitive to gender specific issues. Ideologically, policies seem to be more a reflection of gender, culture, and race stereotypes than actual everyday interactions. Externally, sentencing laws have altered the female prison experience. Internally, the "prison friend" is not well defined as originally assumed and "pseudo-families" are not as productive as observers assumed. As noted by one researcher, "We saw the family as palliative, as keeping the women happy and failed to see that this keep-them-happy philosophy was to keep-them-down. All was in the present, the here-and-how, without any thought for the past or the future" (Van Wormer, 1987:269–270). More fundamentally, "The penalization of women parallels the subjugation of women in the society. Women are to be first and foremost wives and mothers . . . not to act. So, if surrogate family roles are functional in preserving the roles and statuses of the sex, they are dysfunctional for the same reason" (Van Wormer, 1987:270).

STRIP SEARCHES

Of the many different issues confronting women in prison, either because of fear, intimidation, humiliation, or some other feeling of injustice, strip searches seem to be the most sensitive and controversial primarily for the manner in which they are conducted, the reasons for conducting them, and the people who participate in these searches. Amnesty International (1999:1), for instance, reports that "rape and other forms of sexual abuse—including sexually offensive language and male staff touching women's breasts and genitals during searches or watching them when they are naked—are widespread in US prisons and jails." These findings appear consistent with findings from the Human Rights Watch Project (1996). For inmates who refuse being stripped search, the experience can be even more detrimental. A 52-year-old Caucasian woman in California reports that when she refused to be stripped searched before going to court, the administration sends in an "extraction team" to conduct the search. "The team consists of eight men in riot gear who enter her cell and hold her down while a female guard rips off her clothes and conducts the search in their presence . . . [while] the male guards make vulgar comments and threats. . ." (Shaylor, 1998:392).

Historically, strip searches were utilized as a method of social control, but then they began to lose popularity under claims of brutality, injustice, and inhumane treatment. Still, at the same time that correctional policies are being implemented or modified to control for excessive searching or prevent unnecessary strip searches altogether, the female prison population is drastically increasing, mostly for drugs that seem to "justify" strip searches. In fact, vaginal searches are frequently utilized to discover contraband. To Coramae Mann (1984), "What is ironic about this procedure is that these vagina examinations are frequent, yet the preventive Pap test for cervical cancer is not often given."

Logically, these types of experiences not only influence the nature of social relationships between correctional officers and inmates while incarcerated, but continue to shape perceptions about life in prison and society once women are released (Young, 2000). In the words of former antiwar activist Jane Kennedy, "In my way of thinking prison, at least as we know it, is like a war. Both situations cause evil by the very nature of their being. I grew up believing the middle-class idea that anyone who is in prison deserves it. They were antisocial people who wouldn't play by the rules of society. By experiencing prison, I have learned this just isn't so" (DeClue, 1981:37).

Given that strip searches are gender, age, and culture sensitive, we provide three recommendations. First, institutions should hire more female officers, placing these officers in carefully selected areas. For example, even though female inmates rather have male correctional officers than female officers, the majority of women object to having male officers in assignments that require direct physical contact or visual observation, such as pat or strip searches as well as toilet and shower areas (Zupan, 1992).[26] Second, strip searches should be conducted only under extreme situations and properly justified cases. Third, continuous outside review must be implemented in all correctional institutions to increase compliance, avoid injustices, and ensure accountability for failure to follow institutional protocol, state laws, and constitutional mandates.

THE WISCONSIN EXPERIENCE

This section reports findings for female prisoners in the state of Wisconsin. A central objective was to obtain information regarding their interactions and social relationships with correctional officers, particularly information that might be of assistance in policy development. Ultimately, the objective is to establish interactions and relationships that will be more peaceful, respectful, and promising for female offenders as they are being released back to the community.

Interactions and Relationships in Wisconsin Female Prisons

Male vs. Female Officers

As noted above, under harsh criticisms of "male operated" institutions, the prison system has been hiring more female officers, a move that is likely to continue in the future. Additionally, there is evidence that indicates negative relationships and interactions between correctional officers and female prisoners. Surprisingly, when inmates in

Wisconsin were asked if they had a preference for male or female officers, over half (287 or 62.9%) of the participants said no and only 159 (34.9%) women said yes (see Table 22). Of those indicating a preference for correctional officers, 111 women preferred male officers and 44 women preferred female officers, consistent with Zupan (1992).

Table 22
INTERACTION BETWEEN FEMALE INMATES AND CORRECTIONAL
OFFICERS IN WISCONSIN (N=456)

	Frequency	Percent
Preference for male or female officers		
Yes	159	34.9
No	287	62.9
Correctional officer preference		
Males	111	24.3
Females	44	9.6
Respected by officers		
Yes	212	46.5
No	231	50.7
Inappropriate language by officers		
Yes	243	53.3
No	198	43.4
Respect for correctional officers		
Yes	416	91.2
No	19	4.2
Verbally abused by officers		
Yes	253	55.5
No	180	39.5
Emotionally abused by officers		
Yes	168	36.8
No	247	54.2
Physically abused by officers		
Yes	30	6.6
No	347	76.1
Sexually abused by officers		
Yes	15	3.3
No	355	77.9
Strip-searched by officers		
Yes	363	79.6
No	84	18.4

Continued on next page

Table 22 (cont.)

	Frequency	Percent
Who strip-searched		
Female officers	350	76.8
Both male and female officers	14	3.1
Other people	1	0.2
Privacy respected by officers		
Yes	100	21.9
No	147	32.2
I have no privacy	199	43.6
Good communication with officers		
Yes	317	69.5
No	127	27.9
Main goals of officers		
Peace keeping (order)	34	7.5
Providing direction to inmates	9	2.0
Sharing info with inmates	2	0.4
Avoiding violence	15	3.3
Providing material resources	4	0.9
Other duties	47	10.3
Don't know	31	6.8
Multiple duties	293	64.3
Relationship with officers		
Mostly cooperative	266	58.3
Sometimes cooperative	79	17.3
Mostly problematic	44	9.6
Sometimes problematic	50	11.0

Respect in Female Prisons

Considering that perceptions, attitudes, and behaviors are in large part governed by the level of respect between officers and prisoners, inmates were asked some specific questions. As reported in Table 22, slightly over half (231 or 50.7%) of the women reported that officers, in general, do not respect them, with slightly less than half (212 or 46.5%) of the respondents reporting that they do not feel respected. Similarly, over half (243 or 53.3%) of the participants reported being called degrading names and inappropriate language by correctional officers, with 198 (43.4%) reporting otherwise. Most (416 or 91.2%) women reported showing respect for correctional officers, and only 19 women noted that they do not respect officers. In which case, a significant future research question is "why." Is it because of fear, intimidation, oppositional culture, power differentials, obedience to authority, or simply social norms?

Abuse in Female Prisons

Social relationships in prison are influenced by how people are treated. As reported in Table 22, over half (253 or 55.5%) of the participating inmates reported being verbally abused, and over one-third (168 or 36.8%) of the women said that they had been emotionally abused by correctional officers. In terms of actual physical contact, 30 women reported being physically abused, and 15 women reported being sexually abused by correctional officers. Even though the reported rates of physical and sexual abuse are significantly lower than the rates of verbal and emotional abuse, this type of behavior is detrimental to prison reform—not only complicating institutional innovations, like medical treatment and efforts to alleviate the trauma of losing a child, rape, or some other drastic life event, but also efforts that seek to prepare inmates to be "reintegrated" into the community upon release.

Strip Searches in Female Prisons

As one of the most controversial issues in corrections, strip searches continue to present a major challenge to both inmates and the correctional system. To this end, Wisconsin is one of the many states that allow male officers to supervise living units in female prisons, and it is one of the few states that permit pat down searches by male officers without restrictions. As shown in Table 22, the majority (363 or 79.6%) of participating inmates reported being strip-searched by officers. Of those conducting the search, 350 involved female officers and only 14 involved both male and female officers. Logically, as in other type of behavior in prison, strip searches (where abuse may be more likely to happen) are likely to shape future interactions and to influence the nature of relationships between inmates and correctional officers. Last, even though laws are being implemented to place restrictions on when, how, and by whom strip searches can be conducted, it is unlikely that the rate of strip searches will significantly be reduced in the future, at least as long as the drugs and weapons are brought into correctional facilities.

Privacy in Female Prisons

As an original element of corrections (Foucault, 1995), the concept of "privacy" in female prisons remains vague, controversial, and constitutionally unresolved. Yet, based on the authors' observations, privacy in prison is one of the most pressing concerns for female offenders. As shown in Table 22, of the incarcerated women in Wisconsin, only 100 (21.9%) reported having their privacy respected by officers, with 147 (32.2%) women reporting that officers do not respect their privacy and 199 (43.6%) stating that they have no privacy whatsoever.

Considering modern organizational and constitutional changes of the prison system (Flanagan, Marquart, and Adams, 1998), the concept of privacy will continue to be a challenge for these prisoners. Practically, though, the level of privacy in prison is likely to decrease due to the various technological innovations such as that are being implemented (see Chapter 8). More fundamentally, lack of privacy, seen by some female prisoners as a sign of no respect for inmates, is likely to become more significant as the prison population becomes larger.

Communication in Female Prisons

The level of communication between inmates and officers in prison is influential in how interactions and relationships develop. Honest and peaceful communication, for instance, creates an environment where inmates might want to express their deepest concerns about issues such as health, pregnancy, drug addiction, treatment, work, and their children, alleviating intimidation and fear. Further, communication enables inmates to better understand and, perhaps, appreciate the roles of correctional officers, leading to more positive interactions and relationships. Therefore, inmates were also asked about communication, perceptions about officers' main goals, and actual relationships. Table 22 outlines that even though the majority (317 or 69.5%) of inmates reported having good communication with officers, 127 women reported otherwise. In regards to what they perceived to be the primary goals of correctional officers, they reported: multiple duties (293), peace-keeping (34), avoiding violence (15), providing directions to inmates (9), providing material resources (4), sharing information with inmates (2), other duties (47), and "don't know" (31). Last, even though the majority (345 or 75.6%) of respondents had a cooperative relationship with correctional officers, 94 (20.6%) women reported having a problematic relationship with officers.

Good communication in prison depends on patience and understanding, especially related to addictions (see Chapter 3) and mental health problems (see Chapter 6). In addition, changes in demographic characteristics are beginning to present an additional challenge to the correctional system. For example, a growing number of minorities like Latinas, Native Americans, and Hmong (see Chapter 2) is likely to create significant language barriers (see Chapter 8), similar to the Wisconsin court system (Urbina, 2004a).

CONCLUSION

Documented in various prior investigations, and supported by the Wisconsin study, it is not uncommon for women to express feelings of frustration, humiliation, intimidation, and to report being treated unjustly or cruelly by correctional officers or administrators. Even though institutional changes have been made to improve living conditions, and relationships between women and correctional staff, a significant gap remains to be bridged. Such a gap, though, requires changes that go beyond structural modifications that focus on social control. First, the prison system must hire a more diverse prison staff. The racial and ethnic composition of inmates in the United States is mostly Caucasian (but disproportionately minority), followed by African Americans, a growing number of Latinas, and a few of other races (respectively). Yet, the racial and ethnic composition of correctional officers and administrators is predominately Caucasian, followed by a significantly smaller percentage of African Americans, a lesser percentage of Latinas and Latinos, and tiny fraction of other races (respectively) and ethnicities. Second, the prison system must provide continuous training for staff, focusing on gender, race, ethnicity, and cultural understanding (Aguirre, 2003). Third, policies must be based on empirical investigations and not on historical stereotypes. Fourth, the legislature needs to take an active role in ensuring that the correctional system allows for independent outside review, especially in questionable cases that involve issues like strip-searches. Finally, as one of the most significant factors in everyday social interactions and relationships, communication in the prison system must be viewed as a priority. Good communication between inmates and correctional officers has the potential of reducing fear, intimidation, disturbances, assists staff in becoming positive role models for the prisoners, and educates inmates about expectations, consequences, and final outcomes.

Chapter 8

CRITICAL ISSUES:
TWENTY-FIRST CENTURY CHALLENGES

The first part of this chapter examines some of the most significant critical issues that historically have influenced the prison experience, as well as the more contemporary issues facing women in American prisons. Based on the existing literature, not only is the woman experience different from the male experience, but the prison experience is not constant. A major challenge facing both female offenders and correctional staff are correctional policies themselves, which tend to be based on male-oriented needs. For years, investigations have explored a wide range of issues, such as overcrowding, access to rehabilitation or recreation, institutional structure, and medical care. However, other critical issues, such as hate, have received limited attention. For instance, the traditional U.S. prisoner (i.e., African American or Caucasian) is now being joined by other racial and ethnic individuals, particularly Latinas. With these demographic changes, though, also come additional concerns, such as language barriers, gangs forming on racial/ethnic divides, and hatred among inmates. The second part of this chapter will report the findings, to include visitors, racial/ethnic divisions, violence, gangs, and hatred among inmates, for the Wisconsin study.

LEADING CRITICAL ISSUES IN CORRECTIONS

The number of challenges facing women in prison is high, all which deserve special attention. Among the various issues, the authors have identified the following 12 issues as possibly the most pressing concerns that must be addressed properly and in a timely manner to avoid prejudice, discrimination, brutality, lawsuits, and injustice, while increasing efficiency and safety.

Visitors

Visitation remains as one of the most difficult challenges to address even though prison officials, legislators, and other policymakers are making changes for maintaining family contact to better facilitate visitation to all prisons (see Chapters 2 and 5). For example, with visitation as one of the main objectives, Wisconsin officials announced the return of females imprisoned out of Wisconsin in 2000 (see Chapter 6). Realistically, though, this approach has minimal impact without the consideration and reformation of other influential factors, such as economics, employment, institutional issues during visits, transportation, travel distance, and child care (see Raimon, 2000).

The consequences of not maintaining a well-structured visitor network in female prisons (Schoenbauer, 1986), is the continuation of the very same problem that we are trying to solve: the cycle of deviance and crime. Studies have shown that the "maintenance of strong family ties during imprisonment influence future criminal activity" (Hairston, 1988:51). Logically, the loss of a parent to incarceration, divorce or death, often leaves children confused, sad, depressed, angry, vulnerable, and feeling abandoned. As noted by one observer, "In addition to coping with feeling of grief, anger and rejection they must deal with the stigma associated with having a relative in prison" (Fishman, 1983:89). In the end, not well adapted to the school system, children drop out of school, and some end up in the streets involved in a life of drugs, prostitution, violence, and crime (Rodriguez, 1993) and eventually detention centers, jails, and prisons.

In the future, there are two other issues to consider: the historical demon of discrimination and isolation. First, with an increase in the female prison population, particularly minority women, African American and Latina women are likely to suffer the worst injustices, creating another layer of indirect discrimination (Bresler and Lewis, 1983; Browne, 1996). One study found ethnic variation in visitation, with 84.6 percent, 62.5 percent, and 54 percent of Latino/a, African

American, and Caucasian (respectively) visitors visiting females in prison. Also, African American visitors traveled further than Caucasians and Latinas (Fuller, 1993). Second, as the minority prison population increases, so does the pool of family relatives (and possibly friends) with a criminal record, suggesting that visitation will become even more difficult for minority prisoners in that their relatives will be "afraid" or not allowed to make prison visits (Allen, 1982). In short, to avoid isolation, and the destruction of family ties (Bresler and Lewis, 1983), further distance between women and society, visitation must be a high priority.

Race and Ethnic Relations among Female Prisoners

A popular subject of television shows and movies, race and ethnic relations in prison (Hawkins, 1998; Urbina, 2003a, 2007) continues to be a focal subject of investigation, and widely talked among policymakers and the general public. Yet, until recently, the focus has been primarily on African Americans and Caucasians (Carroll, 1974; Fox, 1982), to the exclusion of other races and ethnicities, creating a knowledge gap in the understanding of the female prison experience. First, "male penal models," some of which distort true prison experiences, do not capture the true essence of the female prison experience. Second, with great cultural and circumstantial variation in female prisons, traditional penal models fail to show the realities of minority prisoners, like Latinas and Native Americans.

In regards to gender, race, and ethnic variation, one Minnesota study found racial tensions, but conflict between African Americans and non-Caucasians was not a predominant aspect of life in female prisons (Fox, 1982; Kruttschnitt, 1983; Larson and Nelson, 1984). Consistent with earlier studies, more recent investigations have found that female prisons do not typically have the racial tensions found in men's prisons (Greer, 2000; Owen, 1998). To this end, one Caucasian woman doing time in a California prison stated, "Not that I'm aware of; it doesn't seem real prevalent. I've got Mexican friends, Black friends. . . . Women are different from men. We don't care. . . . Oh sure, there is always going to be the exception to the rule, but I think basically the rule is it makes no difference" (Kruttschnitt, Gartner, and Miller 2000:696). As a whole, ". . . racial issues play some part in the culture and everyday life of the prison, but not to the extent found among male prisoners. . . . The conflict here is age, not race like with the men" (Owen, 1998:13, 177).

Negative race and ethnic relations in female prisons seem to be between inmates and prison staff and not among prisoners (Carroll, 1996). Relations between staff and prisoners have received limited empirical attention, but there is some evidence indicating that Caucasian staff exhibit prejudice and discrimination toward minority prisoners (Diaz-Cotto, 1996; Owen, 1998). For example, some minority female prisoners at the California Women's Facility felt that prison jobs were unfairly distributed to Caucasian inmates (Owen, 1998).

In short, as the racial and ethnic prison population increases (each group with its unique concerns, needs, and views), racial divisions and tensions are likely to escalate, not so much because of power, control, gang formation, or safety (typically found in male prisons), but differential treatment in services and prison employment. Evidently, as a brutal and often bloody historical concept, race and ethnic relations are likely to worsen in the future if the prison system does not take the necessary precautions to avoid chaos, hostility, hate, violence, and discrimination (Aguirre, 2003; Aguirre and Turner, 2006).

Gangs

Traditionally viewed as a "homogenous" female prison population, there seemed to be little need for gang creation. In fact, a recent study found that compared to male prisons, women prisons are less violent and less involved in gang activity (Greer, 2000). Some investigators report that a lack of gangs in female prisons is partially explained by the social power of older inmates in that older women have reputations and respect that allows them to exist without constant challenges to daily life while institutionalized. Thus, fearful of possible consequences, like loss of peace, some elder prisoners do not tolerate gang activities (Moyer, 1980; Owen, 1998). At some level, women are self governing themselves to avoid some of the most feared consequences of gang behavior such as violence, attacks, murders, and riots and response of corrections, such as lockdowns.

Yet, with so many penal changes, it is probable that gangs will become a major concern to both prison staff and female inmates in the future. In particular, with an increase in young prisoners, some of whom are searching for power, identity, or protection, and an increase in minority prisoners, the prison population will become much more heterogeneous. As the inmate population becomes more heterogeneous, variation in diversity, culture, and opportunity will also increase. For example, in fierce competition for limited resources, gang formation might be a natural response.

Violence

Without the abundance of two of the most powerful elements of prison violence (i.e., hostile and antagonistic race and ethnic relations among inmates and a low rate of gang creation), violence in female prisons has not yet reach alarming proportions (*Corrections Digest*, 1985c; Farnworth, 1984). One Minnesota study found that less than one-quarter of the incarcerated women engaged in aggressive behavior against fellow inmates (Kruttschnitt and Krmpotich, 1990). As whole, while assaults, normally for minor things, in female prison exists (Lerner, 1989), research shows that the majority of female prisoners try to avoid "the mix . . . behavior that can bring trouble and conflict with staff and other prisoners" (Owen, 1998:179; see also James and Glaze, 2006).

Findings point to a low level of violence; yet, we must have a clear understanding of female behavior for policy implementation and modification. As suggested in prior studies, female criminal behavior does not begin at the time of a criminal act, arrest, prosecution, or incarceration, Female criminality is a product of the time she was born, socialization, and afterwards (see Chapter 3). Studies show that characteristics, experiences, and early behavior of female offenders before incarceration influence their prison behavior (Roundtree, Mohan, and Mahaffery, 1980). For example, one study found that childhood family structure is associated with female aggression in prison (Kruttschnitt and Krmpotich, 1990). The Minnesota study also found that drug use had no effect on violence among female prisoners, but found childhood family structure to have the strongest influence on aggressive behavior among female inmates (see Chapter 3).

Logically, without a sound understanding of female criminality, the development and implementation of an efficient, humane, and just correctional system is likely to fail. In which case, the female correctional system might resemble the male prison system, as Hans Toch (1977:53) observers, "Jails and prisons . . . have a climate of violence which has no free-world counterpart. Inmates are terrorized by other inmates and spend years in fear of harm. Some inmates request segregation, others lock themselves in and some are hermits by choice. Many inmates injure themselves."[27]

Aging in Prison

Historically, racism and sexism have been two central themes of prison research. However, with the warehousing of inmates, particularly for drug offenses (see Chapter 2), other factors are becoming obvious: aging in prison. Coined in 1969 (Butler, 1969) as a parallel to racism, "ageism" has brought the attention of some investigations and policymakers (Goetting, 1984a, 1985; Sommers and Baskin, 1992), but it remains to be studied by the totality of age circumstances, expectations, and implications. One researcher proclaimed: "People who manage to survive to old age know that the present system is destroying them. They experience discrimination, intolerance and isolation based on the sad fact that they are old. Their oppression stems from an irreversible biological condition, as surely as the black person faces oppression because of color and women experience oppression based on sex" (Curtain, 1972:193).

Mostly attributed to the "war on drugs" and changes in sentencing such as determinant sentences, sentence enhancement, and truth in sentencing, female prison rates are increasingly drastically, creating a elderly prison population (see Chapters 1 and 2). However, the penal system has not properly corresponded with the array of services required to be an elderly population. In particular, the medical health care system in female prisons lags behind the needs of women in prison (see Chapter 6). For instance, due to the deterioration of eye sight, hearing, chronic illnesses, memory, teeth, and reflexes, older inmates require exercise, special diets, and preventative health care on a regular basis. This gap, particularly as it pertains to health care delivery services, is likely to increase if confronting aging prison population is not made a priority. As a consequence, the prison system could be confronted with additional demands, like litigation to provide appropriate health care for older female prisoners (see Barry, 1991; Schlanger, 2003).

Language Barriers

With a prison population that was mostly African American and Caucasian, investigators and policymakers have relied on "dichotomous penal models" to explore the female prison experience, giving other minority groups and their concerns limited attention. Nationally, though, we are now witnessing a sharp increase in the incarceration of other minorities, most notably Latinas, and in states like Wisconsin, Native Americans and Hmong. As in the general population, minority defendants show up in prison with their own unique experiences, ideologies, and concerns (Urbina, 2004a, 2007).

Yet, there is probably no specific minority concern with severe ramifications than language barriers. As documented in a recent investigation, language barriers are influential in the entire legal process, from the time of the arrest until the individual is released from prison (Urbina, 2004a). From a constitutional standpoint, if defendents do not *understand* what they are being asked by police officers, what is being said in court proceedings, what is being said by correctional staff, or understand what they are signing, what they are agreeing to, what they are being asked to to (or not do) during the lengthy legal process, they, practically, have no constitutional rights, since legal rights are conveyed in words (Urbina, 2004a). Thus, with significant changes in demography of the prison population, language barriers must be made a priority.

Lesbianism

For some time, investigations (Foster, 1975; Propper, 1981) have examined the nature, implications, and consequences of prison relationships, a form of inmate interactions in which participants play given or selected roles (see Chapter 7). Researchers have documented that surrogate families help cope with the daily pains of life behind bars (Van Wormer, 1981), but they have also found ". . . political, social, and personal dysfunctions" (Van Wormer, 1987:263).

The manifestation of surrogate families is lesbianism in female prisons, a topic that has received little academic attention. Ironically, whether it is in the general population or institutional settings, dialogue about lesbian relationships are normally fused with stereotypes, prejudice, political and religious ideology, and ignorance, with little reliance on reality. Consequently, lesbian relationships in prison continue to be poorly understood. When studies are conducted, they often contradict historical misconceptions. In particular, there seems to be greater emotional involvement in lesbianism than in gay relationships among men in prison (Ford, 1979). From a legal standpoint, one study found that self-identified lesbians had histories of previous imprisonment, longer sentences, arrested at earlier ages, served more time in prison, higher endorsement of feminist values, and higher rates of conflict and aggression (Leger, 1987). According to the author, "the most criminalistic, feministic, aggressive, and homosexually active women in the institution were those whose first gay experience preceded their initial arrest" (Leger, 1987:448). To this end, one investigation "found virtually no evidence of predatory sexual behavior among . . ." female prisoners (Kruttschnitt and Krmpotich, 1990:384). Further, contrary to our historical stereotypes, gays in prison were better educated, more urbanized, had lower number of children, and were more likely to be single or divorced (Leger, 1987), not supporting deprivation theory as an explanation of lesbianism in correctional institutions.

Lesbianism, though, is likely to increase in the coming years (see Leger, 1987) because of societal and correctional changes. First, the female prison population is increasing, and with it, an increased opportunity to develop these relationships. Second, the prison population is becoming more heterogeneous, making it "easier" to engage in diverse activities and less worries of alienation. Third, when females enter prison, some women are finding bonds that perhaps did not exist before they were incarcerated. As noted earlier, the typical female offender has a long history of raising children on her own. However, as lesbianism increases, so will the corresponding ramifications (e.g., looks of disdain, hostility, and even outright discrimination). For these reasons, the prison system must implement mechanisms, like education and sensitivity training to prevent differential treatment. Education, for example, might be of assistance in developing higher tolerance for the "other," the "outsider," and the "stranger" (see Chapter 10 and Epilogue).

Hatred Among Inmates

Hate in the United States has not only been one of the biggest "demons," but one that refuses to die, like an immortal demon in a Hollywood horror movie (Acuna, 2004; Almaguer, 1994). Civil activists have spoken against hate, particularly hate crimes, academics have studied the subject, developed theories, and advocated policies, and policymakers have passed legislation to prevent and sanction hatred-based offenses (Feagin and Sikes, 1994; Feagin and Vera, 1995). Combined, these efforts have produced positive results. But, as in a Hollywood horror movie, the "demon" always manages to make a comeback. For example, the latest comeback is seen in the World Wide Web, where the demon attacks, anonymously.

In the context of female correctional institutions, though, the subject of hate has received little attention. Logically, hate, as a mentality or emotional element, does not end when people enter prison. If hatred has not been a critical issue in female prisons, it is likely to become a major issue due to changes in prison demographics, leading to possible racial tension and all the conflict that this tension creates.

Female Political Prisoners

While women political prisoners have received some attention in the popular media, they have received little attention in the academic literature (Zwerman, 1988). In fact, pre-September 11, 2001, Puerto Rican Nationalists, the Cuban Marielitos, and civil activists of African American, Mexican, or Caucasian origin were normally the only ones who were often caught in the center of controversy, investigation, and public discussion (Urbina, 2005a). In this regard, investigations have shown that these groups of female political prisoners have been subjected to unjustified punishment, like solitary confinement, which has been characterized by some investigators as cruel and unusual punishment (see Chapter 5).

Case in point: The Lexington Federal Prison in Kentucky, the only control unit designed specifically for female political prisoners opened in 1986, and it has housed political prisoners like Alejandrina Torres (Puerto Rican nationalist), Susan Rosenberg (North American anti-imperialist), and Silvia Baraldini (Italian national and anti-imperialist). In this unit they have endured some of the cruelest injustices, without logical reasoning, but devastating consequences. Some investigators report that prisons like Lexington are designed to meet a number of objectives beyond social control for the purpose of security: "The first of these is to reduce prisoners to the state of submission essential for their ideological conversion. That failing, the next objective is to reduce them to a state of psychological incompetence sufficient to neutralize them as efficient, self-directing antagonists. That failing, the only alternative is to destroy them, preferably by making them desperate enough to destroy themselves" (Korn, 1988b:18-19; *Nation*, 1988). In a follow-up investigation, Richard Korn (1988a:25-26) found that the physical and psychological and physical state of female prisoners at Lexington had deteriorated to the point of absolute danger, as evidence by: loss of weight, loss of appetite, dehydration (requiring hospitalization and intravenous feeding), heart palpitations, intractable insomnia, decreasing ability to concentrate, severe anxiety, obsessive ideation (focusing on dying or being killed in prison), increasing difficulty in communicating with people out of prison, increasing fears of loss of impulse-control, anger and rage at perceived injustices and harassment, intrusive re-experiencing of previous prison traumas, a decreasing ability to direct the flow of their own ideation, obsessive fears of mental and physical breakdowns, and increases in hallucinations.

In *Cages of Steel: The Politics of Imprisonment in the United States* (Churchill and VanderWall, 1992:143), Fay Dowker and Glenn Wood quote Ralph Arons, former Warden of Marion, as saying: the real purpose of correctional institutions like the Marion Control Unit is ". . . to control revolutionary attitudes in the prison system and in the society at large." Martin Guevara Urbina and Leslie Smith (2007) argue that this type of social control against female political prisoners is more a reflection of an historical mentality unwilling to change, fear of instability, a perception of national solidarity, but most significantly, the aftermath of colonialism (see also Agozino, 1997; Chowdhry and Beeman, 2007). Considering the various changes in prosecutorial practices as well as sentencing and correctional laws (see Chapter 2), the experience of female political prisoners is not likely to improve significantly. In fact, violations of human rights have become more systematic because of an increasing state and national surveillance in combination with punitive sanctions (Shaylor, 1998). Logically, post-September 11, 2001, criminal laws and punishments are likely to become more globally defined, unified, and prosecuted (Welch, 2006; see Chapter 10).

Death Penalty

When lynching, a form of illegal executions, came to a near end in the United States (Aguirre and Baker, 1997), death sentences dropped to a low point, legal executions were moved behind closed doors, and the subject of capital punishment and female offenders almost ceased to exist. However, as a consequence of the war on drugs, changes in prosecutorial and sentencing laws, changes in the American public option, capital punishment is once again being viewed as a vital option for social control and safety (Aguirre and Baker, 1997; Urbina, 2003a).

At the present time, few women are being executed (Urbina, 2003a), but the correctional system is pushing for death row (Wares, 1990), a critical situation as the prison population continues to rise (*Corrections Digest*, 1987b; Dreifus, 1984). In 2003, 47 women were under sentence of death, up from 38 in 1993. For females who end up under the sentence of death, few women are actually executed, but the rest serve long prison terms before their sentence is commuted (MacKenzie, Robinson, and Campbell, 1989; Urbina, 2002b). Yet, considering that the majority of women are mothers of young children, ". . . the practical concerns of those women whose lives are constrained and organized around living under the sentence of death" (Coontz, 1983:97; Dreifus, 1984). For instance, the poverty in which their children live, the high mortality rate, and the death of a child can be a traumatic event for women on death row (Kaplan, 1988). When this happens, the state is victimizing young innocent children whose only "sin" is to be born to a criminal mother.

Under the rationalization of public security, social control, and world order, this horrible sanction is not likely to disappear for first-degree murder. Logically, it is highly probable that we will witness significant race discrimination, ethnic discrimination, and violations of civil rights and international treaties, as in the case of males on death row (Urbina, 2004b). Further, as in the case of political prisoners, executions have typically been rationalized as the elimination of a threat to social order, though in reality it has more to do with the historical effects of colonialism, and with current efforts to preserve the status quo (see Agozino, 1997; Chowdhry and Beeman, 2007; Urbina and Smith, 2007).

In *Capital Punishment and Latino Offenders* (2003), Martin Guevara Urbina argues that capital punishment in the United States persists mostly for historical, political, ideological, religious, economical, and social reasons–having little to do with safety or practicality. Fundamentally, Urbina considers capital punishment one of the biggest demons that the world has ever invented. Now, what is the driving force behind this demon? The most powerful single driving force is *indifference* (see Epilogue).

Executions are brutal, vicious, expensive, irreversible, like an everlasting struggle against cancer that continues to get worse and worse. And, at the very bottom of its motive, there lies an historical mystery. As the harshest criminal sanction, capital punishment has been promoted by promising political language, which is designed to make lies sound truthful, government action logical and honorable, murder by the state legal (with a notion of legitimacy and justice), and to a fragile, feared, and mal-informed society, an appearance of global power and solidarity.

The executioners are part of the legal system and its laws, which are assumed to be unalterable, like the word of God. The executioners are serving the state, which has the power to absolve them from this elusive demon. Yet, they do not even know why they are executing. But, of course, they are *not* supposed to. The executioners accept the law almost as they accept the weather, which is, of course, unpredictable by nature. When questioned, the executioners are likely to reply with: "respect for constitutionalism and legality!" No one would support capital punishment if one were not psychologically and emotionally driven on by some powerful demon whom s/he can neither resist nor understand its truth and reality (Urbina, 2003b).

Women in Supermax Prisons

The expanding use of prisons (see Chapter 2) and punitive punishments, like solitary confinement (see Chapter 7), reflect the repressive nature of female correctional institutions in the United States. Along with an increase in the prison population and possibly executions, female "supermax" prisons are likely to become the designated facilities for hardcore criminals, those who present a major threat to social order, like terrorists, and those who publicly express their ideologies in contradiction to what the government defines as a "good citizens," like political prisoners (King, 1999; Shaylor, 1998; Sykes and Messinger, 1958; Miller, 2007; see Chapter 10).

Current Trends in Modern Prison Technologies

This last "critical issue" concerns the latest technological innovations in correctional settings, whose realities must be carefully scrutinized in public discussions. In particular, correctional facilities are adopting some of the most advanced and expensive technology. Ironically, just as prisoners were being used as "human subjects" on medical experiments like the Tuskegee Syphilis Study (Dula, 1994; Gamble, 1997; see also Flavin, 2007), female prisoners are now being used as "human trials" for new technology, such as "beanbag" bullets, prior to proper testing and adjustment. Not an isolated event, a California correctional officer fired directly into the back of Maria Hernandez. The tear gas canister exploded, burning Hernandez's skin and leaving large and permanent scars on her back (Shaylor, 1998). Similarly, new security systems like x-ray machines are being tested on visitors in the California prison system. Given that these machines are carcinogenic and can cause birth defects and genetic damage to the human body due to an excessive amount of radiation, protection equipment is not always provided. These experiments led to the isolation of prisoners and secrecy that sets the foundation for the brutal nature of the prison system. Clearly, technology not only has a high economic prize, but also a high human cost.

Of course, the emerging isolationist model needs to be examined and discussed within the context of the economic, political, and ideological effects of global movements, particularly the national investment in militarism, that seek to conquer, control, exploit, and manipulate (Berzins and Cooper, 1982; see Chapter 10). First, high-tech weaponry and military hardware are now being used in correctional institutions (Thomas, 1994), despite the fact that women are rarely violent in prison. Prison staff is being taught military techniques and the use of high-tech weapons. The growing militarism was illustrated in a videotape of the training in a Texas prison which showed officers brutalizing prisoners (Verhovek, 1997). Actually, just about every aspect of guard culture is now being modeled on the military (see Chapter 10). For example, officers dress in fatigues and combat boots, officers force female inmates to march in single file lines around a California prison (Shaylor, 1998). Not surprisingly, companies of all sorts, like Corrections Corporation of America, American Express, General Electric, Merrill Lynch & Company, Inc., Smith Barney Shearson, Inc., Golden Sachs & Company, Que-Tel Corporation, Dial Soap, and AT&T (not to mention health care companies and food service providers such as ARAMARK), are competing for lucrative prison contracts from the state and federal government (Helliker, 1995).

Second, the expanding political economy of prison is also illustrated by the exploitation of prison labor, a concept that was presumed to be an exploitive industry of the past. Under the "new and *voluntary* prison labor," female prisoners work (i.e., producing shrink-wrap packages) for companies such as Microsoft, arrange reservations for TWA, and produce eyeglasses for LensCrafters (Shaylor, 1998). More fundamentally, the introduction RFID (Radio Frequency Identification) technology is crucial in that ". . . a device such as a bar code is the ultimate material semiotic manifestation of the marriage of economy and technology in the prison–the prisoner's body symbolically inscribed as commodity" (Shaylor, 1998:408). Third, the federal government is currently selling surplus surveillance equipment and weapons, such as armored personnel carriers, to law enforcement agencies (Cassidy, 1998), creating the perception of social threat by those who break the law and instilling fear in the community. Fourth, as an effective mechanism of silencing people, it is also common to prohibit face-to-face interviews by journalists, preventing the public from knowing the reality of life behind bars.

In short, these actions clearly indicate that the American prison system is not taking a rehabilitative approach, but an abusive, exploitive, and combative one towards inmates. The new military ideology and exploitation of labor is illustrated by the mission statement of a state agency (Prison Industry Authority) in California, where rehabilitation is no longer the primary institutional objective, but maximizing profits (Browne, 1996). (Though California PIA, Prison Industries Authority, inmates are paid minimum wage.) In Wisconsin, one female prisoner quoted: "Wisconsin is a prison state, prisons have become an industry of crime for this state." To this end, a conference was organized by World Research Group, a New York investment firm, with the motto: "While arrests and convictions are steadily on the rise, profits are to be made—profits from crime. Get in on the ground floor of this booming industry now" (Silverstein, 1997:1)! Unfortunately, modern technologies and their use are not being designed for the safety of the institution, but to induce intimidation and fear among prisoners. In the context of new labor practices in the states and international free trade agreements, "Prison labor practices in the United States are analogous to neo-imperialist, transnational corporate practices in the world outside" (Shaylor, 1998:409; see also So, 1990).

THE WISCONSIN EXPERIENCE

This section contains findings for female prisoners in the Wisconsin correctional system. A central objective was to expand the investigation of issues that have been identified as critical in female prisons, particularly those carrying fundamental implications to the correctional system, female offenders, and society. Another objective was to gain insight into issues that we see as potential challenges in the near future.

Visitation

Visitation is one of the most important issues not only to inmates, but also to the prison system and society. The degree of visitation influence the relationship between inmates and their children, family, friends, and community. For instance, with few visits, it is probable that the bond attachment to a prisoner's loved ones will be lessened when she is released from prison. In which case, she will find herself without children, husband, friends, or social support, which is vital for reintegration back into the community. Table 23 contains reported findings for female prisoners in Wisconsin.

Of the female inmates who participated in the study, only six inmates reported not being allowed to receive visitors. However, the dynamics of prison visits are not so pleasing. Most (349 or 76.5%) inmates reported receiving visitors, but 95 women reported no visitation. Among those visiting include: children (18), friends (15), parents

(12), boyfriend (10), clergy (6), husband (3), girlfriend (3), multiple visitors (271), and "other" people (14). For those who received visitors, there was significant frequency variation: weekly (125), monthly (109), every few months (79), once a year (21), and over a year (15). In regards to physical contact during visits, most (265 or 58.1%) female reported being allowed to have contact during visitation time, and only 95 women reported otherwise.

Table 23
VISITORS IN WISCONSIN'S CORRECTIONAL SYSTEM (N=456)

	Mean	*Frequency*	*Percent*
Allowed to receive visitors			
Yes		443	97.1
No		6	1.3
Receive visitors			
Yes		349	76.5
No		95	20.8
Frequency of visitor visits			
Weekly		125	27.4
Monthly		109	23.9
Every few months		79	17.3
Once a year		21	4.6
Every so often (over a year)		15	3.3
Physical contact allowed during visits			
Yes		265	58.1
No		95	20.8
Travel distance for visitors*	140.1		
Influence of travel distance on visits			
Yes		232	50.9
No		96	21.1
Don't know		27	5.9
Visitors			
Husband		3	0.7
Friends		15	3.3
Boyfriend		10	2.2
Parents		12	2.6
Girlfriend		3	0.7
Children		18	3.9
Clergy		6	1.3
Other people		14	3.1
Multiple visitors		271	59.4

Continued on next page

Table 23 (cont.)

	Mean	Frequency	Percent
Wished to see visitors more often			
Yes		357	78.3
No		9	2.0
Not sure		11	2.4

* Range: 1 to 2000 miles.

Considering the influence of traveling distance for visitors, most of whom are poor, respondents were asked about travel distance from prison to their communities. As shown in Table 23, women reported a mean of 140.1 miles, and slightly over half (232 or 50.9%) of the inmates noted that travel distance to facility influence the number of visits that visitors wish to make. Lastly, 357 (78.3%) women stated that they wished to see their visitors more often, and only nine women reported otherwise.

Inmate Assaults in Prison

As noted earlier, increases in the prison population and institutional diversity also led to increases in new penal dilemmas, some of which could be of critical importance for institutional management and inmate survival. For example, one specific issue is inmate assaults, possibly leading to more violence, riots, or homicides. Table 24 contains the reported findings for Wisconsin female prisoners. Of those responding, 96 women reported having been attacked by another inmate while incarcerated. Almost half (47) of these 96 inmates reported that the "attacker" was punished, and 46 women claimed that the attacker was not sanctioned. Interestingly, 51 inmates reported having started a fight with another inmate. Of these 51 inmates, 45 reported that they were actually punished for starting the fight.

Table 24
INMATE FIGHTS IN THE WISCONSIN CORRECTIONAL SYSTEM (N=456)

	Yes	*No*
Attacked by another inmate	96 (21.1)	349 (76.5)
Attacker was punished	47 (10.3)	46 (10.1)
Starting a fight with another inmate	51 (11.2)	385 (84.4)
Punished for starting a fight	45 (9.9)	7 (1.5)

Hatred in Wisconsin Prisons

As an historical American phenomenon (Acuna, 2004; Almaguer, 1994; Feagin and Sikes, 1994; Feagin and Vera, 1995), hate continues to be one of the most critical, damaging, and controversial concepts in the United States. In fact, with the advent of the Internet hate is not only returning from its "suppressed" state, but it is returning in more sophisticated ways, making it more difficult to define, detect, and prosecute. Logically, since the female prison population is being transformed into a more heterogeneous population, hatred in prison is likely to become a serious concern to both inmates and correctional staff. Table 25 contains the reported findings for a series of questions regarding this demoralizing concept in the context of the female prison system.

Table 25
HATE IN THE WISCONSIN CORRECTIONAL SYSTEM (N=456)

	Yes	*No*
Inmates hated by other individuals	299 (65.6)	45 (9.9)
Reasons for hate against certain inmates		
Class (SES)	71 (15.6)	126 (27.6)
Criminal record	147 (32.2)	87 (19.1)
Type of offense	191 (41.9)	60 (13.2)
Skin color	211 (46.3)	56 (12.3)
Age	75 (16.4)	127 (27.9)
Language	78 (17.1)	130 (28.5)
Religion	67 (14.7)	136 (29.8)
Race/ethnicity	196 (43.0)	59 (12.9)
National origin	83 (18.2)	116 (25.4)
Other factors	35 (7.7)	2 (0.4)

Continued on next page

Table 25 (cont.)

	Yes	No
Individuals displaying hate		
Other inmates	257 (56.4)	23 (5.0)
Correctional officers	211 (46.3)	53 (11.6)
Administrators	138 (30.3)	87 (19.1)
Race divisions as a problem	240 (52.6)	111 (24.3)
Gang formation in facility	93 (20.4)	236 (51.8)
Gang problems	58 (12.7)	14 (3.1)

As shown in Table 25, over half (299 or 65.6%) of the incarcerated women reported either witnessing or experiencing some form of hatred by other inmates (257), correctional officers (211), or prison administrators (138). Reasons for hatred include: skin color (211), race/ethnicity (196), type of offense (191), criminal record (147), national origin (83), class (71), language (78), age (75), religion (67), and other unspecified factors (35). Consistent with prior investigations, skin color and race/ethnicity seem to be the two most influential factors, followed by type of offense and criminal record. One important caveat here is the observation that skin color, which has received little attention in the academic literature in comparison to race and ethnicity, seems to be a more influential indicator of hate than either race or ethnicity. As Martin Guevara Urbina (2003c, 2007) suggests, as the prison population becomes more heterogeneous, skin color is likely to become more significant in the administration of punishment.

Last, since hate is correlated with race/ethnicity and gangs, inmates were asked about race/ethnic divisions and gang formation. As shown in Table 25, 93 inmates reported gang formation in prison, but only 58 women viewed gangs in prison as a problem. However, as younger inmates enter the prison system, many of them with drug problems and low tolerance for indifference, gang formation in female prisons is likely to increase. Slightly over half (240 or 52.6%) of the respondents viewed race and ethnic divisions among inmates as a problem in the prison system. With an increase in the minority inmate population, particularly African Americans, Latinas, and Native Americans, we predict a significant increase in race and ethnic divisions, as prisoners compete for limited services like jobs, and, by extension, conflict and hatred.

CONCLUSION

Prior to the start of the war on drugs in the 1980s, the female prison population was relatively small and thus with the exception of racism, sexism, and inmate mothers, the female prison experience received minimal empirical investigation. With changes in prosecutorial policies as well as sentencing, and correctional laws, women are not only confronting issues of racism and sexism, but multiple historical, political, ideological, and structural issues, some of which are woven characteristics of the American society (see Chapter 10 and Epilogue). Consistent with prior investigations, the female experience in the Wisconsin prison system points to the emergence and expansion of a wide array of critical factors in the correctional system, some of them having safety, legal, moral, religious, political, and justice implications. Therefore, the prison system must take a serious and honest approach in the investigation of critical issues for the purpose of knowledge, planning, resolving, and preventing future chaos, disturbance, and injustice.

Chapter 9

LIFE AFTER PRISON

The first part of this chapter provides a discussion of "life after prison" for the typical adult female offender. The second part of the chapter reports the findings about inmates' plans and perceptions from the Wisconsin study. It is argued that the most crucial gap to the establishment of social control remains to be bridged: from prison to the community. Otherwise, with limited resources, little hope, a chaotic environment, and a hostile community, women offenders are likely to return to prison. Then, a discussion of major challenges facing reformers in the twenty-first century is provided. The chapter will conclude with recommendations for the creation of a more understanding, tolerant, and forgiving society, while securing public safety.

METHODS OF RELEASE

The combination of tougher sentences has led to a drastic increase in the female prison population (see Chapter 2). Additionally, female prisoners are serving longer prison terms for a wider array of criminal activity. Yet, most female inmates are eventually released back into the community because the majority of offenders are incarcerated for non-violent crimes (Bureau of Justice Statistics, 2001a). Typically, incarcerated individuals are released from prison to the community, normally under parole supervision through various means, depending on state laws. These categories include discretionary release, mandatory release, expirational release, or some other form of conditional release. A very small percentage of people are "removed" from prison as a result of escapes, executions, or deaths.

Once offenders have been punished for their crimes, served their sentences, and released from prison, they are back in the community to begin a new life, with the expectation, that they will never return to prison.[28] In this context, there are several essential questions that must be addressed to facilitate reentry planning for those who are still in prison, and, ultimately, to avoid recidivism. Morally, what will become of female offenders once they are released from prison? Will they be able to find legal employment with the skills that they learned while incarcerated? Considering the wide range of problems facing female offenders, will they be able to pay for their basic needs, like health care, and not return back to illegal activities like prostitution and drugs? If they do not have the necessary skills, will they be able to acquire credentials and qualifications that will allow them to survive in a competitive job market? Will they be able to reunite with their children, partner, husband, friends, or other loved ones? Will they be accepted by the community? Or, will they be treated with disdain, mistrust, rejection, or hostility? And, what is the probability that those released from prison will end up back in the correctional system? A recent study reports that about 75 percent of inmates return to prison (Langan and Levin, 2002).

COMMUNITY INTEGRATION OR BACK TO SURVIVAL DAYS?

Theoretically, female offenders should be able to regain their lives they left when they entered the prison system. In fact, if an inmate took advantage of available resources while in prison, she should be in a better position than those who did not to begin the community (re)integration process. Practically, though, life after prison is more a reflection of "back to survival days," than it is of "community (re)integration."

Female offenders are not provided with a smooth transition from prison to their next living shelter. Likewise, the existing mechanisms do not provide a smooth transition back into the community. To begin with, when inmates are released, often in the middle of the night, the typical ex-prisoner is confused, scared, and has little idea about what lies ahead. Normally, women express concerns as to whether they will be able to turn their lives around after being released (Chesney-Lind and Pasko, 2004; Kruttschnitt, Gartner, and Miller 2000). Stable housing is essential for female offenders to regain custody of their children (Collins, 1997; Henriques, 1996), a permanent address for legal employment to avoid the temptations of the streets, continuation of health care, and substance abuse treatment after release (Women's Prison Association, 2003). Yet, 60 to 70 percent of women released from prison have nowhere to go (Women's Prison Association, 2004). In essence, the typical female offender leaves prison economically, politically, socially, and morally bankrupt.

Economically, the typical inmate has no place to go, limited resources, and has little knowledge of whatever resources might be available in the community. Independent of how long she was in prison, her level of education remains low, lacking the skills to compete in a competitive and technological job market. When unemployment is high, the situation is even more drastic for ex-prisoners who are often perceived by society as "undeserving." For minority parolees, the situation could be even more devastating in that they are not only being marginalized for breaking the law, but for taking the few jobs available (Chesney-Lind and Pasko, 2004; Collins, 1997).

Politically, the typical female ex-prisoner has no ties to appointed or elected officials. Consequently, either because their right to vote has been taken away as a result of a criminal conviction or because they simply fail to exercise their vote, female ex-prisoners are forgotten or neglected by local, state, and federal politicians. As a general rule, politicians' main objective is to address the concerns of the "voting class," and thus the views and concerns of ex-prisoners are not likely to be addressed in a proper and efficient manner, if at all. In the case of minority ex-prisoners, like Latinas, the situation is even more problematic in that their friends and relatives might not be voting if they are not U.S. citizens.

Socially, the typical female ex-prisoner often has no social support when she is released from prison. To the contrary, former prisoners are usually viewed as undeserving criminals who should not be entitled to voice their experiences, views, or concerns. Further, as people who have violated the law, community norms, or challenge the status quo, they are viewed and treated as third or fourth class citizens. In the case of minority ex-prisoners, the post-prison experience might be more consequential if they do not have friends or relatives to rely on for social support, like cultural understanding, appreciation, and, ultimately, reintegration. For instance, studies show that weak family ties or complete separation from their children creates a severe problem for reintegration (Collins, 1997; Goetting and Howsen, 1983; McCarthy, 1980).

Morally, some female prisoners leave the prison system energized and motivated to start their new lives. However, for the typical female offender, the prison experience is disheartening and demoralizing. Once released, they are scared about having to interact with a judgmental society, and morally fragile to diverse and punitive gender stereotypes. Even though the United States is often characterized as a sensitive, understanding, ethical, and moral society, the community is not very forgiving against those who are considered as strangers, outsiders, different, or threatening (Urbina, 2003b, 2003d; see also Epilogue). In a sense, ex-prisoners continue to pay, economically, politically, socially, or morally, for their criminal acts long after they are released from prison.

Evidently, having a population of ex-prisoners that is absolutely bankrupt carries a very high consequence in that it leads to the very same problem that we are arguably trying to solve: crime. In this regard, studies show that female recidivism has been attributed to economic need (Chesney-Lind and Pasko, 2004; Jurik, 1983) as well as discriminatory policies and lack of support in the community (Chesney-Lind and Pasko, 2004; Lewis, 1982). Consider, for instance, the experience of one released person: "I really tried to stay out of trouble, but it's very difficult, you know. Like once you're into a routine and the people you're hanging about with and everything, and plus you're always getting hassled by the police. . . . Its was about this time that I left home . . . and I was on the streets for a very long time . . . because I was homeless, I couldn't get a . . . job . . . but I still had . . . fines that I had to pay. . . . So I am stuck in this rut. I've got to pay these fines or go to jail, and I've got to live as well. So I was committing more crimes, going back to court and getting more fines, and it was just a vicious circle. So the next thing I ended up back in prison again" (Maruna, 2001:71).

To some degree, all inmates are older when they are released from prison. If women have served lengthy sentences, they might experience additional difficulties, like more severe health problems (see Chapter 6). More fundamentally, since the typical female offender leaves prison economically, politically, socially, and morally bankrupt, most offenders will return to prison. Unfortunately, each time a women returns to prison, her situation becomes more devastating and consequential. For example, her chances of obtaining a legitimate job are further tarnished with an increase in apprehensions, prosecutions, convictions, and incarcerations. Of course, re-entry also presents a critical situation for the prison system in various areas of daily prison life, like management, service delivery, and rehabilitation. For instance, re-entry makes it difficult to maintain a reliable medical history, which is vital for community treatment. Still, the majority of women have hopes, dreams, and they wish to stay out of trouble and become productive members of society (Gittelson, 1982).

THE WISCONSIN EXPERIENCE

This section reports findings for female prisoners in the state of Wisconsin. The main goal was to ask inmates about "survival" issues regarding life after prison, like their plans for living arrangements and employment, as well as their most significant concerns. Ultimately, the objective is to obtain a better understanding about forming programs that will keep recidivism rates low. Likewise, by gaining insight into their plans, concerns, and goals, we are able to obtain an appreciation for the realities of female offenders as they try to (re)integrate back into the community.

Life After Prison in Wisconsin

Upon release, women face multiple problems (Richie, 2001). In some respect, life after prison for the typical female offender is an overwhelming challenge at times, especially if she has no where to go and unable to find a job. Further, after being in prison for some time and making few decisions, she is now being forced to make major life decisions, which, if not properly planned and carried out, could result in a return to imprisonment.

Shelter after Prison

Considering that future planning, especially in the area of community resources, is vital for the purpose of continuing rehabilitation and treatment, safety, and (re)integration, inmates were asked where they planned to live after being released from prison. As shown in Table 26, over two-thirds (310 or 68.0%) reported that they would be living in the state of Wisconsin, 121 inmates reported living outside Wisconsin, and three planned to live outside the United States. In addition, since having a place to live is critical to "community survival," women were asked who they planned to live with upon release. Interestingly, these people included: husbands (34), other family members (140), friends (18), halfway house (33), and multiple individuals (34). However, 178 women reported not knowing who they would live with. Not knowing who they will live with, these group of ex-prisoners are possibility the most vulnerable in that they are likely to end up in the streets in a "survival" situation. Considering that economic need has a significant influence on crime, these individuals are likely to recidivate soon after their release from prison and eventually end up back in prison.

Table 26
LIFE AFTER BEING RELEASED FROM THE WISCONSIN
CORRECTIONAL SYSTEM (N=456)

	Frequency	Percent
Living location after release		
In the state of Wisconsin	310	68.0
Outside the state of Wisconsin	121	26.5
Outside the United States	3	0.7
Living with others after release		
Husband	34	7.5
Other family members	140	30.7
Friends	18	3.9
Halfway house	33	7.2
Don't know	178	39.0
With multiple people	34	7.5
Employment after being released		
Yes	313	68.6
No	42	9.2
Not sure	84	18.4
Possession of skills to perform job once released		
Yes	310	68.0
No	46	10.1
Not sure	60	13.2

Continued on next page

Table 26 (cont.)

	Frequency	Percent
Plans to obtains job skills once released		
Yes	213	46.7
No	11	2.4
Not sure	41	9.0
Will be supported by others if no job		
Family members	156	34.2
Friends	8	1.8
The state	33	7.2
Don't know	159	34.8
Other people	69	15.1

Employment after Prison

Besides not having a place to live after being released, employment could possibly be the second most crucial factor in a "street survival" situation because it impacts whether she will be able to secure shelter for her and possibly her children. Employment might also be important for meeting the conditions of parole. Further, legitimate employment is likely to reduce deviance and crime, which in turn increases public safety and community integration. In addition, employment is key for stereotype control; that is, refuting the notions that female offenders would rather be on welfare.

As shown in Table 26, most (313 or 68.6%) women believed that they would be able to find a job after being released from prison. However, 42 women thought that they would not be employed, and 84 were not sure. Similarly, most (310 or 68.0%) women believed that they had the necessary skills to perform a job, but 46 thought otherwise, and 60 women were not sure if they had the proper skills. Almost half (213 or 46.7%) of the inmates reported that they planned in learning the necessary job or life skills once released from prison. However, 11 reported that they would not be trained and 41 reported not being sure if they would obtain employment training. Last, inmates were asked who would support them if they were not able to find a job once released from prison. Persons who would likely provide support included: family members (156), friends (8), the state (33), and "other people" (69). Ironically, consistent with the number of women who reported not knowing who whey would live with, 159 women report-ed not knowing who would support them if they were not able to find a job.

Planning Ahead

One of the most essential things is knowing what female inmates feel and think, as they are about to be released from prison (Doege, 2006). First, knowing and understanding their views, concerns, and objectives enables the Department of Corrections to get a sense as to whether the inmate will make an honest effort to stay out of trouble and thus out of prison. For instance, if an inmate shows little indica-tion that she is motivated to be (re)integrated back into the communi-ty, chances are that she will return to prison. Likewise, if inmates have "vested interest" in staying out of trouble, there is a possibility that they will try their best to be law-abiding citizens and stay out of trou-ble. For example, if a female inmate finishes her education, finds a job, and obtains housing, the inmate might work towards that end. Therefore, as a final set of questions, female prisoners in Wisconsin were inquired about their biggest concerns.

Inmates were asked to indicate the most important person in their lives at the present time. As shown in Table 27, female prisoners iden-tified a wide range of individuals: Children (148), mother (38), hus-band/partner (11), father (8), brother (4), sister (3), grandparents (2), doctor (2), clergy (2), and multiple people (156). Even though several inmates cited mothers, fathers, and partners as the most important per-son in their lives, their children seem to be the single most important person (see Chapter 2). Logically, women who consider their children as the most important person could possibly be facing the most diffi-cult challenge once released from prison in that they will have to con-front social, economic, and political barriers to get their children back. However, these women are also the ones who might have a better chance of staying out of trouble.

Table 27
MOST SIGNIFICANT ISSUES CONFRONTING FEMALE PRISONERS
IN WISCONSIN (N=456)

	Frequency	*Percent*
Most important person at the time		
Children	148	32.5
Husband/partner	11	2.4
Mother	38	8.3
Father	8	1.8
Sister	3	0.7
Brother	4	0.9
Grandparents	2	0.4
Doctor	2	0.4
Clergy	2	0.4
Other people	72	15.8
Multiple people	156	34.2
Biggest concern at the time		
Not having the children	104	22.8
Poor relationship with children	25	5.5
Poor relationship with husband/partner	6	1.3
Not having an education	19	4.2
Lack of economic resources	30	6.6
A long prison sentence	50	11.0
Other concerns	83	18.2
Multiple concerns	121	26.5
Most important short-term goal while in prison		
Getting an education	82	18.0
Staying healthy	47	10.3
Staying away from alcohol and drugs	24	5.3
Staying out of trouble	101	22.1
Maintaining a good relationship with inmates	6	1.3
Maintaining a good relationship with officers	6	1.3
Other goals	33	7.2
Multiple goals	146	32.0
Most important long-term goal once released		
Getting an education	51	11.2
Getting a good legal job	59	12.9
Staying away from alcohol and drugs	82	18.0
Providing for children	52	11.4
Owning a home	14	3.1
Other goals	37	8.1
Multiple goals	147	32.2

Respondents were also asked about their biggest concern at the time of the survey. Again, they pointed to diverse concerns: not having their children (104), a lengthy prison sentence (50), lack of economic resources (30), poor relationship with children (25), lack of education (19), poor relationship with husband/partner (6), and multiple concerns (121). Consistent with the previous finding, children seem to be the biggest concern of female prisoners. In such a case, it is reasonable to argue that these women are likely to seek employment and possibly get an education to care for the well-being of their children. In this context, with the exception of long prison sentences, social agencies in the community can be of great assistance to mothers in prison. In particular, by identifying who these mothers are before they are released from prison, social agencies can better plan to assist in the transition and thus bridge the gap between prison and the community.

Female prisoners were then asked two questions that could possibly give us an indication of future recidivism. First, they were asked about their most important short-term goal while in prison. Their responses include: staying out of trouble (101), getting an education (82), staying healthy (47), staying away from alcohol and drugs (24), maintaining a good relationship with other inmates (6), maintaining a good relationship with correctional officers (6), and multiple goals (146). In regards to their most important long-term goal once released, inmates reported issues that are consistent with previous findings: staying away from alcohol and drugs (82), getting a "good" legal job (59), providing for their children (52), getting an education (51), owning a home (14), and multiple goals (147). Again, with the possible exception of owning a home, social agencies in the community can be a valuable resource for women as they try to achieve their goals. Ultimately, higher rates of goal achievement among released female offenders could result in lower recidivism. For the community, a well-planned transition could result in continuity in community integration and, above all, public safety.

BUILDING BRIDGES BETWEEN PRISON AND SOCIETY

Understanding female offenders requires that we explore their lives by the totality of circumstance, experiences, events, and situations (see

Chapters 1 and 2). This includes the investigation of not only life while incarcerated, but life before (see Chapters 2, 3, and 4), during (see Chapters 5, 6, 7, and 8), and after incarceration. In the context of the prison system, a central objective is to "rehabilitate" inmates so that they can be productive members of society upon release. However, too often, policymakers, politicians, social activists, and others with vested interest in "prison reform" concentrate on offenders who are going into prison and pay little attention to inmates who are about to be released, basically isolating women who are just released from prison.

Once female offenders are released into the community, they are disconnected from conventional society, and so they are confused and scared. Without well-established bridges between prison and society, the typical female offender is prone to "fail" as a citizen, re-offend, and end up in prison for a minor crime, or simply breaking their parole conditions; that is, technical revocation of parole. Because of limited resources, though, African Americans, Latinas, and Native Americans are prone to experience greater challenges (Leonard, Pope, and Feyerherm, 1995; Winfree and Griffiths, 1975). To this end, Raymond Michalowski (1985:240) documents, "Prisons in America exist as a kind of distorted mirror image of American society. Like the mirrors in a carnival funhouse, prisons exaggerate and expand some of the characteristics of the society they reflect. Yet, like fun-house mirrors, what they show is based in the very real object they are reflecting. The parallel between free society and prisons exists at both the organizational and the social level." Barbara Owen (1998:192) argues that "Women in prison represent a very specific failure of conventional society–and public policy–to recognize the damage done to women through the oppression of patriarchy, economic marginalization, and the wider-reaching effects of such short-sighted and detrimental policies as the war on drugs and over reliance on incarceration as social control."

Yet, part of the solution could possibly be found prior to release from prison, as they are being released, and shortly after their release into the community. The focus should be immediately upon release and not after they have engaged in illegal behavior, and thus the challenge is trying to find ways to keep them in the community and not send them back to prison, especially for issues that can be addressed in the community. In this regards, some of the most detrimental issues facing female prisoners are possibly best addressed in the community and not in prison or jail. For example, substance and alcohol abuse, domestic violence, employment skills, stress and depression, and parenting responsibilities are best addressed outside the correctional setting. However, under current penal policies, these problems are deferred to the correctional system by a society unable, but mostly unwilling, to confront the problems of marginalized and neglected women (Owen, 1998). Female offenders confined to prisons are warehoused in a system that is not well-prepared to deal with the many challenges they confront, which include the problems that brought them to prison, like addictions (see Chapter 3), and the problems that they confront while incarcerated, like depression (see Chapter 6). The correctional system, with its priority on security and control, and little emphasis on treatment and rehabilitation, is left to deal with the failures of society. In fact, some investigators argue that we expect too much from the prison system and are disappointed when they fail to meet our expectations (Owen, 1998).

In sum, particular attention should be given to the views and concerns of female inmates that are about to be released to avoid chaos, ruptures, isolation, and fear. A well-established bridge between prison and society should insure proper planning, continuity, and ties to the community. For instance, for women who opted to have their children, "the interruption in their mothering caused by imprisonment is traumatic to their mother-child relationship and causes many problems they must face along when they go back into the community and begin reintegrating with society and their families" (*Corrections Digest*, 1980:7). Therefore, instead of isolating, neglecting, and marginalizing these women, community agencies and conventional society should work together, share resources, and exchange information to create a "road map" for released offenders so that they have realistic established goals, motivation, and hope.

Family Ties

In the context of building bridges between prison and conventional society, positive family ties are essential to prevent recidivism. In the case of mothers in prison, a weak or nonexistent mother-child relationship tends to lower self-esteem, self-confidence, motivation, and hope (see Chapter 2). Logically, lack of family ties could result not only in detachment from society, but create difficulties for both inmates while they are incarcerated, and make it difficult to be reintegrated into the community upon release. Of course, some critics might argue that the correctional setting is no place for bonding with family. Yet, the penal system is becoming a "way of life" for thousands of people in the United State (see Chapters 1 and 2). With a sharp increase of prison rates, the United States has to realize that isolation and detachment could possibility be contributing to the very same problem that we are trying to solve. This proposition might sound illogical to some people, but not new in the context of "world imprisonment." Describing a Guatemalan prison, one investigator documents: "Prison life can be reflective of life as it exists in the general population. The beliefs and values held dear by society can be recognized in a variety of ways, including the manner in which they deal with their institutionalized and dependent members. The importance of family ties in Guatemala is evident by the familistic policies and practices that prevail behind prison walls. The facilities for children including playground and schoolhouse, the prevalence of family industry and the provisions for intimacy all reflect a climate and tone suggesting that family life is the natural mode of human existence, not to be disturbed by government rule" (Goetting, 1984b: 167; Silverstein, 1990).

Conjugal Visits

Some countries have promoted family stability by allowing conjugal visits as a continuation of family life while in prison. However, conjugal visits in the United States have been a controversial issue, only a small number of states allow inmates to engage in overnight visits with their spouses while incarcerated (Goetting, 1984b). Considering the various penal changes of the last 25 years (see Chapter 2), it is unlikely that conjugal association becomes a serious proposition to the U.S. correctional system. Yet, as noted above, to thousands of female offenders, life in prison is becoming a way of life, to some offenders, "their natural environment." Therefore, conjugal visitation should be carefully studied, and allowed under well-structured situations.

Historically, critics have suggested that conjugal visitation in prison is not a right, but a privilege. In particular, opponents argue that conjugal association is immoral, unpractical, and possibly illegal (Goetting, 1982). Yet, others suggest that it is just as immoral not to allow it. Consider, for instance, the following expression: "Of all possible forms of starvation, surely none is more demoralizing than sexual deprivation. . . . To be starved month after month, year after endless years. . . . [T]his is the secret quintessence of human misery. . . . [Prisoners have] a hunger not only for sexual intercourse, but . . . for the voice, the touch, the laugh, the tears, the tears of Woman; a hunger for Woman Herself" (Nelson, 1933:143). In a well-structured and organized prison system, conjugal association has not showed significant burden to the correctional system. Some investigations report that "Conjugal visitation could be instituted in many prison settings without disruption of proper procedures and with a lessening of tension and frustration. Complete isolation of men and women from all sexual activities of a heterosexual nature is completely unrealistic and results in . . . other displacement of sexual drive in hostile, aggressive and sometimes dangerous behavior toward other inmates and prison personnel" (Sheldon, 1972:20–21). Conjugal association is prone to raise legal challenges. Yet, some observers have noted that "The convict is sent to prison to be deprived of this liberty and compelled to labor as an expiation of his crime, and any other punishment besides that which is absolutely necessary to accomplish this and enforce the discipline of the prison is not only unlawful but inhuman" (Lamott, 1972:47).

Community Programs

Considering that the typical female offender suffers from a series of complicated problems, particularly childhood abuse (see Chapters, 2, 3, and 4), alcohol and drug addiction (see Chapter 3) and health issues (see Chapter 6), community-based treatment programs are probably the single most essential element in the creation of bridges between prison and the community. Upon release, female offenders typically end up in the same physical environment where they grow up: plagued with physical contamination, air pollution, drugs, guns, violence, and crime. This time, however, ex-female offenders are burdened with a criminal record (or with additional convictions) and few social, political, and economic resources to rely on while they find a legal job to survive or meet the requirements of parole. In fact, their influence will become even more significant in the future: the female prison population is increasing sharply, and resources in prison for treatment and rehabilitation are not likely to become a high priority in the future.

Taken together, there are five fundamental issues that need to be taken into consideration so that proper, solid, and lasting bridges are built between prison and the community: female offenders are very fragile when they are released from prison, especially mothers of young children, some women have no place to go, women tend to suffer from serious problems, they are confronted with a very competitive job market, and they face a community that tends to have little tolerance, and is often prejudicial, judgmental, or unforgiving (see Chapter 10).

Even though community programs are often under scrutiny by advocates of punitive sanctions, they can be effectively utilized to bridge the gap between prison and society (Hodge, 1982, 1988; Jurado, 1986; *Justice Assistance News*, 1982; Nichollas, 1987). Case in point: Since 1972, the Benedict Center in Milwaukee, Wisconsin has worked with ex-offenders who are looking for another chance. Assisted by dedicated professionals, the Benedict Center provides alternatives to incarceration, including alcohol and drug treatment programs and family counseling (see Chapter 3), two of the most critical issues facing female prisoners. Additionally, the Benedict Center assists female offenders in learning how to rebuild and restructure their lives and reclaim their young children. It is also a place where female offenders with a prior criminal record can learn life skills and find legitimate employment. From a practical standpoint, the Benedict Center provides vital alternatives for people who in actuality do not need to be behind bars, avoiding excessive expenses to the prison system and the community, particularly taxpayers. Socially, the center creates the social benefits of lower imprisonment costs, such as less need for additional prisons, and lower crime rates, making the community safer for everyone (Kane, 2004). Overall, the main objective of community-based programs is for ex-prisoners to take care of their legal and even moral issues without risking future arrest, re-arrest, prosecution, conviction, or incarceration, while keeping the community safe.

Even though community programs have proved to be an effective and beneficial mechanism for the (re)integration of female ex-prisoners into the community, programs have struggled to keep their doors opened because of limited funds, lack of volunteers as well as social and political willingness to support these agencies. As the ones, who are arguably helping the local criminals, community programs do not get proper recognition by the media, making it difficult to convince the community and policymakers that (re)integration is vital for controlling recidivism. In the future, the biggest challenge facing community programs will continue to be lack of resources and community resistance due to stereotypes and fear.

Recommendations

Even though the following recommendations are not politically appealing, they can serve as a first step to breaking the revolving door cycle of prison admissions and discharges, which tends to get more vicious and consequential every time a female re-enters the prison system.

1. Community programs should be given the highest priority. Female offenders need better delivery service because they are the ones with the greatest demand for basic health care (see Chapter 6), education (see Chapter 2), job-seeking skills (see Chapters 2 and 3), and pre-release planning.
2. As the female prison population continues to increase, expansion of service delivery among existing programs and the development of additional programs is essential to avoid chaos, reduce medical and rehabilitation deficiencies, and secure a smooth transition from prison into the community. For instance, for women who have limited employment skills, their chances of obtaining a good paying job in a competitive job market are low. Consequently, they are likely to engage in property crimes (Simon and Landis, 1991), and thus end up back in prison. In the case of non-English speakers and those who do not have the necessary documentation to obtain a social security number or a driver's license, the situation is even more detrimental (Urbina, 2004a). Also, new policies require that undocumented offenders be deported after their release from prison, a critical situation for undocumented mothers (Johansen, 2005). Therefore, considering the importance of transportation, driver's license reinstatement programs are essential not only for the purpose of transportation, but control or regulation, and, above all, ensuring public safety.

3. Community programs often discriminate against indigent people through examinations, by withholding information about available resources, or negligence. Therefore, female offenders should be fully informed of the programs in their communities long before they are released from prison. And, for those who are released on parole, parole officials should insure that women continue to receive information regarding resources in the community.

4. A transition team, including correctional staff, community agencies, community organizers, and volunteers could provide advice, counseling, services, and referrals.

5. Local governments, the media, and the community should advocate for a volunteer program in which people from the community would offer mentoring and one-on-one or group assistance to female ex-offenders.

A TWENTY-FIRST CENTURY CHALLENGE

For the twenty-first century, critical questions remain to be answered, from a theoretical, research, and policy perspective (see Chapter 10 and Epilogue). Likewise, the correctional system, the female offender population, and conventional society are likely to confront serious challenges. Globally speaking, though, the biggest challenge boils down to one question: How do we change the public option of American citizens, particularly the "voting class," so that they can be more tolerant to a population that historically has been perceived and treated with "indifference" (see Chapter 10 and Epilogue)?

The question of such magnitude, of course, will not be resolved overnight in that it will require restructuring of the American society. What follows are a few recommendations that can be used as a "road map" for a more inclusive and just America. First, we must come to the realization that from whatever angle the situation is analyzed (cost-benefit, economically, politically, morally, ethically, or legally), we cannot continue to marginalize, discriminate, manipulate, subjugate, isolate, and neglect female offenders. Second, we must acknowledge the "true" utility of the prison system in the context of those who are being arrested, prosecuted, convicted, and sentenced, and sent to prison. In the words of one critic, "What to do with those whom society cannot accommodate? Criminalize them. Outlaw their actions and creations. Declare them the enemy, then wage war. Emphasize the difference—the shade of skin, the accent in the speech or manner of clothes. Like the scapegoat of the Bible, place society's ills on them, then 'stone them' in absolution. Its convenient. Its logical. It doesn't work" (Rodriguez, 1993:250). Third, we need to be more sensitive to the experiences and realities of female offenders in the context of society as a whole. As observed by some investigators, ". . . the disturbing expansion of prisons and jails as a means of social control for the poor. . . . Now, all of these crises—the crises of class, the crises of race, the crises of prisons and the crises of education—are all interconnected . . . . the have-nots are disproportionately black and brown (Marable, 1999:41; Salholz, 1990). Taken together, "The prisons of the U.S. are vast warehouses for the poor and the unemployed, for low wage workers and the poorly educated, and most particularly . . . in a racist society . . . " for minorities (Marable, 1999:46; see also Zinn and Dill, 1994). These statements are not simply unfounded ideological statements. For instance, we are finding more minorities (both women and men, particularly African American and Latinas/os) locked up in state prisons than those enrolled in the entire State University of New York system (Marable, 1999). Fourth, the American society must acknowledge and accept responsibility for the implications and ramifications of neglecting the "undeserving" members of society or simply warehousing them in prison. In the same way that an alcoholic must accept the "problem and responsibility" before an effective treatment takes its course, we must acknowledge that the prison systems yield very few benefits at the cost of many negative consequences. Fifth, in a highly judgmental and prejudicial society, prison-based education must be made a high priority. The fact that states like California are spending more money on corrections than education, and states like New York are sending more minorities to prison than to universities has long-term consequences. Realistically, education is not only significant to compete in the job market, but it influences the level of ignorance, which in turn governs the level of stereotypes and fears about certain members of society. Sixth, female offenders must have better access to employment opportunities. As part of the restructuring process, policymakers must keep in mind not only the implications of low wages and highly advanced job requirements, but that jobs in the areas where the typical female offender, who most likely lacks transportation, lives are scarce. As noted earlier, re-arrests are tied to failures in economic support, including employment. It is ironic that the prison system is adopting some of the latest "safety technologies" (see Chapter 8), yet advanced educational and vocational training for women in prison is minimal or nonexistent. As we enter the twenty-first century, how can it be possible that when it comes to quality and up-to-date technology, safety technologies stand on one end of the spectrum, and innovations that will prepare females for after release stand on the other end of the spectrum? Lastly, fueled by notions of colonialism, slavery, conquest, stereotypes, hate, and the perception of threats, the history of race and ethnic relations in the United States has been vicious, vindictive, and bloody (Acuna, 2004; Almaguer, 1994; Bosworth and Flavin, 2007). Yet, we argue that no single historical element has been more influential in unjustifiable behavior, believes, apathy, and feelings than "indifference" (see Epilogue). In this context, we argue that the educational system, starting in preschool, must play a more active role in advocating and developing more tolerance for indifference.

CONCLUSION

Invariably, female offenders are economically, politically, socially, and morally bankrupt when they are released from prison. And, of course, they are confronted with great uncertainty and confusion. Morally, what will become of female offenders once they are released from prison? Will they be able to find legal employment with the skills that they learned while incarcerated? Considering the wide range of problems facing female offenders, will they be able to pay for their needs, like health care, and not return to illegal activities, like prostitution and drugs? If they do not have the necessary skills, will they be able to acquire credentials and qualifications that will allow them to survive in a competitive job market? Will they be able to reunite with their children, partner, husband, friends, or other love ones? Will they be accepted by the community? Or, will they be met with looks of disdain, mistrust, rejection, or hostility? Last, what is the probability that those released from prison will end up back in the correctional system?

In a sense, like the offender, the female prison system as well as conventional society lack significant "rehabilitation." Yet, the majority of female offenders have dreams and goals for their lives after prison. Data from Wisconsin female prisoners indicate that women wish to stay out of trouble and become productive members of society once released from prison. Therefore, instead of creating further isolation and detachment, the female prison population, the correctional system, and conventional society should work together to create a more inclusive, understanding, and just America. Above all, society must take steps towards the creation of a more tolerant and forgiving society, while advocating public safety.

Chapter 10

CONCLUSION

In this final chapter, we draw together essential issues of the previous chapters to point toward a new approach of female imprisonment in the United States that is sensitive to the interweaving historical and modern forces that extend beyond race, ethnicity, gender, class, culture, and borders. First, the modern logic of imprisonment will be discussed, followed by the "evolution of female criminals." Then, threats, fear of crime, and scapegoats in the context of criminalization and incarceration will be analyzed, followed by a discussion on the global nature of imprisonment and a detailed analysis of the militarism of corrections. The chapter concludes with a reference to key critical issues to consider in future research and criminal justice policy.

THE MODERN LOGIC OF IMPRISONMENT

In 2001, the Sentencing Project reported that with mass releases of prisoners in Russia, the U.S. became the country with the highest prison rates in the developed world (men and women combined). From a global standpoint, the U.S. has 10 times the population of its northern neighbor, Canada, yet about 35 times the prison population (Bureau of Justice Statistics, 2004a, 2004b). Although criminal behavior in the U.S. has been declining for about 20 years, the incarceration rate continues to climb. At the end of 2005, one in every 32 adults was in prison, jail, on probation or parole (Harrison and Beck, 2006). The United States not only has the largest prison population and the highest rate of imprisonment in the world, but the gap in relation to other countries continues to widen sharply. More than seven million people (about 3% of the U.S. adult population) were under the control of the criminal justice system at the end of 2005. Of the 7 million, nearly 2.2 million (approximately 1 in every 136 U.S. residents) were in jail or prison at the end of 2005 (Harrison and Beck, 2006). China, with a population of approximately 1 billion people, ranks second with 1.5 million prisoners, followed by Russia with 870,000 prisoners, indicating a significant gap. Similarly, the U.S. has the highest imprisonment rate, with 737 per 100,000 people, followed by Russia with 611 and St. Kitts and Nevis with 547. According to Ethan Nadelmann of the Drug Policy Alliance, the U.S. has approximately 5 percent (300 million in 2006) of the world's population (over 6.87 billion in 2006) and about 25 percent of the world's incarcerated population (*Time*, 2006; Vicini, 2006).

As of 2003, the correctional budget was estimated to be over $60 billion.[29] Five states, including Wisconsin, now have correctional annual budgets of more than $1 billion (Donziger, 1996; *Milwaukee Journal Sentinel*, 2002). In several states, more money is spent on corrections than on higher education. In 1998, New York spent $275 million more on prisons than on state colleges and universities (Ziedenberg, Gangi, and Schiraldi, 1998). In California, the higher education budget dropped 3 percent while spending for correctional facilities rose 60 percent from 1990 to 1998 (*New York Times*, 1998).

From the development of the prison, there has been a notion, at least in theory, that the prison system is to serve in the best interests of society and offenders through strategic approaches, like treatment, rehabilitation, public safety, fear of crime reduction, elimination of the criminal stigma, education, and community integration. The figures above, however, point to a very different story: (1) the U.S. has the highest prison rates, but also the highest homicide rates in the developed world; (2) crimes rates have declined in the last two decades, but while state imprisonment rates have stabilized, federal imprisonment continue to increase; (3) state and national corrections budgets have skyrocketed with no signs of staying constant. To the contrary, everything indicates that state and national prison budgets will continue to increase significantly each year; and (4) some states are spending more money on corrections than they are on programs for health, education, or welfare, a trend that is likely to continue.

Evidently, the modern logic of the U.S. correctional system can be summed in one word: *imprisonment*. In what seems to be a race as to how many people can be placed behind bars, the modern logic of the prison system has become a top priority, at the expense of factors, like education, which is vital to treatment, rehabilitation, community integration, and thus crime reduction. More fundamentally, the new logic becomes a leading force in the very same problem we are trying to solve: crime. The next sections explore historical, behavioral, social, ideological, political, and economic forces that account for these trends.

FROM GOOD CITIZENS TO VICIOUS CRIMINALS

Historically, the female experience in the United States has been shaped by male-oriented mentalities, governing not only behavior, but analytical thoughts, emotions, and even the nature of their soul. In a sense, as long as women stayed within the boundaries of male-imposed demands and expectations, women were perceived and treated paternally, with leniency. It was only when women disobeyed the "rule of law," or perhaps I should say, the "rule of man," that women were harshly punished either informally or formally.

The good citizen's mentality and its corresponding treatment, however, began to significantly redefine itself in the last 50 years or so due to a series of social, legal, political, ideological, and economic changes in society. In particular, with the advent of the war on drugs in the early 1980s and the subsequent introduction of crack cocaine into poor neighborhoods, the transformation of "good citizens" to practically "vicious criminals" manifested itself into a punitive movement against female offenders, which punishes not only individual offenders but their families, especially their children, friends, and society, who end up paying for the high cost of incarceration.

The process is further complicated for females who overtly resist or wish to alter the status quo and for minority offenders. That is, for the typical female offender, the process of criminalization starts with early victimization and running way from home and living in the streets, and culminates in structural dislocation and being labeled as delinquent or criminal. Along the way, women who resist male-imposed norms and expectations are view as "lascivious and . . . a threat to society" (Sargent, 1984:38), and thus in need of strict social control. For African Americans, Mexicans, and Puerto Ricans, the process is more punitive (Collins, 1997; Urbina, 2007; Urbina and Smith, 2007). Regina Arnold (1994:171), for instance, reports that African American "females, as young girls, are labeled and processed as deviants, and subsequently as criminals, for refusing to participate in their own victimization." Some investigators report that "the criminality of black women appears to be more directly tied to structural forces" (Hill and Crawford, 1990:621). As a whole, expectations and stereotypes of African American females (see Young, 1986), have been used as justifications for denying them equal treatment in law enforcement encounters, prosecutorial proceedings, incarcerations, and ultimately opportunity after release. In the words of one Wisconsin female prisoner: "There is the stereotype of us all being terrible rotten people because we are in prison." From a moral standpoint, ". . . when the poor or socially undesired people become discardable because they are deemed useless, we must retain our sense of alarm about such a state" (Williams, 1997:67).

In short, as one of the most vulnerable segments of society, female prisoners are often a product of racism, sexism, and poverty in all the ways that these forces intersect with one another historically, politically, economically, culturally, religiously or symbolically. From an early history of childhood abuse to their admission to prison and ultimately life on parole, the realities of female offenders are a result of negligence, isolation, marginalization, and powerful oppressive policing and control practices (Mill, 1997).

Last, independent of their race or ethnicity, upon release, the typical female offender is often morally, socially, politically, and economically disadvantaged.[30] More fundamentally, not being able to vote because of a conviction, female offenders are virtually silent in a punitive, unforgiving, and vindictive society. In essence, female offenders have no voice, which will result in further marginality, negligence, and isolation in the future (Collins, 1997). As recently documented by Adalberto Aguirre and David Baker (2007), structured inequality in the United States must be eliminated to avoid its manifestations, such as discrimination, and corresponding ramifications.

THREATS, FEAR OF CRIME, AND SCAPEGOATS

As lawmakers, legislatures have certain conformity expectations, which are often shaped and governed by practitioners, like police officers, prosecutors, judges, juries, and prison staff. Seldom, however, do legislatures reference what could possibly be the most powerful force in shaping and reshaping the everyday experiences of female offenders, the American society. Typically, society is perceived to be the one experiencing the threats of crime and the fear it creates. In retrospect, society responds by stereotyping those who have been defined as criminal, and, for critical reasons, use them as scapegoats for the problems of the day.

To begin with, as observed by Christopher Jencks (1994:27), "even in the world's most commercialized society, blame is still free. That means there is still plenty for everyone." However, not only is blame seldom, if ever, evenly distributed among those "responsible" for wrongdoing, but it has a multiplicative and amplification effect. In particular, in a free-market economy where cut-throat competition and institutionalized greed are the norm, those who are most vulnerable become scapegoats and easy targets of blame during periods of economic hardship, social instability, or political uncertainty. Second, the perceived threat to public safety contributes to the enactment of punitive sanctions and strict social control. Actually, personal safety is such an intense concern to society that the need to ward off potential criminals spreads the safety fears even further. For example, treating young girls like adults conveys the message to the mainstream population that girls in general are acting more like adult criminals and not the presumed "naïve risk takers" of earlier times (Bernard, 1992). Even worse, society is then under the impression that young females are indeed posing a serious threat to social order. Threats, whether they are actual, imagined, exaggerated, or displaced, then lead to feelings of revenge. Even though the feelings are a mixture of fear, anger, vindictiveness, and disapproval, fear may be one of the most important elements in the labeling and scapegoating process. Here again, institutionalized scapegoating is useful in that it functions as a general object of revenge when trying to reduce public fear of crime.

Third, ideologically, satisfactory "explanations and solutions" are often easier and cheaper to find in already available theoretical models and statistics from which unwelcomed behavior and irrational motives can be inferred (Urbina, 2003b). To some critics, it is even easier and more satisfying to argue that personal beliefs are more accurate than empirical data, or, as Representative William McCollum of Florida once remarked in a discussion on capital punishment, "While statistics might not indicate that it deters crime, it's common sense that it does" (cited in Seelye, 1994:23). Fourth, it is even possible to suggest that it is not the behavior by young delinquent girls and adult female offenders or the resulting threats, actual or imaginary, to the mainstream population. Instead, what may energize feelings of fear, terror, anger, and, above all, revenge is the perceived insolence of females behaving in ways that contradict male imposed norms and expectations. Fifth, these seeming inconsistencies in the handling of crime are in part the "normal" differential treatment, which carries into the prison system, of those high and low in the class, gender, race, and ethnic hierarchies. The harsh treatment of women in prison is not only for their low status, however, but for the existence of crime itself in a modern democracy.

Last, notice that concern with personal safety and its identification with street crime has suppressed threats to safety stemming from so-called "elite" crimes—i.e., economic crimes committed with the pen instead of the gun. For instance, no one has yet created stereotypes of the "threatening" members of the business industry, such as pharmaceutical companies. Hence, safety threats connected to crimes committed by females must also be understood as particular cases of more general insecurities and fears that go far beyond issues of personal safety. As argued by Barbara Owen (1998:15), "When women's imprisonment itself is examined separately, it may well be that the rising numbers of women in prison are a measure of the society's failure to care for the needs of women and children. . . ." Only when society acknowledges that labeling, blaming, scapegoating, and harshly punishing female offenders, particularly mothers, only supply symptomatic temporary relief but solve little, if anything, can both crime and all the problems it wakes, be soundly explained, discussed, and remedied.

THE GLOBAL NATURE OF IMPRISONMENT

A holistic analysis of the nature and motive of incarceration requires an appreciation of historical forces and ideologies that shape modern female imprisonment (Lundstrom-Roche, 1985; Ohlin, 1956; Rafter, 1983, 1985). Further, the structural and cultural forces that have governed the criminalization process, punishment, and imprisonment must be examined from a global perspective. What follows, then, is a discussion of six vital factors that have shaped and reshaped beliefs, attitudes, and criminal justice policy: slavery, colonialism, race, ethnicity, threats, and globalized sanctions.

Slavery and Colonialism

From a global perspective, the roots of slavery and colonialism continue to shape justice policies (Agozino, 1997; Bales, 2004, 2005). In the case of African Americans, the old form of slavery, which became illegal in 1865 with ratification of the 13th Amendment, has manifested itself into a new form of slavery (Messerschmidt, 2007; Young and Spencer, 2007). With a life-long history of isolation, neglect, and marginalization, African Americans are enslaved in a system that few protest because of its legality, efficiency as a form of social control, and the political economy of crime. Consider, for instance, the following statistics: in 2004, the government classified 40 million men, women, and children—12.7 percent of the population—as poor. The typical poor family, though, had to survive on $12,000 in 2004. Of all families living below official poverty level ($19,307 for a family of four), 51 percent were headed by women in 2004. Of all poor African American families, 74 percent were headed by women; for Latinas, the figure was 44 percent, and non-Latina Caucasians, 43 percent (U.S. Census Bureau, 2005a, 2005b). With little education, lack of skills to compete in a competitive and technological job market, crime becomes a survival mechanism for many female offenders. Logically, savage poverty leads to crime, which in turn leads to arrests, prosecutions, convictions, and prison (Reiman, 2006). Imprisonment then diminishes the probability of obtaining a well-paying job, which in turn further increases the probably of ending *back* in prison, resulting in a cycle of poverty and crime that gets worse each time a person gets arrested, prosecuted, convicted, and sentenced to prison.

In the case of Latinas, particularly Mexicans, the historical roots of conquest and colonialism remain institutionalized in the American society (Acuna, 2004). The Treaty of Guadalupe Hidalgo in 1848 did not stop the bitterness between Mexico and the United States

(Almaguer, 1994), but instead it gave birth to a "legacy of hate" (Acuna, 2004:59). Scholars further document that "the conquest set a pattern for racial antagonism, viciousness, and violence, justified by the now popular slogans such as 'Remember the Alamo!'" (Urbina, 2003c:109; Urbina and Smith, 2007). To this day, as Earl Shorris (1992) points out, the Alamo has been a shrine to anti-Mexican sentiment, the ultimate symbol of the glorious victory of the moral character of "white" over "brown."

The Origins of Race and Ethnicity

As reported by Paul Gilroy (1993), the ideologies of race (and ethnicity) are historically linked, and race, as we perceive it today, is a modern construct dating back to the late eighteenth century when the prison was invented (Acuna, 2004; Almaguer, 1994; Foucault, 1995). Historically contingent and constructed, and ideas of race and ethnicity are necessary for the prison system to survive and expand. In essence, the United States would have difficulties sustaining its current prison system, if one out of four African American men were not under some form of incarceration or surveillance (Irwin and Austin, 1997; Tonry, 2004).

Similarly, the prison system would have difficulties surviving and growing without the "new minority," Latinas and Latinos, who recently bypassed the African American population in the U.S. for the first time in history (Urbina, 2007). Likewise, the prison system would struggle to survive and continue to grow without the newly "targeted" population, women, particularly African Americans and Latinas. Above all, the prison system would struggle to survive, grow, and prosper without the "intergenerational connection," female offenders and their children, especially minority children. From an economic standpoint, it is possible that the prison system would not survive economically without the African American and Latina/o population. In short, just as it has been documented that punishment is an expression of historically contingent sensibilities (Garland, 1990), ideas of race, of ethnicity, of difference, and of "other," play into our strategies of when and how we respond to criminal behavior (Urbina, 2003a, 2007; Bosworth and Flavin, 2007). In this context, what if young Caucasian women (and men) were being imprisoned at the same rate? Would the American society support such practices of confinement?

Threat Differentials in Modern Times

Theoretically, penal sanctions have been rationalized under politically and media driven concepts like social control, safety, and rehabilitation (Faith, 1993b; Sohoni, 1989). The unspoken objective of the criminal justice system, though, has been to control anyone and everyone who is perceived as a threat not only to social order, but the status quo (Urbina, 2003c). It is in this context that the nature and motive of imprisonment need to be understood, within a historical framework. For instance, for most of the twentieth century conflict theorists argued that dominant groups within market economies used penal sanctions to control populations when their interests are threatened (Quinney, 1977; Rusche, 1933/1978; Rusche and Kirchheimer, 1939/1968; Spitzer, 1975). To this end, some scholars document that political and economic domination in the United States is rooted in colonial times (Acuna, 2004; Almaguer, 1994; Knepper, 1989).

Yet, as suggested by minority threat theories, as the ethnic and racial landscape begins to change, so does the nature of punishment and imprisonment (Blalock, 1967; Bonacich, 1972, 1976, 1979; Crawford, Chiricos, and Kleck, 1998; Liska, 1992; Turk, 1969). In particular, changes in the size of racial or ethnic minority groups threatens the status quo in that competition for economic and political power and social standing becomes a focal concern (Jacobs and Wood, 1999). Ian Taylor (1999) reports that as cultural differences increase, political practices become more exclusionary. These exclusionary practices might also include the enhanced use of prison for minorities, most notably, African Americans, Mexicans, Native Americans, and Puerto Ricans (as reflected by the disproportionate number of minority populations being processed by the penal system), or those defined as the *other*–i.e., the "outsider," the "stranger" (Wacquant, 1999). Martin Guevara Urbina (2003a) argues that variation in punishment is largely attributed to threat differentials, suggesting that the female prison experience is governed by threat differentials. As a whole, threat theories suggest that in response to perceived racial, ethnic, social, political, or economic threats, powerful groups support the "prison boom" (see Chapter 2) to control those who pose a threat to the status quo– e.g., when living standards decrease or unemployment increases.

THE MILITARISM OF CORRECTIONS

The political and economic nature of imprisonment becomes evident when one analyzes the current practices of militarism and globalized penal sanctions (Bennett, 2004; Sanchez, 2007). The last 20 years have brought many changes in so-called "First World Countries," like the U.S., Spain, and Great Britain, "want-to-be First World Countries," like Mexico, and "Third World Countries," like Colombia, ranging from anti-crime legislation to anti-terrorism laws. In the process, we have seen movements that come near political anarchy (see Bosworth, 2007; Calavita, 2007; Welch, 2007).

From a legal standpoint, the United States spearheaded the "war on drugs" during the 1980s with a series of anti-drug laws, and it coerced other countries to participate in what became an aggressive international "drug fight" that continues today (see Diaz-Cotto, 2007). Yet, few advocates acknowledge that the transcontinental war on drugs has had significant ramifications. In the United States, for instance, the drug war has been overwhelmingly targeted at the poor, especially poor minorities (Currie, 1993; Inciardi, 2001; Irwin and Austin, 1997; Tonry, 1995).

Globally, just south of the U.S. border, Mexican politicos are taking advantage of the U.S. economic aid since 1986 to fight a drug war that appears be more related to political rhetoric and manipulation than public safety. Since the aid is not free of strings, Mexico has to demonstrate progress by placing "drug dealers" behind bars at whatever cost, even if they have to bend the already questionable laws. Logically, arrests for drug dealing have increased in recent years just as Washington demands, but, as in the U.S., the largest impact has been on the poor, powerless, and those with little political influence. From a practical standpoint, independent of whether governments are fighting a legitimate drug war, policing the world, or keeping the peace, negative consequences are not evenly distributed; the majority land on the already disadvantaged—e.g., those with little political power. Worse, transcontinental anti-drug movements are even more apparent in places where democracy is "fragile." In countries like Columbia, for example, the notorious fighting between the military and drug dealers has been so intense that not even the safety or security of the Columbian President is guaranteed. Hence, a war philosophy to meet

U.S. expectations has created a situation that resembles a "war zone" in some parts of the world.

A war philosophy, though, underlies some modern legal practices, especially in countries that are classified as "fully democratic," like the United States (see Ruddell and Urbina, 2007). Further, the language of warfare, propagated by politicians and the media, permeates efforts to reduce criminal behavior. For example, politicians, legislators, and others responsible for implementing anticrime legislation may describe crime as threatening the peace, social order, and national security of the nation and its citizens. As a result, politicians and policymakers often describe new anti-crime strategies as wars against those who threaten the security of a country. In this context, beginning in the 1990s drug czars in the United States directed anti-drug efforts from high-tech headquarters that rivaled those of the U.S. Department of Defense. In 2001, the director of the newly created Office of Homeland Security coordinated military units, federal law enforcement, and other intelligence-gathering agencies assigned to detect and destroy terrorism in the United States and abroad. With law violators as "the enemy," the United States and other countries are using sophisticated war weapons, including armored personnel carriers, and resort to military tactics in situations like crowd control, drug-related situations, and uprisings by rebels, who are not satisfied with a country's political system.

The September 11, 2001 incident gave advocates of "law-and-order" what they have been waiting for years: a rationalization for strict and punitive social control. In the aftermath of the September 11, 2001 attacks on the United States, state governments also created their own homeland security agencies, mimicking initiatives of federal authorities. Of course, not all of the targets of modern anti-terrorism efforts are foreign-born enemies (see Bosworth, 2007; Welch, 2006, 2007). The war on terrorism is unquestionably a policing strategy as well as a military effort, further blurring the boundary and distinctions between civilian law enforcement and military participation in maintaining social order. Further, it is highly probable that the September 11, 2001 incident will raise questions regarding constitutional issues, limit economic development, resulting in a rise in issues like infant mortality and poverty. On a related vein, in the late 1990s elite U.S. Marine Corp units operated on the U.S.-Mexico border as ancillaries in the war on drugs (see Dunn, 1996). Such operation, however, required the bending of the 100-year-old Posse Comitatus Act, which prohibits the use of military troops in domestic police activities, an ironic action for a country that advocates democracy and civil liberties.

Most recently, on October 26, 2006 President Bush signed into law a bill allowing the construction of a 700-mile U.S.-Mexico border fence, at an estimate cost of 6 to 8 billion dollars. Democratic Senator Ted Kennedy slammed the bill as a "bumper-sticker solution that Republicans hope will provide cover for their stunning failure to produce comprehensive immigration reform." Mexican President Vicente Fox referenced the move as an "embarrassment to the United States," and Foreign Minister Luis Ernesto Derbez cited the wall as an "insult." Mexican President-elect Felipe Calderon deplored the move because "the fence doesn't resolve anything," it will just cause more misery and deaths. Televised from Mexico City, Amnesty International condemned the move as "criminalizing migration (and) a step backward on human rights."

Evidently, there are critical problems associated with the application of this type of language to crime-fighting strategies throughout the world. Democratic countries tend to have great difficulty using paramilitary units and strategies against their own citizens, and when they do, some groups and individuals compare them to totalitarian regimes. Within countries, the enemy is usually targeted from the same population as those being protected. That is, most law violators are citizens of the country that seeks to apprehend and destroy them, or at least to reduce the actual or perceived threat they pose. In essence, then, by utilizing the language of war against lawbreakers, a country has declared war against itself. More fundamentally, the language of war in a given country, or against members of a particular country, is also exclusionary. In order for a nation to declare war against an enemy, members of that group—in this case classified as criminals—must be identified and viewed as outsiders. This practice, though, has two significant ramifications. First, it is easier to violate the civil and constitutional rights of those considered outsiders, individuals who should not be entitled to the same constitutional protections as law-abiding people (Sanchez, 2007; Urbina, 2004b). Second, once they are identified and treated as outsiders—as enemies of the state or country—reintegration of classified criminals into mainstream society becomes a very difficult mission (see Urbina, 2005a; Welch, 2006, 2007).

In sum, countries like the U.S., Great Britain, and Spain now seem to worry about personal safety and to favor costly anti-crime punitive laws, but present social control laws are fueled as much by the expression of popular anger and the desire for revenge as by the honest attempt to develop and implement mechanisms of reducing crime and the fear it creates. Therefore, investigations of imprisonment need to be sensitive to modern structural shifts and historical ideological factors. Finally, given the current tactics of militarism and globalized punishments, using comparative frameworks to better understand the nature of female imprisonment might yield fruitful results.

CRITICAL ISSUES: LOOKING AHEAD

As we seek to better understand the experience of female offenders before, during, and after incarceration, there are a series of issues that must be considered, addressed, and prioritized:

- As depression rates continue to increase, will the prison system be able to treat and cope with a depressed prison population?
- As alcohol and drug addiction becomes more complicated among female offenders, will the system be able to treat, cope, and prioritize addiction and the various related issues?
- What kind of services and treatment should prisoners infected with communicable diseases, such as HIV or AIDS, receive?
- Will the correctional system be able to incarcerate, rehabilitate, treat, and educate female offenders in a just fashion?
- Will the correctional system push for improvements, such as bilingual staff, as more minorities enter the prison system?
- Is placing surveillance devices (e.g., electronic monitoring) in homes of released female offenders, most of whom are nonviolent offenders, a logical idea or an invasion of privacy?
- With a high concentration of African Americans and Latinas in prison, what influence will these trends have on politics? As observed in the last state and national elections, minority voting can shift elections. Yet, as the number of minorities in the prison system increase, the number of minorities who cannot vote due to felony convictions increases. Is this fair or Democratic?

• With hundreds of thousands of children with mothers in prison, will the prison system make an honest effort to prioritize family ties, which includes visitations? As noted by Sylvia Ann Hewlett, "We think of ourselves as a nation that cherishes its children, but, in fact, America treats its children like excess baggage. Our tax code offers greater incentives for breeding horses than for raising children. We slash school budgets and deny working parents the right to spend even a few weeks with their newborns. We spend 23 percent of the federal budget to the elderly but less than 5 percent on children" (cited in Macionis, 2007:480). In 1992, Congress passed the Family Leave Act, by which the U.S. joined more than 100 nations in guaranteeing maternity leave (but not pay) for all working women.

SUMMARY

The data show that the simultaneous interaction of historical and ideological factors has resulted in a *new class of offenders*: a surplus population of poor female offenders. Then, as reported by Richard Quinney (1977:136), "a way of controlling this unemployed surplus population is simply and directly by confinement in prisons." Indeed, if incarceration trends continue, 6.6 percent of residents born in 2001 will go to prison at some point during their lifetime (Bonczar, 2003). Reported findings from the Wisconsin study suggest that we continue to ". . . live in a classist, racist, and sexist society and nowhere is that more apparent than in a women's prison" (Rierden, 1997:xvii). Consistent with prior investigations, before, during, and after incarceration, female offenders continue to experience regimentation and control resulting from what Goffman calls "trimming and programming" of sex-role stereotypes (Moyer, 1984), a practice that is likely to continue (see Shaw, 1996).

As a whole, the lives of female prisoners are shaped by the influence of patriarchy, social, cultural, political, and economic marginalization, and the stigma of being labeled criminal. As suggested by economic marginalization and feminists theories, ". . . female criminality is based on the need for marginalized women to survive under conditions not of their own making . . . many women struggle to survive outside legitimate enterprises" (Owen, 1998:9). Isolated and neglected, the typical female offender is condemned by society to live in savage poverty, as they are trying to care for their young children. Ironically, not only does poverty lead to higher rates of delinquency and crime, but because imprisonment disrupts working careers, prison time increases the risk of poverty (Western, 2002). Hence, future studies of women in prison must be viewed through the lens of slavery, colonialism, patriarchy, class, stereotypes, globalized sanctions, fear as well as racial, ethnic, social, political, cultural, and economic threats. As noted herein, this writing is by no means a scientific treatment of the subject matter. However, the experience of Wisconsin female prisoners suggests that future investigations must also consider not only life before, during, and after incarceration, but that the experience of female offenders must be analyzed by the totality of issues, events, and circumstances, which tend to shape and reshape final outcomes in and outside the prison system.

EPILOGUE: THOUGHTS FOR THE FUTURE

Sara Nieling and Martin Guevara Urbina

WOMEN BEHIND BARS: BREAKING THE SILENCE

Until recently, few studies considered the views of women in prison (Scheffler, 1986; Alarid and Cromwell, 2006). In addition, some studies relied heavily on quantitative methodologies that failed to fully capture the reality of the prison experience (Scheffler, 1984a, 1984b). Eloquently stated by one investigator, "The pains of imprisonment are tragically underestimated by conventional [i.e., quantitative] methodological approaches to prison life. Prison is all about pain—the pain of separation and loss, the wrench of restricted contact in the context of often fragile relationships, of human failings and struggles" (Liebling, 1999:165; see also Johnson, 2003). In this context, in an attempt to underscore the "human side of female prisoners" in academic literature and public discussions (see Chapter 9), a detailed discussion of qualitative anecdotal data from the Wisconsin study is included.

The Prison Experience: Shadow of the Night

In an attempt to capture the multiple truths and realities, particularly their emotional state, we asked female prisoners in Wisconsin to share their concerns, views, fears, and emotions from their standpoint. As reported by the respondents, life behind bars is not a reflection of media propagated images of "life in Holiday Inns." As noted below, life in prison is a story of continuous struggle.

Psychological Impact

One of the most cited concerns by female prisoners is the psychological impact that the prison has on inmates from the time they enter the institution until they are released from prison (see Chapters 5, 7, and 8). Consider, for instance, the following statements by Wisconsin female prisoners:

- "If someone has a low self-esteem upon entering a correctional facility, expect it to be worse upon leaving."
- "We have no privacy . . . you lose your freedom of speech and respect."
- "The way they treat us in this place is so disrespectful and they talk to us like we are animals."
- "This is the most dehumanizing place one can ever experience."
- "You are made to feel that you are nothing, not even human."
- "I will tell my children prison is hell."
- "This place will drive you crazy."
- "When inmates look through bars, some see mud, others see stars!"

Another common concern is loneliness and fear, especially at night, and the difficulty of staying sane while in prison. Considering the powerful psychological impact of the prison system (Foucault, 1995; Liebling and Arnold, 2004; Mahan, 1984), legislators must ensure that proper outside review is implemented to control for unjustifiable psychological punishment on all prisoners.

Health Care

Health care was among the biggest concerns for female inmates in Wisconsin (see Chapter 6), as illustrated in the following statements:

- "One time I fell down playing volleyball and the nurse wouldn't come and see me, she said I would have to walk to HSC. I was finally able to walk down there 2 days later. The nurse gave me ibuprofen and an ice bag for a badly sprained ankle, and left me on the top bunk."
- "I have been fighting to have surgery on my right foot . . . I can't wear a shoe on my foot until I have the surgery. I have to wear a

Velcro cast and I've been wearing the Velcro cast for two years and six months now."

- "Being HIV and being in prison is really poor . . . the officers discuss your business with each other and the mistreatment that they do to me is very wrong and this needs to stop."
- "As a disabled person, someone needs to look at the blatant way prison officials are violating the American with Disabilities Act."

Women also reported not being able to see medical staff due to high expenses. The health care co-pay went from $2.50 to $7.50, as substantial amount for those who do not have the money. For inmates who are working, their hourly wage is only a few cents an hour.[31] Jim Greer, the Department's health services director, reports that Wisconsin has one of the highest co-pays for inmates in the country. Indeed, Greer confirms that ". . . you have people not showing up until they're really, really sick. And guess what? Then they're a $1,000 ER visit" (Marley, 2004:5A). Last, some women pointed to the lack of female doctors and reported that they wished to be examined by female doctors, who might be more sensitive to women health care issues.

A Question of Innocence

The typical practitioner in the United States normally argues that no person is convicted until proven guilty in a court of law (Urbina, 2005b; Urbina and Kreitzer, 2004). Unfortunately, theory often clashes with reality (Acuna, 1998; Bell, 1992; Feagin and Vera, 1995). In fact, studies show that innocent people are being arrested, prosecuted, convicted, sentenced to jail/prison, and some are executed without a fair trial (Urbina, 2004a, 2004b; Vandiver, 1999; Woffinden, 1985). In the words of one female inmate in Wisconsin, "We aren't innocent until proven guilty, we are guilty until proven innocent." Another female prisoner reported, "There are too many women here who are innocent."

Differential Treatment

As an historical topic of heated debate (Bosworth and Flavin, 2007; Free, 2001; Mann, 1993; Urbina, 2007), differential treatment in the prison system continues to be a matter of concern for female prisoners, as reported in the following statements:

- "There is a lot of racial tension . . . serious racial problems, and accusations from staff to African American inmates."
- "There is . . . racial discrimination toward the African American inmates."
- "Also . . . lot of prejudice and pressure by security against lesbians."
- "Half the problems occur due to officers' actions and treatment of inmates."
- "Officers lie about inmates on conduct reports, show favoritism in dealing with inmates."
- "There is major racial inequality in this facility . . . that begins in the administration."
- "I feel as though my civil liberties are denied and to give that a voice would subject me to punishment."

Evidently, from the standpoint of female prisoners in Wisconsin, differential treatment exists, it is significant, it is unjustifiable, and it adds to the very same problem that reformers are trying to remedy: cruel and excessive punishment. As eloquently, documented by Adalberto Aguirre and Jonathan Turner (2006), the consequences of discrimination are detrimental and long-lasting.

Correctional Competence

Some women also expressed concerns about the ability of correctional staff and social workers to work in a prison setting. Some female prisoners stated that either correctional officers do not know the rules or they blatantly violate correctional policies on a regular basis. Some inmates also reported that correctional officers lack skills in handling certain inmates, like those who are sick or disabled. Further, some inmates reported that some correctional officers show up to work with serious problems. In the words of one female prisoner, "A lot of these officers are mentally disturbed."

Rehabilitation

Historically, rehabilitation has served as a primary rationalization for the expansion of the prison system. The "rehabilitation thesis," however is not well-supported by empirical investigations, a position that is also shared by some female inmates. According to one female prisoner, "Prison is not for rehabilitation." Aware of the competitive job market, inmates recommended that better educational and vocational programs be offered, especially computer skills, and access to college courses.

Items in Prison

Another common concern among female prisoners in the state of Wisconsin is the lack of proper hygiene items, like soap, toothpaste, and toilet paper, to stay healthy, clean, and safe. One inmate, for example, stated: "females should be allowed to purchase their undergarments and bra. The facility does not supply supportive bras. That could become a health issue for large breasted females."

Meals

Some female prisoners reported that dietary needs are becoming a critical concern in that medical conditions are getting worse for some inmates (see Chapter 6). For instance, because of medical problems, some inmates are supposed to follow a very strict diet and exercise. Yet, inmates have no choice but to eat what the rest of the inmates are given to eat. Unlike patients in the community, inmates are not given the opportunity to follow proper exercise to remedy their medical conditions (Kort, 1987).

Prison as a Way Out

Considering the lives of the typical female prisoner (see Chapters 2, 3, and 4), it is not surprising that some women see the prisons system as a "way out" of their violent, dangerous, and chaotic home environment (see Chapter 5). When everything is falling apart, prison serves as a refuge and, at time, as an educational experience that enables some female inmates to reintegrate back into the community upon release. In the words of one female prisoner in Wisconsin, "Although prison isn't a great place to be, but it will help you get your life back on track if you are willing to make a positive change in your life."

Uncertain Dilemmas

As reported by female prisoners in Wisconsin, there are various dilemmas that female offenders confront before their conviction, during their incarceration, and after their release. For instance, before prison, some women have to decide between being homeless and committing a crime (see James and Glaze, 2006). While in prison, women have to decide between keeping their children and giving up parental rights. After prison, women have to decide between committing another crime to survive and a life of isolation, negligence, and uncertainty (see Petersilia, 2003). Consider the following statement by Wisconsin female prisoners:

- "I would rather be homeless with my kids then in prison without them. I committed a forgery to save us from being homeless."
- "No one to help me go the right route so I just go back to my old lifestyle."
- "There is a large number of women who leave and come back again and again due to recidivism because they didn't get any real help and support in solving their issues."

The Human Side of Female Prisoners

Considering their turbulent history with the criminal justice system (see Chapters 3, 4, 5, and 7), the majority of female prisoners in Wisconsin did not take the opportunity to make vindictive or vicious statements. In the contrary, the majority of inmates reported that we need to work together to resolve the "correctional crises" and its various manifestations. The majority of women acknowledge that they have serious problems, but, as noted by one inmate, we "need more help reintegrating into society."

Voices From Prison

Considering the phrase "it takes a criminal to catch a criminal," we opted to ask female prisoners in Wisconsin for their recommendations, not to "catch a criminal," but "to prevent people from becoming criminals." What follows is a list of the most common recommendations, particularly for young people:

• Stay in school.
• Practice safe sex.
• Stay away from drugs.
• Stay away from alcohol.
• Stay away from gangs.
• Stay away from bad influences.
• Stay away from violence.
• Think of the consequences.
• Stay away from street fights.
• Stay away from deviance and crime.

Perhaps because of their low levels of education (see Chapter 2), school was the most recommended by our respondents, followed by stay away from drugs, and think of the consequences. Consistent with prior investigations, one female inmate reported, "once you commit a crime it haunts you forever" (Harris, 1988).

RECOMMENDATIONS TO CONSIDER

Given the historical and modern issues, events, and circumstances governing the lives of female offenders before, during, and after incarceration, the lives of female offenders must be made a top priority. As eloquently documented by Elliot Currie (1993), the United States has tried virtually everything, but "improving lives." What follows, then, is a list of recommendations, with the objective of developing and implementing a strategic plan that will reduce differential treatment, prejudice, fear, brutality, negligence, and isolation. Ultimately, the correctional system must be restructured so that it will be able properly and ethically function, cope, and rehabilitate one of the most vulnerable segments of society.

Litigation

Even though male offenders have made use of litigation to resolve some of their concerns, females are still reluctant to select litigation for solutions (Aylward and Thomas, 1984; Barry, 1991; Schlanger, 2003).[32] In addition to gender and organizational constraints, some inmates worry about being labeled "troublemakers," and thus the resulting consequences. In the words of one inmate, "The administration has more total control of the inmate population because of the 'ideology'–if you f . . k up, back [to maximum security] you go" (Aylward and Thomas, 1984:270; *Nation*, 1988; Sykes and Messinger, 1958).

Realistically, though, access to the courts is vital (Alpert, 1982; Urbina, 2003a), especially since "violations fall within the scope of the eighth Amendment prohibition" of cruel and unusual punishment (Rippon and Hassell, 1981:460). Marginalized, neglected, and isolated, litigation is a "means of fighting oppression and combating the passivity and paternalism rampant in women's prisons" (Leonard, 1983:55; Schlanger, 2003).

Strengthening of Family Ties

As a way of improving lives, lowering the momentum of crime and imprisonment, and eventually breaking the cycle of delinquency and crime, family ties must be made a priority, especially between mothers in prison and their children (Hairston, 1988). From a cost-benefit analysis, governments must make use of the necessary resources upfront to ensure continuity, efficiency, and safety, and thus avoid having to spend millions of dollars for issues that could of been resolved early on.

Accessibility and Quality of Health Care

From a legal and moral standpoint, health care issues must be addressed early on to avoid the spread of contagious diseases, deaths, lawsuits, and possibly a health care crisis in prisons (Kohn, 1986; Kornhauser, 1989; McGaha, 1987). The correctional system must also be sensitive to gender, ethnic, and age variation in the examination, prevention, and treatment of female offenders.

Enforcement of Correctional Standards

Prison administrators must ensure that correctional standards are being enforced by correctional officers and other staff members to protect the constitutional rights of female prisoners. In this context, correctional staff should be trained properly and on a regular basis so that they are up-to-date on the policies pertaining to female prisoners. For example, seminars, say every three months, could be a productive approach for the sharing of information, expressing concerns, and remedying current issues and concerns.

Changes in the Mentality of the American Society

Since the majority of female prisoners are institutionalized for non-violent crimes, the punitive and vindictive American mentality must change in regards to the high volume of people that are being sentenced to prison and jail. As noted by Eldrin Bell, Police Chief of Atlanta, "If we started to put white America in jails at the same rate that we're putting black America in jail, I wonder whether our collective feelings would be the same, or would we be putting pressure on the President and our elected officials not to lock up America, but to save America" (cited in Shaylor, 1998:413)? Putting the historical stereotypes aside, the United States needs to be more sensitive, tolerant, and understanding of the *actual reality* of female offenders.

Applying the Global Perspective

In our efforts to improve the correctional system, cross-national research might assist us in better understanding the lives of female offenders as well as the structure, organization, policies, procedures, and innovations of the U.S. prison system by exploring the prison systems in other countries (Cook and Davies, 1999; King and Maguire, 1994).[33] For instance, recent cross-national studies by Rick Ruddell and Martin Guevara Urbina suggest that applying a "global" perspective not only allows us to apply a more holistic investigative approach, but it enables us to see the many gaps that need to be bridged.

Outsider Review of the Prison System

For over 200 years, the U.S. prison system has been resistant to outsider review, suggesting that outside review is not the most vital mechanism for investigating or addressing internal issues of the prison system. Wisconsin Department of Corrections Secretary Jon Litscher, for example, argued that "corrections employees 'can investigate ourselves' and do a thorough and honest job" (Zahn and McBride, 2000a:16A). Empirical investigations, however, indicate otherwise. Logically, many of the current problems could possibly be addressed with the proper implementation of outsider review. Therefore, we argue that the correctional system must strive for the implementation of outside review.

Priority of Social Programs

The United States needs to make social programs, including those dealing with education, employment, poverty, urban development, health care, and childcare, in the community a priority. The traditional argument of limited resources should no longer be used to maintain the status quo.[34] In particular, local, state, and the federal government need to invest in long-term economic development in communities where most of the offender population comes from. Without a well-structured economic development plan in poor neighborhoods, the cycle of negligence and isolation will continue, and, in a sense, we are telling these citizens that they do not have the right to exist.

THE PRACTICALITY OF PRISON REFORM

At the end of the day, we must question ourselves whether we are actually rehabilitating female prisoners, or simply redefining crime, displacing crime, recalculating crime statistics, and "reinventing" punishment. To this end, Graeme Newman (1995:12–13) argues that "By denying that force, liberal penologists who will not punish, simply create a greater demand for it. . . . But the responsibility for the excesses of prison today lies squarely with the liberal reformers who have fiddled with the punishment processes in society. The liberal reformers of the eighteenth and nineteenth centuries created prisons as we know them today. Ashamed of punishing, they have swept punishment behind the secret walls of prison. There it has grown and festered like a huge ulcer. Guilty about punishing, they have invented programs to negate the punitive might of prison. Deeply concerned with control, they have invented community programs of nonpunishment to add on to prison."

DE QUE COLOR ES EL ALMA?: A FINAL NOTE

Perhaps because the United States considers itself a "moral" and "law-and-order" society, the U.S. has a phobia of the *outsider*, the *different*, and the *stranger*. As an institutionalized state of feeling and thinking, such phobia has manifested itself into ignorance, which in turn has resulted in viciousness and vindictiveness. Likewise, fear of those who threaten our interests or the status quo, has manifested itself into low levels of tolerance. In this context, in the words of internationally renowned Mexican intellectual, Carlos Fuentes, "What the U.S. does best is understand itself. What it does worst is understand others." Consequently, instead of understanding, forgiving, and integrating outsiders, the U.S. tends to retaliate against those whom society does not wish to understand, tolerate, or accommodate. Lastly, we argue that "hate" and fear are not the driving forces, as often suggested in public and academic discussions, but *indifference.*

Following the advice of legendary sociologist Georg Simmel (1971), before we can deal with anyone, we need to know who the person is, in the same way that we need to know who we are. In the process, we should never forget that cruelty has a human face. We should be thankful and excited about living in a democratic country. Yet, we should not forget that when people experience injustices, democracy is of little utility. Finally, it is our hope that this project inspires understanding, righteous anger, tolerance and respect for indifference, and hope. Ultimately, we hope that someday we all realize *que el alma es de todos colores,* as we seek to achieve universal justice and peace.

Sara Nieling graduated from the University of Wisconsin-Madison with a B.A. in psychology and Social Welfare and from the University of Wisconsin-Milwaukee with a M.S. in criminal justice. Her academic passion lies in the rehabilitation of and advocacy for disadvantaged correctional populations. She has previously worked in Colorado with female offenders on probation, in Wisconsin with offenders diagnosed with severe and persistent mental illnesses, in Minnesota with women involved in prostitution, and in both Illinois and Hawaii with federal offenders. From 2003 through 2005, she served as a member of the Minnesota Advisory Task Force on Female Offenders, a committee formed to promote and advocate for gender and culturally-responsive services for women and girls in the criminal and juvenile justice systems. Sara is currently employed as a United States Probation Officer for the District of Hawaii.

NOTES

1. The Wisconsin study, conducted between July 2003 and December 2003, gave every adult woman in prison who wished to participate an opportunity to voice (via questionnaire) their views, concerns, and experiences. Of the six female Wisconsin prisons, research access was granted for four prisons. However, access was denied to one facility because, arguably, it was being used as a "temporary" housing facility, and access was denied to the other facility for unknown reasons.
2. While the numbers are not as large as those of the California prison population, Oklahoma imprisons a higher percentage of female offenders than any other state.
3. As reported by the U.S. Department of Justice, violent and property crime rates in 2005 were at the lowest since 1973. The rate of every major violent and property crime decreased between 1993 and 2005, with a 58 percent decline in violent crime and a 52 percent decline in property crime. The number of violent crimes dropped from an estimated 11 million in 1993 to 5.2 million in 2005 (Catalano, 2006).
4. In fiscal year 2004, local, state, and federal governments spent an estimated $193 billion for corrections ($61,945,625,000), police ($88,858,664,000), and judicial and legal activities ($42,706,002,000).
5. In the same way that people tend to pay two or three times the purchase price before paying off a home or a motor vehicle, states do the same thing when they finance correctional facilities through long-term bonds.
6. To provide a detailed analysis of the experiences of incarcerated women, we opted to survey all adult women in the Wisconsin correctional system. The goal was not to obtain a random or selected sample, but to include every inmate who wished to participate so

that we could fully explore the lives and experiences of women before, during, and after incarceration in the State of Wisconsin.

7. Cigarette smoking remains the leading cause of death and illness among Americans, yet some fail to mention this deadly fact. In 2001, 46.3 million adults were smokers, nearly one in every four people (or about 25%). Every year, a staggering 440,000 people die in the United States from tobacco use. In fact, nearly one of every five deaths are related to smoking. Cigarettes kill more people than alcohol, motor vehicle accidents, AIDS, homicide, suicide, and illegal drugs combined. Tobacco use costs the nation over $100 billion each year in direct medical expenses and lost productivity (Morbidity and Mortality Weekly Report, 2002; National Center for Health Statistics, 2003).

8. For women who were charged with multiple offenses, the majority of offenses were for nonviolent crimes, like property crime, prostitution, and welfare fraud.

9. In Wisconsin, defendants who earn $250 (or more) a month do not qualify for a public defender. Therefore, indigent defendants must be in savage poverty; that is, defendants must earn below the $250 a month limit to qualify for a public defender.

10. The majority of states do not mention in their legislative codes the issues of pregnant women or inmates with small children, and many states do not mention female incarceration in their state legislative codes (Radosh, 1988).

11. Since 1904, the maximum security Bedford Hills has served as the first live-in nursery for children of inmates. In small rooms on the top floor of an eighteenth century brick building sit 21 cots next to 21 cribs, where mothers care for their children, take parenting courses, and are served by a resident pediatric nurse.

12. The nation's first state-run jail facility for women and their infants was opened on December 12, 1988 in Boston, designed to concentrate more extensively on both prenatal and post-natal health care and social needs. Two federal programs in Texas and California also involve separate jail facilities for mothers during the delivery of the babies.

13. In *Estelle v. Gamble* (1976), the U.S. Supreme Court established the standard in which prisoners may challenge a prison's medical care system as unconstitutional under the 8th Amendment.

14. *Todaro v. Ward* (1977) was the first lawsuit filed by female prisoners challenging the adequacy of medical care at a women's prison.

15. The following statistics represent out-of-state prisoners from Wisconsin (females and males), indicating a rapid return trend: December, 2002 (3,482), December, 2003 (1,890), December, 2004 (68), March, 2005 (53), and May 4, 2005 (none).

16. Including women and men, the situation is much more critical. In 1991, New York City was under federal court order to build 84 communicable disease cells at a cost of $450,000 each for inmates with tuberculosis. In 1994, 25 percent of California's inmates had tuberculosis. Likewise, as early as the mid-1990s, the incidence of AIDS among inmates was 20 times higher than the national average (Morain, 1994; Osborne Association, 1994; Steptoe, 1986).

17. Based on current statistics, depression is the leading cause of disability in the U.S. Over 1 in 20 Americans have a depressive disorder every year, and over 1 in 5 Americans can expect to get some form of depression in their lifetime. By the year 2020, depression is projected to be the second cause of DALY's (after heart disease) estimated for males and females of all ages (Bland, 1997; Murray and Lopez, 1997; World Health Organization, 2006). (DALY's: disability adjusted life years; that is, the sum of years of potential life lost due to premature mortality and the years of productive life lost due to disability).

18. There were early efforts to separate the mentally ill from other institutionalized offenders, but not until 1859 did the first institution open near Auburn Prison, the New York State Lunatic Asylum for Insane Convicts. Today, all states have either separate facilities for mentally ill people or sections of mental hospitals reserved for them (Clear, Cole, and Reisig, 2006).

19. Combined with men, only about 8 percent of convicted or accused individuals in mental hospitals are there because they were found not guilty by reason of insanity; 6 percent are in hospitals because they are judged mentally disordered sex offenders; 32 percent have been found to be incompetent to stand trial; but 54 percent consists of people who become mentally ill after they enter prison (Clear, Cole, and Reisig, 2006).

20. An estimated 191,000 mentally ill men and women are currently in state prisons, making up about 10 percent of the inmate population. In correctional facilities like New York City's Riker's Island, with 3,000 mentally ill inmates, the prison has become the state's largest psychiatric facility. In Los Angeles, 50 percent of those entering the

county jail are identified as mentally ill (Bureau of Justice Statistics, 2001b; Winerip, 1999; Butterfield, 1998).

21. In an interview with David Melby, experienced probation and parole officer, regarding sex offenders in the United States, particularly in Wisconsin, the existing sex offender literature is shortsighted by critical research gaps and grave misconceptions regarding the scope and nature of the subject.

22. In *West v. Manson* (1987), the care and treatment of pregnant women in prison, not addressed in *Todaro*, was challenged. *Harris v. McCarthy* (1989) was the first lawsuit to challenge solely the quality of prenatal and post-partum care given to pregnant prisoners.

23. By state law, inmates have a constitutional right to adequate medical care: "Any person in charge of or employed in a penal or correctional institution or other place of confinement who abuses, neglects, or ill treats any person confined in or a resident of any such institution or place or who knowingly permits any person to do so is guilty of a class E felony."

24. Some investigators report that HIV was introduced to humans around the 1940s or the early 1950s, and still others report that AIDS goes back to the end of the nineteenth century (Boer, 2005).

25. Given that AIDS/HIV is one of the leading institutional problems facing the correctional system, states should ensure that the following are in place: (1) Case management approach to HIV; (2) Upgraded medical facilities to comply with medical standards; (3) Appropriate medical clinics; (4) Staffing needs are properly addressed; (5) Upgraded sero-prevalence reporting, continuous HIV testing, and test counseling; (6) Application of nondiscriminatory policies affecting prisoners with HIV infection; (7) Comprehensive aftercare services; (8) Continuous monitoring; (9) Proper counseling to cope with stress, depression, and trauma; and (10) Available alternative sanctions.

26. Linda Zupan (1992) also reports that female inmates were more obedient to male officers than female officers.

27. Jails in the United States have a history of overcrowding, poor food quality, ineffective medical care, brutal environment, threats of attack, rapes, and suicides (Salholz, 1990). In 1965, Ronald Goldfarb characterized jail conditions in the United States as the "ultimate ghetto" (cited in Clear, Cole, and Reisig, 2006:286). With few exceptions (Wirtzfeld, 1985), women in county jails have remained

invisible, neglected, and marginalized (Connolly, 1983). As noted by some observers, "The general public and the media ignores jails unless there are escapes, fires, suicides, riots, or titillating tales of corruption or wrongdoing by the staff or elected sheriff" (Clear, Cole, and Reisig, 2006:286).

28. Some investigators have suggested that post-prison expectations influence both the prison experience, particularly attitudes, and life after prison (Jensen and Jones, 1976).

29. Of approximately 7 million U.S. adults in the criminal justice system, 59 percent are on probation, 20 percent are on parole, and 10 percent are in local jails. An estimated 12.6 percent of African American males aged 25–29, 3.6 percent of Latinos, and 1.7 percent of Caucasian men are in prison or jail (Bureau of Justice Statistics, 2005).

30. Conservatives, like liberals, point to the welfare state as a way of equalizing their cognitive dissonance, or simply out of ignorance or political rhetoric. Realistically, the welfare state is a mechanism for silencing the masses. Few people, for instance, will mention that it is cheaper to have people on welfare than it is to create decent paying jobs.

31. A Wisconsin inmate may earn 12 cents to 42 cents per hour. Prisoners who have been assigned to a school, vocational training, or other programs are paid an hourly wage of 15 cents. Inmates who are unable to work may be paid an hourly wage of 5 cents. The hourly wages for Badger Industries in medium and maximum security institutions range from 20 cents to 1 dollar. In minimum-security institutions, the range is 50 cents to $1.60, and the hourly wages on the farms range from 20 cents to $1.60 (Sappenfield, 2006:B-6).

32. Investigators report that the Attica incident led to an increase in legal action, but that "even thought hundreds of petitions were filed, only a handful were filed by, or on behalf of women prisoners. . . Since women prisoners have historically been reluctant to file lawsuits themselves their specific problems have continued to go relatively unnoticed. . . . Perhaps it is the nature of the women's prison and the attitudes and the values it fosters which affect the prisoner's behavior" (Alpert, 1982:38; *Corrections Magazine*, 1982; *Criminal Justice Newsletter*, 1983; Kohn, 1986; Kornhauser, 1989)

33. Studies in Canada (Adelberg and Currie, 1993), Great Britain (Carlen, 1990; Dobash, Dobash, and Gutteridge, 1986; Mandaraka-

Sheppard, 1986; Mawby, 1982), France (O'Brien, 1982), Mexico (Pearson, 1993), and Scotland (Carlen, 1983).

34. According to the World Bank, if all private and public wealth in the United States were divided equally, each person would have approximately $425,000 (Macionis, 2007).

REFERENCES

Abdul-Alim, J. (2000). Easing visits to mom in prison. *Milwaukee Sentinel*, October 30. Available at: http://www.jsonline.com/news/state/oct00/ Mama30102900a. asp.

Ace Program of the Bedford Hills Correctional Facility (1998). *Breaking the walls of silence: AIDS and women in a New York state maximum-security prison.* NewYork: The Overlook Press.

Acoca, L. (1998). Defusing the time bomb: Understanding and meeting the growing health care needs of incarcerated women in America. *Crime and Delinquency, 44*: 49–69.

Acuna, R. (2004). *Occupied America: A history of Chicanos.* 5th edition. New York: Pearson Longman.

Acuna, R. (1998). *Sometimes there is no other side.* Notre Dame: University of Notre Dame Press.

Aday, R. (2003). *Aging prisoners: Crisis in American corrections.* Westport, CT: Praeger.

Adelberg, E. and Currie, C. (1993). *In conflict with the law: Women and the Canadian justice system.* Vancouver: Press Gang Publishers.

Adler, F. (1977). Crime, and equal opportunity employer. *Trial Magazine,* January: 31.

Adler, F. (1975). *Sisters in crime: The rise of the new female criminal.* New York: McGraw-Hill.

Agozino, B. (1997). *Black women and the criminal justice system: Towards the decolonisation of victimisation.* Brookfield, VT: Ashgate.

Aguirre, A. (2003). *Racial and ethnic diversity in America: A reference handbook.* Santa Barbara, CA: ABC-CLIO, Incorporated.

Aguirre, A. and Baker, D. (2007). *Structured inequality in the United States: Discussions on the continuing significance of race, ethnicity, and gender.* 2nd edition. Upper Saddle River, NY: Prentice Hall.

Aguirre, A. and Baker, D. (1997). A descriptive profile of Mexican American executions in the Southwest. *The Social Science Journal, 34*: 389–402.

Aguirre, A. and Turner, J. (2006). *American ethnicity: The dynamics and consequences of discrimination.* 5th edition. New York: McGraw-Hill.

Albisa, C. (1989). Sexual abuse and harassment (jailhouse lawyer's manual). *Columbia Human Rights Law Review, 20*: 95–107.

Alarid, L. F. (1997). Female inmate subcultures. In J.W. Marquart and J.R. Sorensen (eds.), *Contemporary and classical readings.* Los Angeles: Roxbury.

Alarid, L. F. and Cromwell, P. F., eds. (2006). *In her own words: Women offenders' views on crime and victimization.* Los Angeles, CA: Roxbury Publishing Company.

Allen, D. (1982). Jail mother has no contact right (California). *The Los Angeles Daily Journal, 95*: 2.

Almaguer, T. (1994). *Racial fault lines: The historical origins of White supremacy in California*. Berkeley: University of California Press.

Alpert, G. P. (1982). Women prisoners and the law: Which way will the pendulum swing? *Journal of Criminal Justice, 10*: 37–45.

American Correctional Association (1990). *The female offender: What does the future hold?* Alexandria, VA: Kirby Lithographic Company.

Amnesty International (1999). Rough justice for women behind bars.

Anglin, M. and Hser, Y. (1987). Addicted women and crime. *Criminology, 25*: 359–394.

Applebome, P. (1992). U.S. prisons challenged by women in prison bars. *The New York Times* (November 30): A10.

Arnold, R. (1994). Black women in prison: The price of resistance. In M. B. Zinn and B. T. Dill (eds.), *Women of color in U.S. society* (pp. 171–184). Philadelphia: Temple University Press.

Arnold, R. (1990). Processes of victimization and criminalization of Black women. *Social Justice, 17*: 153–166.

Ash, P. and Guyer, M. (1982). Involuntary abandonment: Infants of imprisoned parents. *The Bulletin of the American Academy of Psychiatry and the Law, 10*: 103–113.

Atwood, J. E. (2000). *Too much time: Women in prison*. London: Umbrage Editions.

Aylward, A. and Thomas, J. (1984). Quiescence in women's prisons litigation: Some exploratory issues. *Justice Quarterly, 1*: 253–276.

Bales, K., ed. (2005). *Understanding global slavery today: A reader*. Berkeley: University of California Press.

Bales, K. (2004). *Disposable people: New slavery in the global economy*. Berkeley: University of California Press.

Balthazar, M. L. and Cook, R. J. (1984). An analysis of the factors related to the rate of violent crimes committed by incarcerated female delinquents. *Journal of Offender Counseling, Services, and Rehabilitation, 9*: 103–118.

Barlow, D. E. (1999). Police, prisons, and the war on drugs. In *Conference summary: An action plan: Money, education, and prisons: Standing at the crossroads*. Milwaukee, WI: The Benedict Center.

Barry, E. M. (1991). Jail litigation concerning women prisoners. *The Prison Journal, LXXI*: 44–50.

Barry, E. M. (1989). Pregnant prisoners. *Harvard Women's Law Journal, 12*: 189–205.

Barry, E. M. (1987). Imprisoned mothers face extra hardships. *The National Prison Project Journal, 14*: 1–4.

Barton, G. (2002). Bembenek seeks DNA testing. *Milwaukee Journal Sentinel*, August 24: 12A.

Baunach, P. J. (1985). *Mothers in prison*. New Brunswick, NJ.: Transaction Publishers.

Beckett, K. (1997). *Making crime pay: Law and order in contemporary American politics*. New York: Oxford University Press.

Beckett, K. and Sasson, T. (2003). *The politics of injustice: Crime and punishment in America*. 2nd edition. Thousand Oaks, CA: Sage Publications.

Belenko, S. (1999). Research on drug courts: A critical review 1999 update. *National Drug Court Institute Review, 2*: 1–58.

Belknap, J. (1996). *The invisible woman: Gender, crime, and justice.* Belmont: Wadsworth Publishing Company.

Bell, D. (1992). *Faces at the bottom of the well: The permanence of racism.* New York: Basic Books.

Benn, M. and Ryder-Tchaikovsky, C. (1983). Women behind bars. *New Statesman, 106*: 8–11.

Bennett, R. (2004). Comparative criminology and criminal justice research: The state of our knowledge. *Justice Quarterly, 21*: 1–22.

Bergen, D. (1982). A mold that fits Nebraska's mothers in prison. *Corrections Today, 44*: 12, 42.

Bergman, C. (1983). You can't lock up a mother's love. Prison service for inmate mothers. *U.S. Catholic, 48*: 18–26.

Bergsmann, I. R. (1989a). Adolescent female offenders. *Corrections Today, 51*: 98, 100.

Bergsmann, I. R. (1989b). The forgotten few: Juvenile female offenders. *Federal Probation, 53*: 73–78.

Berk, R. A., S. L. Messinger, D. Rauma and J.E. Berecochea (1983). Prisons as self-regulating systems: A comparison of historical patterns in California for male and female offenders. *Law and Society Review, 17*: 547–586.

Bernard, T. (1992). *The cycle of juvenile justice.* New York: Oxford University Press.

Bershad, L. (1985). Discriminatory treatment of the female offender in the criminal justice system. *Boston College Law Review, 26*: 389–438.

Berzins, L. and Cooper, S. (1982). The political economy of correctional planning for women: The case of the bankrupt bureaucracy. *Canadian Journal of Criminology, 23*: 399–416.

Blalock, H. M. (1967). *Toward a theory of minority group relations.* New York: Wiley.

Bland, R. C. (1997). Epidemiology of affective disorders: A review. *Canadian Journal of Psychiatry, 42*: 367–377.

Bloom, B. (1996). *Triple jeopardy: Race, class and gender as factors in imprisonment.* Ph.D. Dissertation, Department of Sociology, University of California-Riverside.

Bloom, B., M. Chesney-Lind and B. Owen (1994). *Women in California prisons: Hidden victims of the war on drugs.* San Francisco: Center on Juvenile and Criminal Justice.

Blount, W., T. Danner, M. Vega and I. Silverman (1991). The influence of substance use among adult female inmates. *Journal of Drug Issues, 21*: 449–467.

Bobo, L. and Hutchings, V. (1996). Perceptions of racial group competition: Extending Blummer's theory of group position to a multiracial social context. *American Sociological Review, 61*: 951–972.

Bodine, L. (1981). Tales of the unborn (attempt to free fetus from jail). *The National Law Journal, 3*: 35.

Boer, B. (2005). The origins of HIV and the first cases of AIDS. Available at: http://www.avert.org/origins.htm.

Bonacich, E. (1979). The past, present, and future of split labor market theory. *Research in Race and Ethnic Relations, 1*: 17–64.

Bonacich, E. (1976). Advanced capitalism and Black/White race relations in the United States: A split labor market interpretation. *American Sociological Review, 41*: 34–51.

Bonacich, E. (1972). A theory of ethnic antagonism: The split labor market. *American Sociological Review, 37*: 547–559.

Bonczar, T. P. (2003). *Prevalence of imprisonment in the U.S. population, 1974–2001.* Washington, D.C.: U.S. Department of Justice.

Bondeson, U.V. (1989). *Prisoners in prison societies.* New Brunswick, NJ: Transaction Publishers.

Bosworth, M. (1996). Resistance and compliance in women's prisons: Towards a critique of legitimacy. *Critical Criminology, 75*: 5–19.

Bosworth, M. (2007). Identity, citizenship, and punishment. In M. Bosworth and J. Flavin (eds.), *Race, gender, and punishment: From colonialism to the war on terror* (pp. 134–148). Piscataway, NJ: Rutgers University Press.

Bosworth, M. and Flavin, J., eds. (2007). *Race, gender, and punishment: From colonialism to the war on terror.* Piscataway, NJ: Rutgers University Press.

Boudouris, J. (1985). *Prisons and kids: Programs for inmate parents.* College Park, MD: American Correctional Association.

Bresler, L. and Lewis, D. K. (1983). Black and White women prisoners: Differences in family ties and their programmatic implications. *The Prison Journal, 63*: 116–123.

Brodie, D. L. (1982). Babies behind bars: Should incarcerated mothers be allowed to keep their newborns with them in prison? *University of Richmond Law Review, 16*: 677–692.

Brownmiller, S. (1975). *Against our will.* New York: Simon and Schuster.

Browne, D. C. (1989). Incarcerated mothers and parenting. *Journal of Family Violence, 4*: 211–221.

Browne, J. (1996). The labor of doing time. In E. Rosenblatt (ed.), *Criminal injustice: Confronting the prison crises.* Boston, MA: South End Press.

Bunch, B. J., L. Foley and S. Urbina (1983). The psychology of violent female offenders: A sex-role perspective. *The Prison Journal, 63*: 66–79.

Bureau of Justice Statistics (2005). *Prison and jail inmates at midyear 2004.* Available at: http://www.ojp.usdoj.gov/bjs/pub/pdf/pjim04.pdf.

Bureau of Justice Statistics (2004a). *Bulletin,* November. Washington, DC: U.S. Government Printing Office.

Bureau of Justice Statistics (2004b). *Bulletin,* May. Washington, D.C.: U.S. Government Printing Office.

Bureau of Justice Statistics (2004c). *HIV in prisons,* 2001. January. Washington, D.C.: U.S. Government Printing Office.

Bureau of Justice Statistics (2003a). *Bulletin,* August. Washington, D.C.: U.S. Government Printing Office.

Bureau of Justice Statistics (2003b). *Bulletin,* July. Washington, D.C.: U.S. Government Printing Office.

Bureau of Justice Statistics (2001a). *Special report.* October. Washington, D.C.: U.S. Government Printing Office.

Bureau of Justice Statistics (2001b). *Mental health treatment in state prisons.* July. Washington, DC: U.S. Government Printing Office.

Bureau of Justice Statistics (2001c). *Medical problems of inmates, 1997.* January. Washington, D.C.: U.S. Government Printing Office.

Bureau of Justice Statistics (1999a). *Special report: Women offenders.* December. Washington, D.C.: U.S. Department of Justice.

Bureau of Justice Statistics (1992). *Women in jail in 1989.* Washington, D.C.: U.S. Government's Printing Office.

Bureau of Justice Statistics (1991). *Special report: Women in prison.* Washington, D.C.: U.S. Government's Printing Office.

Burden, O.P. (1983). Changing times bring better-than-equal opportunity for growing female-inmate ranks. *Law Enforcement News, 9*: 13.

Burkhart, K.W. (1973). *Women in prison.* Garden City, NY: Doubleday.

Butler, A.M. (1997). *Gendered justice in the American West: Women prisoners in men's penitentiaries.* Chicago: University of Illinois Press.

Butler, R. (1969). Age-ism: Another form of bigotry. *Gerontologist, 9*: 243–246.

Butterfield, F. (2003). Study finds hundreds of thousands of inmates mentally ill. *New York Times*, October 22: A16.

Butterfield, F. (1998). Prisons replace hospitals for the nation's mentally ill. *New York Times*, March 5: A1.

Cade, J. and Elvin, J. (1988). Prisoners with aids in New York live half as long as those on outside. *Journal, 15*: 7.

Cain, M. (1990). Towards transgression: New directions in feminist criminology. *International Journal of the Sociology of Law, 18*: 1–18.

Calavita, K. (2007). Immigration, social control, and punishment in the industrial era. In M. Bosworth and J. Flavin (eds.), *Race, gender, and punishment: From colonialism to the war on terror* (pp. 117–133). Piscataway, NJ: Rutgers University Press.

Carlen, P. (1994). Why study women's imprisonment or anyone else's? *British Journal of Criminology, 24*: 131–140.

Carlen, P. (1990). *Alternatives to women's imprisonment.* Philadelphia, PA: Open University Press.

Carlen, P. (1983). *Women's imprisonment: A study in social control.* Boston, MA: Routledge and K. Paul.

Carmouche, J. and Jones, J. (1989). Two innovative programs. *Federal Prisons Journal, 1*: 23, 26–27.

Carp, S. and Schade, L. (1992). Tailoring facility programming to suit female offenders' needs. *Corrections Today*, August: 152–159.

Carrieri, J. R. (1990). The rights of incarcerated parents (New York). *Law Journal, 203*: 1.

Carroll, L. (1996). Racial conflict. In M. McShane and F. Williams (eds.), *Encyclopedia of American corrections.* New York: Garland.

Carroll, L. (1974). *Hacks, Blacks and cons: Race relations in maximum security prisons.* Lexington, MA: Lexington Press.

Carron, L. R. (1984). Termination of incarcerated parents' rights in Massachusetts. *New England Journal on Criminal and Civil Confinement, 10*: 147–167.

Cassel, R. and Van Vorst, R. (1961). Psychological needs of women in a correctional institution. *American Journal of Correction, 23*: 22–24.

Cassidy, P. (1998). Police take a military turn. *Boston Globe*, January 11: C1, C2.

Catalano, S. M. (2006). *Criminal victimization*, 2005. Washington, D.C.: U.S. Department of Justice.

Cavaiola, A. A. and Schiff, M. (1988). Behavioral sequelae of physical and/or sexual abuse in adolescents. *Child Abuse and Neglect, 12*: 181–188.

Kassebaum, P. A. (1999). *Substance abuse treatment for women offenders: Guide to promising practices.* Rockville, MD: Department of Health and Human Services.

Chandler, E. W. (1973). *Women in prison.* New York: Bobbs-Merrill.

Chesney-Lind, M. (1991). Patriarchy, prisons and jails: A critical look at trends in women's incarceration. *The Prison Journal, 71*: 51–67.

Chesney-Lind, M. (1989). Girl's time and woman's place: Toward a feminist model of female delinquency. *Crime and Delinquency, 35*: 5–29.

Chesney-Lind, M. (1988). Girls in jail. *Crime and Delinquency, 34*: 150–168.

Chesney-Lind, M. and Pasko, L., eds. (2004). *Girls, women, and crime: Selected readings.* Thousand Oaks: Sage Publications.

Chesney-Lind, M. and Rodriguez, N. (1983). Women under lock and key: A view from the inside. *The Prison Journal, 63*: 47–65.

Chesney-Lind, M. and Shelden, R. (2003). *Girls, delinquency, and juvenile justice.* 3rd edition. Belmont, CA: Wadsworth Publishing Company.

Chowdhry, G. and Beeman, M. (2007). Situating colonialism, race, and punishment. In M. Bosworth and J. Flavin (eds.), *Race, gender, and punishment: From colonialism to the war on terror* (pp. 13–31). Piscataway, NJ: Rutgers University Press.

Christopher, M. (1987). When mothers serve time. *Scholastic Update, 119*: 8.

Churchill, W. and Vander Wall, J., eds. (1992). *Cages of steel: The politics of imprisonment in the United States.* Washington, D.C.: Maisonneuve Press.

Clark, J. (1995). The impact of the prison environment on mothers. *Prison Journal, 75*: 306–329.

Clear, T. R., G. F. Cole and M. D. Reisig (2006). *American corrections.* 7th edition. Belmont, CA: Wadsworth/Thomson Learning.

Colley, E. and Camp, A. T. (1992). Creating programs for women inmates. *Corrections Today,* April: 208–209.

Collins, C. F. (1997). *The imprisonment of African American women: Causes, conditions and future implications.* Jefferson, NC: McFarland & Company.

Connolly, J. E. (1983). Women in county jails: An invisible gender in an ill-defined institution. *The Prison Journal, 63*: 99–115.

Cookson, H. M. (1977). A survey of self-injury in a closed prison for women. *British Journal of Criminology, 17*: 332–347.

Cook, S. and Davies, S. (1999). *Harsh punishment: International experience of women's imprisonment.* Boston: Northeastern University Press.

Coontz, P. D. (1983). Women under sentence of death: The social organization of waiting to die. *The Prison Journal, 63*: 88–98.

Corrections Digest (1989). Minnesota women's prison meets all standards. 20: 8.

Corrections Digest (1988a). Massachusetts opens jail for new mothers, babies. 19: 10.

Corrections Digest (1988b). Supreme court agrees that New Jersey county jail must provide abortion option for inmates. 19: 6.

Corrections Digest (1987a). N.J. (New Jersey) county told to pay for abortions for inmates. 18: 10.

Corrections Digest (1987b). N.C. (North Carolina) warden says executing women is hard on staff. 17: 3–4.

Corrections Digest (1985a). N.Y.C. (New York City) women's prison needs immediate improvements, correctional association says. 16: 9.

Corrections Digest (1985b). Senate kills proposal to prevent federal funding of abortions for women inmates. 16: 4.

Corrections Digest (1985c). Women behave better, BJS finds in study of who ends up behind the prison walls. 16: 3–4.

Corrections Digest (1982). Substance abuse common among women inmates. 13: 1, 9.

Corrections Digest (1980). Mother-child relationship in prison needs attention. 11: 1, 7.

Corrections Magazine (1982). Kentucky officials appeal sex bias ruling: Female inmates strike. 8: 3–4.

Covington, S. S. (2003). A woman's journey home: Challenges for female offenders. In J. Travis and M. Waul (eds.), *Prisoners once removed: The impact of incarceration and reentry on children, families, and communities* (pp. 67–103). Washington, D.C.: Urban Institute Press.

Crawford, C., T. Chiricos and G. Kleck (1998). Race, racial threat, and sentencing of habitual offenders. *Criminology, 36*: 481–512.

Creighton, L. L. (1988). Nursery rhymes and hard time (infants in women's prisons). *U.S. News & World Report, 105* (August 8): 22–25.

Criminal Justice Newsletter (1983). Mothers in prison (projects to help them). 14: 4.

Criminal Justice Newsletter (1982). Women inmates sue Kentucky prisons. 13: 7.

Culbertson, R. G. and Fortune, E. P. (1986). Incarcerated women: Self concept and argot roles. *Journal of Offender Counseling, Services, and Rehabilitation, 10*: 25–49.

Curtain, S. (1972). *Nobody ever died of old age.* Boston: Atlantic Monthly Press.

Curtis, T. (1992). The origin of aids. *Rolling Stone, 628*: 54–59, 61, 106, 108.

Currie, E. (1993). *Reckoning: Drugs, the cities, and the American future.* New York: Hill & Wang.

Currie, E. (1985). *Confronting crime: An American challenge.* New York: Pantheon.

Dahmer, L. (1994). *A father's story.* New York: William Morrow & Company.

Daley, B. and Przybycin, C. (1989). Cocaine-dependent women have unique treatment needs. *Addiction Letter, 5*: 1–3.

Daly, K. and Chesney-Lind, M. (1988). Feminism and criminology. *Justice Quarterly, 5*: 497–535.

Daly, K. and Maher, L. (1998). *Criminology at the crossroads: Feminist readings in crime and justice.* New York: Oxford University Press.

Damousi, J. (1997). *Depraved and disorderly: Female convicts, sexuality, and gender in colonial Australia.* Cambridge: Cambridge University Press.

Datesman, S. K. and Cales, G. L. (1983). I'm still the same mommy: Maintaining the mother/child relationship in prison. *The Prison Journal, 63*: 142–154.

Davidson, R. T. (1974). *Chicano prisoners: The key to San Quentin.* New York: Holt, Rinehart & Winston.

Deck, M. V. (1988). Incarcerated mothers and their infants: Separation or legislation? *Boston College Law Review, 19*: 689–713.

DeClue, D. (1981). Prison was almost like death. *Student Lawyer, 9*: 32–37.

Diaz-Cotto, J. (2007). Latina imprisonment and the war on drugs. In M. Bosworth and J. Flavin (eds.), *Race, gender, and punishment: From colonialism to the war on terror* (pp. 184–199). Piscataway, NJ: Rutgers University Press.

Diaz-Cotto, J. (1996). *Gender, ethnicity, and the state: Latina and Latino prison politics.* Albany, NY: State University of New York Press.

DiIulio, J. J. (1991). Understanding prisons: The new and old penology. *Law and Social Inquiry, 16*: 65–114.

Ditton, P. M. (1999). *Mental health and treatment of inmates and probationers.* Washington, D.C.: U.S. Department of Justice.

Dobash, R. P., R. E. Dobash and S. Gutteridge (1986). *The imprisonment of women.* New York: Basil Blackwell.

Dodge, M. (1999). One female prisoner is of more trouble than twenty males: Women convicts in Illinois prisons, 1835–1896. *Journal of Social History, 32*: 907–930.

Doege, D. (2006). Early release is no easy task for female prisoners. *Milwaukee Journal Sentinel,* January 3: B1, B5.

Donziger, S., ed. (1996). *The real war on crime: The report of the national criminal justice commission.* New York: HarperCollins.

Dowker, F. and Wood, G. (1992). From Alcatraz to Marion to Florence: Control unit prisons in the United States. In W. Churchill and J. Vander Wall (eds), *Cages of steel: The politics of imprisonment in the United States* (pp. 131–151). Washington, D.C.: Maisonneuve Press.

Downing, D. S. (1989). The incarcerated mother's rights with respect to her children. *Columbia Human Rights Law Review, 20*: 75–93.

Dreifus, C. (1984). Lady lifers: What it's like to live behind bars. *Mademoiselle, 90*: 178–183.

Dunn, T. (1996). *The militarization of the U.S.-Mexico border, 1978–1992: Low intensity conflict doctrine come home.* Austin: University of Texas Press.

Dula, A. (1994). African American suspicion of the healthcare system is justified: What do we do about it?" *Cambridge Quarterly of Healthcare Ethics, 3*: 347–357.

Durose, M. R. and Langan, P. A. (2005). *State court sentencing of convicted felons, 2002.* Washington, D.C.: U.S. Department of Justice.

Dyer, C. (2000). Women in prison: Their family relationships and their depiction in the media. Available at: http://www.fsu.edu/~crimdo/dyer.html.

Epp, J. (1996). Exploring health care needs of adult female offenders. *Corrections Today, 58*: 96–97, 105, 121.

Epperson, D. L., T. E. Hannum and M. L. Datwyler (1982). Women incarcerated in 1960, 1970, and 1980: Implications of demographic, educational, and personality characteristics for earlier research. *Criminal Justice and Behavior, 9*: 352–363.

Faily, A., G. A. Roundtree and R. K. Miller (1980). A study of the maintenance of discipline with regard to rule infractions at the Louisiana correctional institute for women. *Corrective and Social Psychiatry and Journal of Behavior Technology Methods and Therapy, 26*: 151–155.

Faith, K. (1993a). *Unruly women: The politics of confinement and resistance.* Vancouver: Press Gang Publishers.

Faith, K. (1993b). Media, myths, and masculinization: Images of women in prison. In E. Adelberg and C. Currie (eds.), *In conflict with the law: Women and the Canadian justice system.* Vancouver: Press Gang Publishers.

Farnworth, M. (1984). Male-female differences in delinquency in a minority-group sample. *Journal of Research in Crime and Delinquency, 21*: 191–212.

Farrington, K. (1992). The modern prison as total institution? Public perception versus objective reality. *Crime and Delinquency, 38*: 6–26.

Feagin, J. and Sikes, M. (1994). *Living with racism: The Black middle class experience.* Boston: Beacon Press.

Feagin, J. and Vera, H. (1995). *White racism: The basics.* New York: Routledge.

Fearn, N. and Parker, K. (2005). Healthcare for women inmates: Issues, perceptions, and policy considerations. *Californian Journal of Health Promotion, 3*: 1–22.

Fearn, N. and Parker, K. (2004). Washington state's residential parenting program: An integrated public health, education, and social service resource for pregnant inmates and prison mothers. *Californian Journal of Health Promotion, 2*: 34–48.

Feeley, M. M. and Simon, J. (1992). The new penology: Notes on the emerging strategy of corrections and its implications. *Criminology, 30*: 449–474.

Feinman, C. (1983). An historical overview of the treatment of incarcerated women: Myths and realities of rehabilitation. *The Prison Journal, 63*: 12–26.

Festervan, E. (2003). *Women probationers: Supervision and success.* Alexandria: VA: American Correctional Association.

Fishman, S. (1983). The impact of incarceration on children of offenders. *Journal of Children in Contemporary Society, 15*: 89–99.

Flanagan, T. J., J. W. Marquart and K. G. Adams, eds. (1998). *Incarcerating criminals: Prisons and jails in social and organizational context.* New York: Oxford University Press.

Flavin, J. (2007). Slavery's legacy in contemporary attempts to regulate Black women's reproduction. In M. Bosworth and J. Flavin (eds.), *Race, gender, and punishment: From colonialism to the war on terror* (pp. 95–114). Piscataway, NJ: Rutgers University Press.

Fletcher, B., L. D. Shaver and D. Moon, eds. (1993). *Women prisoners: A forgotten population.* Westport, CT: Praeger.

Fletcher, G. (1988). *A crime of self defense.* Chicago: The University of Chicago Press.

Fogel, D. (1979). ". . . *we are the living proof": The justice model of corrections.* Cincinnati: Anderson.

Ford, C. (1979). Homosexual practices of institutionalized females. *Journal of Abnormal and Social Psychology, 23*: 442–448.

Forer, L. G. (1982). Medical services in prisons: Rights and remedies. *ABA Journal, 68*: 562–565.

Foster, T. W. (1975). Make-believe families: A response of women and girls to the deprivations of imprisonment. *International Journal of Criminology and Penology, 3*: 71–78.

Foucault, M. (1995). *Discipline and punish: The birth of the prison.* New York: Vintage Books.

Fox, J. G. (1984). Women's prison policy, prisoner activism, and the impact of the contemporary feminist movement: A case study. *The Prison Journal, 1*: 15–36.

Fox, J. G. (1982). *Organizational and racial conflict in maximum security prisons.* Lexington, MA: D.C. Heath and Company.

Frankl, V.E. (1992). *Man's search for meaning.* Boston: Beacon Press.

Franklin, C. A., N. E. Fearn and T. W. Franklin (2005). HIV/AIDS among female prison inmates: A public health concern. *Californian Journal of Health Promotion, 3*: 99–112.

Free, M. D. (2001). Racial bias and the American criminal justice system: Race and presentencing revisited. *Critical criminology: An International Journal, 10*: 195–223.

Freedman, E. B. (1981). *Their sisters' keepers: Women's prison reform in America.* Ann Arbor: University of Michigan Press.

French, L. (1983). A profile of the incarcerated Black female offender. *The Prison Journal, 63*: 80–87.

Fuller, L. (1993). Visitors to women's prisons in California: An exploratory study. *Federal Probation, 57*: 41–47.

Gaarder, E. and Belknap, J. (2002). Tenuous borders: Girls transferred to adult court. *Criminology, 40*: 481–518.

Gabel, K. and Johnston, D., eds. (1995). *Children of incarcerated parents.* New York: Lexington Press.

Gamble, V. N. (1997). Under the shadow of Tuskegee: African Americans and health care. *American Journal of Public Health, 87*: 1773–1778.

Gans, H. (1995). *The war against the poor: The underclass and antipoverty policy.* New York: Basic Books.

Garbarino, J. and Plantz, M. C. (1986). Child abuse and juvenile delinquency: What are the links? In J. Garbarino and C. Schellenbach (eds.), *Troubled youth, troubled families* (pp. 27–39). New York: Aldine-DeGruyter.

Garland, D. (1990). *Punishment and modern society.* Chicago: University of Chicago Press.

Gauch, S. (1988). When mothers go to prison: When you're behind bars, does your family life have to crumble? One model program discovers some surprising answers. *Human Rights, 16*: 32–35.

Geballe, S. and Stone, M. (1988). The new focus on medical care issues in women's prison cases. *The National Prison Project Journal, 15*: 1–7.

Gelsthorpe, L. and Morris, A., eds. (1990). *Feminist perspectives in criminology.* Philadelphia: Open University Press.

Genders, E. and Player, E. (1990). Women lifers: Assessing the experience. *The Prison Journal, 80*: 46–57.

Genty, P. M. (1989). Protecting the parental rights of incarcerated mothers whose children are in foster care: Proposed changes in New York's termination of parental rights law. *Fordham Urban Law Journal, 17*: 1–26.

Giallombardo, R. (1966). *Society of women: A study of women's prison.* New York: Wiley.

Gido, R. and Alleman, T., eds. (2001). *Turnstile justice: Issues in American corrections.* 2nd edition. Upper Saddle River, NJ: Prentice Hall.

Gilfus, M. (1992). From victims to survivors to offenders: Women's routes of entry and immersion into street crime. *Women and Criminal Justice, 4*: 63–89.

Gilroy, P. (1993). *The Black Atlantic: Modernity and double consciousness.* Cambridge, MA: Harvard University Press.

Ginsburg, C. (1980). Who are the women in prison? *Corrections Today, 42*: 56–59.

Girshick, L. B. (1999). *No safe haven: Stories of women in prison.* Boston: Northeastern University Press.

Gittelson, N. (1982). What sustains me is the hope of getting out (interview with Jean Harris). *McCall's, 109*: 72–74.

Glaser, J. B. and Greifinger, R.B. (1993). Correctional health care: A public health opportunity. *Annuals of Internal Medicine, 118*: 139–145.

Glaze, L. E. and Bonczar, T. P. (2006). *Probation and parole in the United States, 2005.* Washington, D.C.: U.S. Department of Justice.

Goetting, A. (1985). Racism, sexism, and ageism in the prison community. *Federal Probation, 49*: 10–22.

Goetting, A. (1984a). The elderly in prison: A profile. *Criminal Justice Review, 9*: 14–24.

Goetting, A. (1984b). Conjugal association practices in prisons of the American nations. *Alternative Lifestyles, 6*: 155–174.

Goetting, A. (1982). Conjugal association in prison: Issues and perspectives. *Crime and Delinquency, 28*: 52–71.

Goetting, A. and Howsen, R.M. (1983). Women in prison: A profile. *The Prison Journal, 63*: 27–46.

Goffman, E. (1961). *Asylums: Essays on the social situation of mental patients and other inmates.* Garden City, N.Y.: Anchor Books.

Goode, E. and Ben-Yehuda, N. (1994). *Moral panics: The social construction of deviance.* Cambridge, MA.: Blackwell.

Greenwood, L. (1997). *Sex offenses and offenders: An analysis of data on rape and sexual assault.* Washington, D.C.: U.S. Government Printing Office.

Greer, K. (2000). The changing nature of interpersonal relationships in a women's prison. *The Prison Journal, 80*: 442–468.

Gutierres, S. and Reich, J. (1981). A development perspective on runaway behavior: Its relationship to child abuse. *Child Welfare, 60*: 89–94.

Gutierrez, D. G., ed. (1997). *Between two worlds: Mexican immigrants in the United States.* Wilmington, DE: Scholarly Resources Inc.

Haft, M. (1973). Women in prison: Discriminatory practices and some legal solutions. In M. G. Hermann and M. G. Haft (eds.), *Prisoner's rights sourcebook.* New York: Clark Boardman Company.

Hairston, C. F. (1988). Family ties during imprisonment: Do they influence future criminal activity? *Federal Probation, 52*: 48–52.

Haley, K. (1977). Mothers behind bars: A look at the parental rights of incarcerated women. *New England Journal on Prison Law, 4*: 144–155.

Hammett, T. (1988). 1988 update: AIDS in correctional facilities. In *Issues and practices in criminal justice.* National Institute of Justice.

Hannah-Moffat, K. (1995). Feminine fortresses: Women-centered prisons. *The Prison Journal, 75*: 135–164.

Hannum, T. E., F. H. Borgen and R. M. Anderson (1978). Self-concept changes associated with incarceration in female prisoners. *Criminal Justice and Behavior, 5*: 271–279.

Hansen, P. (2005). Life-changing words. *Research profile, 27*: 16–19. University of Wisconsin-Milwaukee.

Harlow, C. W. (1993). *HIV in US prisons and jails.* Bureau of Justice Statistics. Washington, D.C.: U.S. Department of Justice.

Harm, N. (1992). Social policy on women prisoners: An historical analysis. *Affilia Journal of Women and Social Work, 7:* 90–108.

Harris, J. (1988). *They always call us ladies: Stories from prison.* New York: Scribner's.

Harrison, P. M. and Beck, A. J. (2006). *Prisoners in 2005.* Washington, D.C.: U.S. Department of Justice.

Hawkins, D., ed. (1998). *Ethnicity, race and crime; perspectives across time and space.* New York: SUNY Press.

Hayes, L. M. (1995). Prison suicide: An overview and a guide to prevention. *Prison Journal, 75:* 431–456.

Heffernan, E. (1972). *Making it in prison: The square, the cool, and the life.* New York: John Wiley and Sons.

Heidensohn, F. (1985). *Women and crime: The life of the female offender.* London: MacMillan.

Helliker, K. (1995). Expanding prison population captivates markets. *Wall Street Journal,* January 19: B1.

Henriques, Z. W. (1996). Imprisoned mothers and their children: Separation reunion syndrome dual impact. *Women and Criminal Justice, 8:* 77–95.

Hill, G. D. and Crawford, E. M. (1990). Women, race, and crime. *Criminology, 28:* 601–626.

Hodge, A. (1982). Bonnie Rateree (assists children of women in prison). *Essence Magazine 13:* 26.

Hodge, J. (1988). Group work with women in a maximum security unit. *Prison Service Journal, 72:* 6–8.

Holt, K. E. (1982). Nine months to life-the law and the pregnant inmate. *Journal of Family Law, 20:* 523–543.

Holtfreter, K. and Morash, M. (2003). The needs of women offenders: Implications for correctional programming. *Women and Criminal Justice, 14:* 137–160.

Hooper, E. (2000). *The river: A journey back to the sources of HIV and AIDS.* Harmondsworth: Penguin.

Howe, A. (1994). *Punish and critique: Towards a feminist analysis of penality.* New York: Routledge.

Hudson, B., ed. (1996). *Race, crime and justice.* Aldershot: Dartmouth.

Hughes, K. A. (2006). *Justice expenditure and employment in the United States, 2003.* Washington, D.C.: U.S. Department of Justice.

Human Rights News (2003). United states: Mentally ill mistreated in prison. New York: Human Rights Watch.

Human Rights Watch Project (1996). *All too familiar: Sexual abuse of women in U.S. state prisons.* New York: Human Rights Watch.

Humphries, D. (1999). *Crack mothers: Pregnancy, drugs, and the media.* Columbia: Ohio University Press.

Hunter, S. M. (1986). On the line-working hard with dignity. *Corrections Today, 48:* 12–13.

Hunter, S. M. (1984). Issues and challenges facing women's prisons in the 1980s. *The Prison Journal, 64:* 129–135.

Inciardi, J. A. (2001). *The war on drugs III: The continuing saga of the mysteries and miseries of intoxication, addiction, crime, and public policy.* Boston: Allyn and Bacon.

Immarigeon, R. (1997). Gender-specific programming for female offenders. *Community Corrections Report on Law and Corrections Practice, 4*: 65–80.

Immarigeon, R. (1987). Few diversion programs are offered for female offenders. *The National Prison Project Journal, 12*: 9–11.

Immarigeon, R. and Chesney-Lind, M. (1992). *Women's prisons: Overcrowded and overused.* San Francisco: National Council on Crime and Delinquency.

Ingram-Fogel, C. (1991). Health problems and needs of incarcerated women. *Journal of Prison and Jail Health, 10*: 43–57.

Irwin, J. and Austin, J. (1997). *It's about time: America's imprisonment binge.* 2nd edition. Belmont, CA: Wadsworth Publishing Company.

Jacobs, D. and Wood, K. (1999). Interracial conflict and interracial homicide: Do political and economic rivalries explain white killings of Blacks or Black killings of Whites? *American Journal of Sociology, 105*: 157–190.

James, D. J. and Glaze, L. E. (2006). *Mental health problems of prison and jail inmates.* Washington, D.C.: U.S. Department of Justice.

Jencks, C. (1994). The truth about the homeless. *New York Review of Books.* April 21: 20–27.

Jensen, G. F. and Jones, D. (1976). Perspectives on inmate culture: A study of women in prison. *Social Forces, 54*: 590–603.

Johansen, P. S. (2005). Incarcerated mothers: Mental health, child welfare policy, and the special concerns of undocumented mothers. *Californian Journal of Health Promotion, 3*: 130–138.

Johnson, P. (2003). *Inner lives: Voices of African American women in prison.* New York: New York University Press.

Johnston, D. (1995). Intervention. In K. Gabel and D. Johnston (eds.), *Children of incarcerated parents* (pp. 199–236). New York: Lexington Press.

Jones, A. (1982). One woman who chose to say no: Sex exploitation behind bars (Carol Ann Wilds). *Nation, 234*: 456–460.

Jones, R. (2000). State ready to bring back many inmates held elsewhere. *Milwaukee Journal Sentinel,* August 14: 1B, 5B.

Jurado, R. (1986). California project stands up for women in prison. *The National Prison Project Journal, 7*: 10–11.

Jurik, N. C. (1983). The economics of female recidivism. *Criminology, 21*: 603–622.

Justice Assistance News (1982). Varied programs aid young women in trouble. 3: 3.

Juvenile and Family Law Digest (1981). Termination-cannot automatically terminate parental rights to child born in prison. 13: 288–290.

Kane, E. (2004). Benedict Center shines in pursuit of justice for all. *Milwaukee Journal Sentinel,* May 2: 3B.

Kaplan, M. F. (1988). A peer support group for women in prison for the death of a child. *Journal of Offender Counseling, Services, and Rehabilitation, 13*: 5–13.

Kappeler, V. and Potter, G. (2004). *The mythology of crime and criminal justice.* 4th edition. Prospect Heights, IL: Waveland Press.

Kennedy, R. (1998). *Race, crime and law.* New York: Vintage Books.

King, R. D. (1999). The rise and rise of super-max: An American solution in search of a problem? *Punishment and Society, 1*: 163–186.

King, R. D. and Maguire, M., eds. (1994). *Prisons in context.* New York: Oxford University Press.

Kiser, G. (1991). Female inmates and their families. *Federal Probation, 55*: 56–63.

Kleck, G. (1991). *Point blank: Guns and violence in America.* New Brunswick, N.J.: Aldine Transaction.

Knepper, P. (1989). Southern-style penal repression: Ethnic stratification, economic inequality, and imprisonment in territorial Arizona. *Social Justice, 16*: 132–149.

Koban, L. A. (1983). Parents in prison: A comparative analysis of the effects of incarceration on the families of men and women. *Research in Law, Deviance and Social Control, 5*: 171–183.

Kohn, A. (1986). State wins appeal of dental-care plan in women's prison (New York). *New York Law Journal, 196*: 1.

Kolman, A. S. (1983). Support and control patterns of inmate mothers: A pilot study. *The Prison Journal, 63*: 155–166.

Korn, R. (1988a). Follow-up report on the effects of confinement in the high security unit at Lexington. *Social Justice, 15*: 20–30.

Korn, R. (1988b). The effects of confinement in the high security unit at Lexington. *Social Justice, 15*: 8–19.

Kornhauser, A. (1989). Male-only club feds hit in suit; female inmates press claims for equal treatment. *Legal Times, 12*: 1.

Kort, M. (1987). A tough assignment-working out inside (prison exercise program). *Ms. Magazine, 16*: 32.

Krasno, M. R. (1982). What prison does to women. *Update on Law-Related Education, 6*: 18–21.

Kruttschnitt, C. (1983). Race relations and the female inmate. *Crime and Delinquency, 29*: 577–592.

Kruttschnitt, C. (1980–1981). Social status and sentences of female offenders. *Law and Society Review, 15*: 247–265.

Kruttschnitt, C. and Krmpotich, S. (1990). Aggressive behavior among female inmates: An exploratory study. *Justice Quarterly, 7*: 271–389.

Kruttschnitt, C. and Gartner, R. (2004). *Marking time in the golden state: Women's imprisonment in California.* New York: Cambridge University Press.

Kruttschnitt, C., R. Gartner and A. Miller (2000). Doing her own time? women's responses to prison in the context of the old and the new penology. *Criminology, 38*: 681–718.

Kuhlmann, R. and Ruddell, R. (2005). Elderly jail inmates: Problems, prevalence, and public health. *Californian Journal of Health Promotion, 3*: 50–61.

Kurshan, N. (1996). Behind the walls: The history and current reality of women's imprisonment. In E. Rosenblatt (ed.), *Criminal injustice: Confronting the prison crisis.* Boston, MA.: South End Press.

Kurshan, N. (1992). Women and imprisonment in the U.S. In W. Churchill and J. Vander Wall (eds), *Cages of steel: The politics of imprisonment in the United States* (pp. 331–358). Washington, D.C.: Maisonneuve Press.

Lamott, K. (1972). *Chronicles of San Quentin.* New York: Ballatine Books.

Langan, P. A. and Levin, D. J. (2002). *Recidivism of prisoners released in 1994.* Washington, D.C.: U.S. Department of Justice.

Langston, S. D. (2003). Commentary: The reality of women of color in the prison system. *Journal of Ethnicity in Criminal Justice, 1*: 85–93.

Larson, J. H. (1983). Rural female delinquents' adaptation to institutional life. *Juvenile and Family Court Journal, 34*: 83–92.

Larson, J. and Nelson, J. (1984). Women, friendship, and adaptation to prison. *Journal of Criminal Justice, 12*: 601–615.

Legal Service Bulletin (1983). Incarcerated mothers and babies. 8: 35–37.

Leger, R. G. (1987). Lesbianism among women prisoners: Participants and nonparticipants. *Criminal Justice and Behavior, 14*: 448–467.

Leonard, E. B. (1983). Judicial decisions and prison reform: The impact of litigation on women prisoners. *Social Problems, 31*: 45–58.

Leonard, K. K., C. E. Pope and W. H. Feyerherm, eds. (1995). *Minorities in juvenile justice.* Thousand Oaks, CA: Sage Publications.

Lerner, S. (1989). Women behind bars. *Cosmopolitan, 206*: 214–219.

Levine, J. (1992). *Juries and politics.* Pacific Grove, CA: Brooks/Cole Publishing Company.

Lewis, D. K. (1982). Female exoffenders and community programs: Barriers to service. *Crime and Delinquency, 28*: 40–51.

Liebling, A. (1999). Doing research in prison: Breaking the silence? *Theoretical Criminology, 3*: 147–173.

Liebling, A. (1995). Vulnerability and prison suicide. *British Journal of Criminology, 35*: 173–185.

Liebling, A. (1994). Suicide amongst women prisoners. *Howard Journal of Criminal Justice, 33*: 1–9.

Liebling, A. and Arnold, H. (2004). *Prisons and their moral performance: A study of values, quality, and prison life.* New York: Oxford University Press.

Lindquist, C. A. (1980). Prison discipline and the female offender. *Journal of Offender Counseling, Service, and Rehabilitation, 4*: 305–318.

Liptak, A. (2006). Prisons often shackle pregnant inmates in labor. *New York Times*, March 2.

Liska, A. (1992). *Social threat and social control.* Albany: SUNY Press.

Logan, G. (1992). Family ties take top priority in women's visiting program. *Corrections Today*, August: 160–161.

Lord, E. (1995). A prison superintendent's perspective on women in prison. *Prison Journal, 75*: 257–269.

Low, P., J. C. Jeffries and R. Bonnie (1986). *The trial of John W. Hinckley, Jr.: A case study in the insanity defense.* New York: Foundation Press.

Lundstrom-Roche, F. (1985). *Women in prison: Ideals and reals.* Stockholm: Universitet Stockholm.

Macher, A., D. Kibble, K. Bryant, A. Cody, T. Pilcher and D. Jahn (2005). Educating correctional health care providers and inmates about drug-drug interactions: HIV-medications and illicit drugs. *Californian Journal of Health Promotion, 3*: 139–143.

MacKenzie, D. L., J. Robinson and C. Campbell (1989). Long-term incarceration: Prison adjustment and coping. *Criminal Justice and Behavior, 16*: 223–238.

Maden, A., M. Swinton and J. Gunn (1994). Psychiatric disorder in women serving a prison sentence. *British Journal of Psychiatry, 164*: 44–54.

Maden, A., M. Swinton and J. Gunn (1992). A survey of pre-arrest drug use in sentenced prisoners. *British Journal of Addiction, 87*: 27–33.

Maden, A., M. Swinton and J. Gunn (1990). Women in prison and use of illicit drugs before arrest. *British Medical Journal, 301*: 1133.

Mahan, S. (1984). Imposition of despair: An ethnography of women in prison. *Journal of Crime and Justice, 7*: 101–129.

Mandaraka-Sheppard, A. (1986). *The dynamics of aggression in women's prisons in England.* Aldershot: Gower.

Mandel, J. (1979). Hispanics in the criminal justice system. The nonexistent problem. *Law and Justice, 3*: 16–20.

Mann, C. R. (1995). Women of color in the criminal justice system. In B. Price and N. Sokoloff (eds.), *Women in the criminal justice system* (pp. 118–135). NY: McGraw-Hill.

Mann, C. R. (1993). *Unequal justice: A question of color.* Bloomington: Indiana University Press.

Mann, C. R. (1984). *Female crime and delinquency.* Tuscaloosa: University of Alabama Press.

Marable, M. (1999). The politics of race. In *Conference summary: and action plan: Money, education, and prisons: Standing at the crossroads.* Milwaukee, WI: The Benedict Center.

Marley, P. (2004). Prisoners' health costs rise 500%. *Milwaukee Journal Sentinel,* June 7: 1A, 5A.

Martinez, D. J. (2004). Hispanics incarcerated in state correctional facilities: Variations in inmate characteristics across Hispanic subgroups. *Journal of Ethnicity in Criminal Justice, 2*: 119–131.

Martinson, R. (1974). What works? Questions and answers about prison reform. *The Public Interest, 35*: 22–54.

Maruna, S. (2001). *Making good: How ex-convicts reform and rebuild their lives.* Washington, D.C.: American Psychological Association.

Masters, B. (1993). *The shrine of Jeffrey Dahmer.* London: Hodder and Stroughton Limited.

Mauer, M. (1999). *Race to incarcerate.* New York: The New Press.

Mawby, R. I. (1982). Women in prison: A British study. *Crime and Delinquency, 28*: 24–39.

Maxey, J.W. (1986). Designing a women's prison. *Corrections Today, 48*: 140–142.

McBride, J. and Zahn, M. (2000). Prison workers find it hard to give good care. *Milwaukee Journal Sentinel,* October 23: 1–11. Available at: wysiwyg://7/http://www.jsonline.com/news/state/oct00/3pris24102300.asp.

McCall, C., J. Castell and N. Shaw (1985). *Pregnancy in prison: A needs assessment of prenatal outcome in three California penal institutions.* Sacramento, CA: Department of Health Services, Maternal and Child Health Branch.

McCampbell, S. and Layman, E. (2000). *Training curriculum for investigating allegations of staff sexual misconduct with inmates.* Tamarac, FL: Center of Innovative Public Policies.

McCarthy, B. R. (1980). Inmate mothers: The problems of separation and reintegration. *Journal of Offender Counseling, Services and Rehabilitation, 4*: 199–212.

Macionis, J. (2007). *Sociology.* 11th edition. Upper Saddle River: Pearson/Prentice Hall.

McClellan, D. (1994). Disparity and discipline of male and female inmates in Texas prisons. *Women and Criminal Justice, 5*: 71–97.

McConnell Clark Foundation (1997). *Seeking justice: Crime and punishment in America.* New York.

McDonald, D. C. (1995). *Managing prison health care and costs.* Washington, D.C.: U.S. Government Printing Office.

McGaha, G. S. (1987). Health care issues of incarcerated women. *Journal of Offender Counseling, Services and Rehabilitation, 12*: 53–59.

McGuire, J. (1995). *What works: Reducing re-offending.* New York: John Wiley.

McHugh, G. (1980). Protection of the rights of pregnant women in prisons and detention facilities. *New England Journal on Prison Law, 6*: 231–263.

McNeely, R. L. and Pope, C.E. (1981). *Race, crime and criminal justice.* Beverly Hills, CA: Sage Publications.

McKenzie, D. L., J.W. Robinson and C.S. Campbell (1989). Long-term incarceration of female offenders: Prison adjustment and coping. *Criminal Justice and Behavior, 16*: 223–237.

McPeters, J. E. (1984). Post-conviction rights of pregnant women under North Carolina law. *North Carolina Law Review, 62*: 1252–1260.

Merlo, A. and Pollock, J. (2005). *Women, law and social control.* 2nd edition. Boston, MA: Allyn & Bacon.

Messerschmidt, J. (2007). We must protect our southern women: On whiteness, masculinities, and lynching. In M. Bosworth and J. Flavin (eds.), *Race, gender, and punishment: From colonialism to the war on terror* (pp. 77–94). Piscataway, NJ: Rutgers University Press.

Messerschmidt, J. (1997). *Crime as structured action: Gender, race, class and crime in the making.* Thousand Oaks, CA: Sage Publications.

Miami Herald (2005). Ex-inmate sues over death of baby born over Tampa jail toilet. Available at: http://www.miami.com.

Michalowski, R. (1985). *Order, law and crime.* New York: Random House.

Mill, J. S. (1997). *The subjection of women.* New York: Dover Publications.

Miller, E. (1986). *Street woman.* Philadelphia: Temple University Press.

Miller, J. (1996). *Search and destroy: African American males in the criminal justice system.* New York: Cambridge University Press.

Miller, J. L., P. H. Rossi and J. E. Simpson (1986). Perceptions of justice: Race and gender differences in judgments of appropriate prison sentences. *Law and Society Review, 20*: 313–334.

Miller, V. (2007). Tough men, tough prisons, tough, times: The globalization of supermaximum secure prisons. In M. Bosworth and J. Flavin (eds.), *Race, gender, and punishment: From colonialism to the war on terror* (pp. 200–215). Piscataway, NJ: Rutgers University Press.

Milovanovic, D. and Schwartz, M., eds. (1999). *Race, gender, and class in criminology.* New York: Routledge.

Milwaukee Journal Sentinel (2002). Corrections: What about policies on prison, sentencing? August 25: 3J.

Milwaukee Journal Sentinel (2000a). A Wisconsin prison term can equal a death sentence. October 22: 1A, 14A–16A.

Milwaukee Journal Sentinel (2000b). Prison demographics. August 16: B3.

Morain, D. (1994). California's prison budget: Why is it so voracious? *Los Angeles Times*, October 19.

Morash, M. and Bynum, T. (1995). *Findings from the national study of innovative and promising programs for women offenders.* Washington, D.C.: U.S. Department of Justice.

Morash, M., R. Haar and L. Rucker (1994). A comparison of programming for women and men in U.S. prisons in the 1980s. *Crime and Delinquency, 40*: 197–221.

Morash, M. and Schram, P. J. (2002). *The prison experience: Special issues of women in prison.* Prospect Heights, IL: Waveland Press.

Morbidity and Mortality Weekly Report (2002). Annual smoking-attributable mortality, years of potential life lost, and economic costs-United States, 1995–1999. 51: 300–303.

Morris, R. (1987). Women in prison. *Canadian Dimension, 20*: 10–13.

Morris, A. and Wilkinson, C. (1995). Responding to female prisoners' needs. *Prison Journal, 75*: 295–305.

Morton, J. B. (2004). *Working with women offenders in correctional institutions.* Alexandria, VA: American Correctional Association.

Morton, J. B., ed. (1998). *Complex challenges, collaborative solutions: Programming for adult and juvenile female offenders.* Lanham, MD: American Correctional Association.

Moss, D. C. (1988). Pregnant? Go directly to jail: Suit hits prenatal care for women inmates. *ABA Journal, 74*: 20.

Moulden, M. (2000). Women prisoners with mental health problems. *Prison Service Journal, 126*: 11–12.

Moyer, I. L. (1984). Deceptions and realities of life in women's prisons. *The Prison Journal, 64*: 45–56.

Moyer, I. L. (1980). Leadership in a women's prison. *Journal of Criminal Justice, 8*: 233–241.

Moyer, I. L. (1978). Differential social structure and homosexuality among women in prisons. *Virginia Social Science Journal*, April: 13–14, 17–19.

Mullings, J., J. W. Marquart and D. J. Hartley (2003). Exploring the effects of childhood sexual abuse and its impact on HIV/AIDS risk-taking behavior among women prisoners. *The Prison Journal, 83*: 442–463.

Mumola, C. J. (2007). *Medical causes of death in state prisons, 2001–2004.* Washington, D.C.: U.S. Department of Justice.

Mumola, C. J. (2005). *Suicide and homicide in state prisons and local jails.* Washington D.C.: U.S. Department of Justice

Mumola, C. J. (2000). *Incarcerated parents and their children.* Bureau of Justice Statistics Special Report. Washington D.C.: U.S. Department of Justice.

Murphy, D. S. (2005). Health care in the Federal Bureau of Prisons: Fact or fiction. *Californian Journal of Health Promotion, 3*: 23–37.

Murray, C. and Lopez, A. (1997). Alternative projections of mortality and disability by cause 1990–2020: Global burden of disease study. *Lancet, 349*: 1498–1504.

Myers, M. (1998). *Race, labor and punishment in the New South.* Columbus, Ohio: Ohio State University Press.

Nation (1988). Follow-up (transferring women prisoners to high security facility for beliefs). 247: 152.

National Center for Health Statistics (2003). Health United States, 2003, with chartbook on trends in the health of Americans. Hyattsville, MD.

Nelson, V. (1933). *Prison days and nights.* Boston: Little, Brown.

Neto, V. V. and Bainer, L. M. (1983). Mother and wife locked up: A day with the family. *The Prison Journal, 63*: 124–141.

Newman, G. (1995). *Just and painful: A case for the corporal punishment of criminals.* 2nd edition. New York: Harrow and Heston.

New Statesman (1985). Mad and bad women (mentally ill women prisoners). 109: 3.

New York Times (1998). October, 2: A17.

New York Times (1996). December, 27: A18.

New York Times (1992). November, 30: A10.

Newton, K. (1980). Researchers find health care lacking for women prisoners. *The Los Angeles Daily Journal, 93* (August 20): 3.

Nichollas, D. (1987). Mothers in prison: How young lawyer Gail Smith fights for their rights. *Barrister, 14*: 14–18.

Norz, F. (1989). Prenatal and postnatal rights of incarcerated mothers. *Columbia Human Rights Law Review, 20*: 55–73.

Oboler, S. (1995). *Ethnic labels, Latino lives: Identity and the politics of (re)presentation in the United States.* Minneapolis: University of Minnesota Press.

O'Brien, P. (1982). *The promise of punishment: Prisons in Nineteenth Century France.* Princeton: Princeton University Press.

O'Connell, J.P. (1995). Throwing away the key (and state money). Winter *Spectrum, 28*: 12–15.

O'Halloran, T. (1984). Women in prison getting dosed to the eyeballs. *New Statesman, 108*: 5.

Ohlin, L. (1956). *Sociology and the field of corrections.* New York: Russell Sage Foundation.

O'Leary, M. and Weinhouse, D. (1992). Colorado facility helps women overcome barriers to education. *Corrections Today*, August: 194–199.

Olsen, F. E. (1995). *Feminist legal theory.* New York: New York University Press.

O'Malley, P. (1999). Volatile and contradictory punishment. *Theoretical Criminology, 3*: 175–196.

Osborne Association (1994). AIDS in prison fact sheet: United States.

Oshinsky, D. (1997). *Worse than slavery: Parchman farm and the ordeal of Jim Crow justice.* New York: The Free Press.

Owen, B. (1998). *In the mix: Struggle and survival in a women's prison.* New York: State University of New York Press.

Owen, B. and Bloom, B. (1995a). *Profiling the needs of California's female prisoners: A needs assessment.* Washington, D.C.: National Institute of Justice.

Owen, B. and Bloom, B. (1995b). Profiling women prisoners: Findings from national surveys and a California sample. *Prison Journal, 75:* 165–185.

Pearson, J. (1993). Centro Femenil: A women's prison in Mexico. *Social Justice, 20:* 85–126.

Petersilia, J. (2006). *Understanding California corrections.* Berkeley, CA: California Policy Research Center. Available at: http://ucicorrections.seweb.uci.edu/pdf/UnderstandingCorrectionsPetersilia20061.pdf.

Petersilia, J. (2003). *When prisoners come home.* New York: Oxford University Press.

Petersilia, J. (1998). *Community corrections: Probation, parole, and intermediate sanctions.* New York: Oxford University Press.

Petersilia, J. (1997). Just for all? Offenders with mental retardation and the criminal justice system. *The Prison Journal, 77:* 358–380.

Peugh, J. and Belenko, S. (1999). Substance-involved women inmates: Challenges to providing effective treatment. *Prison Journal, 79:* 23–45.

Phillips, S. and Bloom, B. (1998). In whose best interest? The impact of changing public policy on relatives caring for children with incarcerated parents. *Child Welfare, 77:* 531–541.

Pollock, J. M. (2002a). *Women, prison, and crime.* 2nd Edition. Belmont, CA: Wadsworth Publishing Company.

Pollock, J. M. (2002b). Parenting programs in women's prisons. *Women and Criminal Justice, 14:* 131–154.

Pollock, J. M. (1998). *Counseling women in prison.* Thousand Oaks, CA: Sage Publications.

Pollock, J. M. (1986). *Sex and supervision: Guarding male and female inmates.* Westport, CT: Greenwood Press.

Pollock, J. M. (1984). Women will be women: Correctional officers' perceptions of the emotionality of women inmates. *The Prison Journal, 64:* 84–91.

Potter, G. and Kappeler, V. (1998). *Constructing crime: Perspectives on making news and social problems.* Prospect Heights, IL: Waveland Press.

Prendergast, M., J. Wellisch and G. Falkin (1995). Assessment of services for substance-abusing women offenders in community and correctional settings. *Prison Journal, 75:* 240–256.

Presser, L. and Gunnison, E. (1999). Strange bedfellows: Is sex offender notification a form of community justice? *Crime and Delinquency, 45:* 299–315.

Pridemore, W. (2000). An empirical examination of commutations and executions in post-Furman capital cases. *Justice Quarterly, 17:* 159–183.

Propper, A.M. (1981). *Prison homosexuality: Myth and reality.* Lexington, MA: D.C. Heath.

Quinney, R. (1977). *Class state and crime.* New York: David McKay Company.

Radosh, P. (1988). Inmate mothers: Legislative solutions to a difficult problem. *Crime and Justice, 11:* 61–73.

Rafter, N.H. (1992). Equality or difference? *Federal Prisons Journal, 3:* 17.

Rafter, N.H. (1990). *Partial justice: Women, prisons, and social control.* 2d edition. New Brunswick, N.J.: Transaction Publishers.

Rafter, N.H. (1987). Even in prison, women are second-class citizens. *Human Rights,* *14*: 28–32.

Rafter, N. H. (1985). *Partial justice: Women in state prisons, 1800–1935.* Boston, MA: Northeastern University Press.

Rafter, N.H. (1983). Prison for women, 1790–1980. In M. Tonry and N. Morris (eds.), *Crime and justice: An annual review of research* (vol. 5, pp. 129–182). Chicago: University of Chicago Press.

Raimon, M. (2000). Barriers to achieving justice for incarcerated parents. *Fordham Law Journal, 70*: 421–426.

Ramsey, M. L. (1980a). Special features and treatment needs of female drug offenders. *Journal of Offender Counseling, Services and Rehabilitation, 4*: 357–368.

Ramsey, M. L. (1980b). GENESIS: A therapeutic community model for incarcerated female drug offenders. *Contemporary Drug Problems, 9*: 273–281.

Rasche, C. E. (1974). The female offender as the object of criminological research. *Criminal Justice and Behavior, 1*: 301–320.

Reaves, L. (1983). Babies in jail: Suit asks rights for moms. *ABA Journal, 69*: 1014.

Reiman, J. (2006). *The rich get richer and the poor get prison: Ideology, class, and criminal justice.* 8th edition. Boston: Allyn & Bacon.

Resnick, J. and Shaw, N. (1980). Prisoners of their sex: Health problems of incarcerated women. In I. Robbins (ed.), *Prisoners rights sourcebook: Theory, litigation and practice* (pp. 339–413). New York: Clark Boardman.

Reuben, W. and Norman, C. (1987). The women of Lexington prison. *The Nation, 244*: 881.

Rice, M. (1990). Challenging orthodoxies in feminist theory: A Black feminist critique. In L. Gelsthorpe and A. Morris (eds.), *Feminist perspectives in criminology.* Philadelphia: Open University Press.

Richie, B. (2001). Challenges incarcerated women face as they return to their communities: Findings from life history interviews. *Crime and Delinquency, 47*: 368–389.

Richie, B. (1996). *Compelled to crime: The gender entrapment of battered Black women.* New York: Routledge.

Rierden, A. (1997). *The farm: Life inside a women's prison.* Amherst, MA: University of Massachusetts Press.

Rippon, M. and Hassell, R.A. (1981). Women, prison, and the Eighth Amendment. *North Carolina Central Law Review, 12*: 434–460.

Roberts, Y. (1989). Abandoned inside. *New Statesman and Society, 2*: 17.

Rock, P. (1996). *Reconstructing a women's prison: The Halloway redevelopment project, 1968–1988.* Oxford: Clarendon Press.

Rodriguez, L. (1993). *Always running: La vida loca: Gang days in L.A.* New York: Simon and Schuster.

Romenesko, K. and Miller, E. (1989). The second step in double jeopardy: Appropriating the labor of female street hustlers. *Crime and Delinquency, 35*: 109–135.

Rosenbaum, J.L. (1993). The female delinquent: Another look at the role of the family. In R. Muraskin and T. Alleman (eds.), *It's a crime: Women and justice* (399–415). Englewood Cliffs, NJ: Prentice Hall.

Roth, R. (2004). Do prisoners have abortion rights. *Feminist Studies, 30*: 353–381.

Roundtree, G. A., B. Mohan and L. W. Mahaffery (1980). Determinants of female aggression: A study of a prison population. *International Journal of Offender Therapy and Comparative Criminology, 24*: 260–269.

Ruddell, R. (2004). *America behind bars: Trends in imprisonment, 1950 to 2000.* New York: LFB Scholarly Publishing.

Ruddell, R. and Urbina, M. G. (2004). Minority threat and punishment: A cross-national analysis. *Justice Quarterly, 21*: 903–931.

Ruddell, R. and Urbina, M. G. (2007). Weak nations, political repression, and punishment. *International Criminal Justice Review, 17*: 84–107.

Rusche, G. (1933/1978). Labour market and penal sanction: Thoughts on the sociology of criminal justice. *Crime and Social Justice*, (Fall-Winter): 2–8.

Rusche, G. and Kirchheimer, O. (1939/1968). *Punishment and social structure.* New York: Russell and Russell.

Runtz, M. and Briere, J. (1986). Adolescent 'acting out' and childhood history of sexual abuse. *Journal of Interpersonal Violence, 1*: 326–334.

Russell, D. (1986). *The secret trauma: Incest in the lives of girls and women.* New York: Basic Books.

Salholz, E. (1990). Women in jail: Unequal justice; an unprecedented influx of female inmates leaves prisons overcrowded and overwhelmed. *Newsweek, 115*: 37–40.

Sametz, L. (1980). Children of incarcerated women. *Social Work, 25*: 298–303.

Sanchez, L. E. (2007). The carceral contract: From domestic to global governance. In M. Bosworth and J. Flavin (eds.), *Race, gender, and punishment: From colonialism to the war on terror* (pp. 167–183). Piscataway, NJ: Rutgers University Press.

Sanford, L. and Donovan, M. (1994). *Women and self esteem.* New York: Penguin Books.

Sappenfield, A. (2006). *Wisconsin legislator briefing book, 2006–2007.* Madison, WI: Wisconsin Legislative Council.

Sargent, J. P. (1984). The evolution of a stereotype: Paternalism and the female inmate. *The Prison Journal, 64*: 37–44.

Scheffler, J. A. (1986). *Wall tappings: An anthology of writings by women prisoners.* Boston, MA: Northeastern University Press.

Scheffler, J. A. (1984a). An annotated bibliography of writings by women prisoners. *The Prison Journal, 64*: 68–83.

Scheffler, J. A. (1984b). Women's prison writing: An unexplored tradition in literature. *The Prison Journal, 64*: 57–67.

Schlanger, M. (2003). Inmate litigation. *Harvard Law Review, 116*: 1555–1706.

Schoenbauer, L. J. (1986). Incarcerated parents and their children-forgotten families. *Law and Inequality: A Journal of Theory and Practice, 4*: 579–701.

Schupak, T. L. (1986). Women and children first: An examination of the unique needs of women in prison. *Golden Gate University Law Review, 16*: 455–474.

Schweber, C. (1984). Beauty marks and blemishes: The coed prison as a microcosm of integrated society. *The Prison Journal, 64*: 3–14.

Seelye, K. (1994). House talks tough on capital punishment as it begins debate on crime bill. *New York Times*, April 15: A23.

Segura, D. A. and Pesquera, B. M. (1998). Chicana feminists: Their political context and contemporary expressions. In A. Darder and R.D. Torres (eds.), *The Latino studies reader: Culture, economy and society* (pp. 193–205). Malden, MA: Blackwell Publishers.

Seymour, C. and Hairston, C. F., eds. (2001). *Children with parents in prison: Child welfare policy, program, & practice issues.* New Brunswick: Transaction Publishers.

Shaylor, C. (1998). 'It's like living in a black hole.' Women of color and solitary confinement in the prison industrial complex. *New England Journal on Criminal and Civil Confinement, 24*: 385–416.

Shaw, M. (1996). Is there a feminist future for women's prisons? In R. Matthews and P. Francis (eds.), *Prisons 2000: An international perspective on the current state and future of imprisonment.* London: Macmillan.

Sheldon, R. (1972). Rehabilitation programs in prison. *Psychiatric Opinion, 9*: 20–21.

Shorris, E. (1992). *Latinos: A biography of the people.* New York: W W Norton & Company.

Silbert, M. and Pines, A. (1981). NIMH study of 200 female street prostitutes in San Francisco.

Silverstein, A. (1990). Mother and child reunion: With the number of women in prison on the rise, corrections officials struggle to make sure children aren't punished too. *Empire State Reporter, 16*: 23–26.

Silverstein, K. (1997). America's private gulag. Available at: http://www.thirdworldtraveler.com/Prison_System/America_Gulag.html.

Simon, R. (1975). *The contemporary women and crime.* Rockville, MD: National Institute of Mental Health.

Simon, R. J. and Landis, J. (1991). *The crimes women commit and the punishment they receive.* Lexington, MA: Lexington Books.

Slater, E. (1995). Pizza thief gets 25 to life. *Los Angeles Times,* March 3.

Smith, C. (1995). *Courts and public policy.* Chicago: Nelson-Hall Publishers.

Simmel, G. (1971). *On individuality and social forms.* Chicago: The University of Chicago Press.

Smykla, J. O., ed. (1980). *Coed prison.* New York: Human Services Press.

Snow, C. (1981). Women in prison (women and poverty: Women's issues in legal services practice). *Clearinghouse Review, 14*: 1065–1068.

So, A. Y. (1990). *Social change and development: Modernization, dependency, and world-system theories.* Newbury Park: Sage Publications.

Sohoni, N. K. (1989). *Women behind bars.* New Dalhi: Vikas Publishing House.

Sommers, I. and Baskin, D. (1992). Sex, race, age and violent offending. *Violence and Victims, 7*: 191–201.

Sorensen, V. (1981). Educational and vocational needs of women in prison. *Corrections Today, 43*: 61–69.

Specter, D. (1994). Mentally ill in prison: A cruel and unusual punishment. *Forum,* December.

Spitzer, S. (1975). Toward a Marxian theory of deviance. *Social Problems, 22*: 638–651.

Spohn, C., J. Gruhl and S. Welch (1985). Women defendants in court: The interaction between sex and race in convicting and sentencing. *Social Science Quarterly, 66*: 178–185.

Stalans, L. J. (2003). Adult sex offenders on community supervision: A review of recent assessment strategies and treatment. *Criminal Justice and Behavior, 31*: 564–608.

Steadman, H. J. and Cocozza, J. J., eds. (1993). *Mental illness in America's prisons.* Seattle, Washington: National Coalition for the Mentally Ill in the Criminal Justice System.

Stefan, S. (1989). Whose egg is it anyway? Reproductive rights of incarcerated, institutionalized and incompetent women. *Nova Law Review, 13*: 405–456.

Steptoe, S. (1986). Careless treatment: Inmates claim prisons are failing to provide adequate medical care; courts order improvements, but states act slowly. *Wall Street Journal, 207* (May 15): 1.

Strasser, F. and Hickey, M. G. (1989). Running out of room for women in prison. *Governing, 3*: 70–71.

Street, D., R. D. Vinter and C. Perrow (1966). *Organization for treatment.* London: Collier Macmillan.

Strickland, K. (1976). *Correctional institutions for women in the U.S.* Lexington, MA: Lexington Books.

Sultan, F., G. Long, S. Kiefer, D. Schrum, J. Selby and L. Calhoun (1984). The female offender's adjustment to prison life: A comparison of psychodidactic and traditional supportive approaches to treatment. *Journal of Offender Counseling, Services and Rehabilitation, 9*: 49–56.

Sykes, G. and Messinger, S. (1958). *The society of captives: A study of a maximum security prison.* Princeton, NJ: Princeton University Press.

Szasz, T. (1987). *Insanity: The idea and its consequences.* New York: Wiley.

Szasz, T. (1963). *Law, liberty, and psychiatry.* New York: Macmillan.

Tanner, A. (2007). Inmates, California officials warn prisons crowded. Available at: http://news.yahoo.com/s/nm/20070215/us_nm/california_prisons_dc&printer=1;_ylt=At_PloJyIqsnwOkAUcCkpdMXIrOF

Taylor, I. (1999). *Crime in context: A critical criminology of market societies.* Cambridge: Polity Press.

Tell, L. (1981). Study finds women prisoners are denied equal facilities and training programs. *The National Law Journal, 3*: 6.

The Sentencing Project (2001). U.S. continues to be world leader in rate of incarceration. Press release, August.

Thomas, P. (1994). Making crime pay: Triangle of interests creates infra-structure to fight lawlessness. *Wall Street Journal,* May 12: A1, A8.

Thompson, D. (2007). Judge: Calif. prison transfer illegal. Associated Press. Available at: http://news.yahoo.com/s/ap/20070220/ap_on_re_us/california_prisons&printer=1;_ylt=ArdUbGOvfH19iesMRwmTjrpH2ocA

Time (2006). Who we are. October 30: 44–45.

Tischler, C. A. and Marquart, J. W. (1989). Analysis of disciplinary infraction rates among female and male inmates. *Journal of Criminal Justice, 17*: 507–513.

Tittle, C. R. (1972). *Society of subordinates: Inmate organization in a narcotic hospital.* Bloomington: Indiana University Press.

Tittle, C. R. (1969). Inmate organizations: Sex differentiation and the influence of criminal subcultures. *American Sociological Review, 34*: 493–505.

Toch, H. (1977). *Police, prisons and the problem of violence.* Washington, D.C.: U.S. Government Printing Office.

Tonry, M. (2004). *The future of imprisonment.* New York: Oxford University Press.

Tonry, M. (1995). *Malign neglect: Crime, race and punishment.* New York: Oxford University Press.

Torrey, E. F. (1988). *Nowhere to go: The tragic odyssey of the homeless mentally ill.* New York: Harper & Row.

Travis, J. and Waul, M., eds. (2003). *Prisoners once removed: The impact of incarceration and reentry on children, families, and communities.* Washington, D.C.: Urban Institute Press.

Turk, A. (1969). *Criminality and legal order.* Chicago: Rand McNally.

Twohey, M. (2004). Prisons not acting to stop sex misconduct. *Milwaukee Journal Sentinel,* August 20: 1A, 10A.

Urbina, M. G. (2007). Latinas/os in the criminal and juvenile justice systems. *Critical Criminology: An International Journal, 15*: 41–99.

Urbina, M. G. (2005a). Puerto Rican nationalists. *Encyclopedia of Prisons & Correctional Facilities,* Vol. 2: 796–798. Edited by M. Bosworth.

Urbina, M. G. (2005b). Transferring juveniles to adult court in Wisconsin: practitioners voice their views. *Criminal Justice Studies: A Critical Journal of Crime, Law and Society, 18*: 147–172.

Urbina, M. G. (2004a). Language barriers in the Wisconsin court system: The Latino/a experience. *Journal of Ethnicity in Criminal Justice, 2*: 91–118.

Urbina, M. G. (2004b). A qualitative analysis of Latinos executed in the United States between 1975 and 1995: Who were they? *Social Justice, 31*: 242–267.

Urbina, M. G. (2003a). *Capital punishment and Latino offenders: Racial and ethnic differences in death sentences.* New York: LFB Scholarly Publishing.

Urbina, M. G. (2003b). The quest and application of historical knowledge in modern times: A critical view. *Criminal justice studies: A critical journal of crime, law and society, 16*: 113–129.

Urbina, M. G. (2003c). History of U.S. race and ethnic relations. In M.G. Urbina, *Capital punishment and Latino offenders: Racial and ethnic differences in death sentences.* New York: LFB Scholarly Publishing.

Urbina, M. G. (2003d). Race and ethnic differences in punishment and death sentence outcomes: Empirical analysis of data on California, Florida and Texas, 1975–1995. *Journal of Ethnicity in Criminal Justice, 1*: 5–35.

Urbina, M. G. (2002a). Death sentence outcomes. *Encyclopedia of Crime and Punishment,* Vol 2: 482–485. Edited by D. Levinson.

Urbina, M. G. (2002b). Furman and Gregg exist death row?: Un-weaving an old controversy. *The Justice Professional, 15*: 105–125.

Urbina, M. G. and Kreitzer, S. (2004). The practical utility and ramifications of RICO: Thirty-two years after its implementation. *Criminal Justice Policy Review, 15*: 294–323.

Urbina, M. G. and Smith, L. (2007). Colonialism and its impact on Mexicans' experience of punishment in the United States. In M. Bosworth and J. Flavin (eds.), *Race, gender, and punishment: From colonialism to the war on terror* (pp. 49–61). Piscataway, NJ: Rutgers University Press.

USA Today (1990). Babies behind bars-innocent victims. 118: 7.

U.S. Census Bureau (2005a). Historical poverty tables-families. Available at: http://www.census.gov/hhes/www/poverty/histpov/famindex.html.

U.S. Census Bureau (2005b). *Income, poverty, and health insure coverage in the United States: 2004.* Washington, D.C.: U.S. Government Printing Office.

Vandiver, M. (1999). An apology does not assist the accused: Foreign nationals and the death penalty in the United States. *The Justice Professional, 12*: 223–245.

Van Wormer, K. (1987). Female prison families: How are they dysfunctional? *International Journal of Comparative and Applied Criminal Justice, 11*: 263–271.

Van Wormer, K. (1981). Social functions of prison families: The female solution. *Journal of Psychiatry and Law, 9*: 181–191.

Verhovek, S. H. (1997). Texas jail video puts transfers programs in doubt. *New York Times*, August 22: A1.

Viadro, C. I. and Earp, J. A. (1991). AIDS education and incarcerated women: A neglected opportunity. *Women and Health, 17*: 105–17.

Vicini, J. (2006). U.S. has most prisoners in world due to tough laws. Available at: http://news.yahoo.com/s/nm/20061209/tsnm/usaprisonersdc&printer=1.

Vitale, A. T. (1980). Inmate abortions-the right to government funding behind the prison gates. *Fordham Law Review, 48*: 550–567.

Vukson, T. M. (1987). Inmate abortion funding in California: A constitutional analysis. *California Western Law Review, 24*: 107–126.

Wacquant, L. (1999). Suitable enemies: Foreigners and immigrants in the prisons of Europe. *Punishment & Society, 1*: 215–222.

Walford, B., ed. (1987). *The stories of eleven women serving life sentences for murder.* Montreal: Eden Press.

Walker, S. (2005). *Sense and nonsense about crime and drugs: A policy guide.* 6th edition. Belmont, CA: Wadsworth.

Walker, S. (1980). *Popular justice: A history of American criminal justice.* New York: Oxford University Press.

Walters, L. (1995). Anticrime wave shackles state educational spending. *Christian Science Monitor*, February.

Ward, D. and Kassebaum, G. (1965). *Women's prison: Sex and social structure.* New York: Aldine-Atherton.

Wares, D. (1990). Equality behind bars: The state's only maximum security prison for women makes plans for a death row (California). *California Lawyer, 10*: 17–18.

Waring, N. and Smith, B. (1991). The AIDS epidemic: Impact on women prisoners in Massachusetts-an assessment with recommendations. *Women and Criminal Justice, 2*: 117–143.

Watterson, K. (1996). *Women in prison: Inside the concrete womb.* Boston: Northeastern University Press.

Watterson, K. (1973). *Women in prison.* New York: Doubleday.

Watts, T. J. (1990). *Experiences and problems of women in prison: A bibliography.* Monticello, IL: Vance Bibliographies.

Weisheit, R. A. (1985). Trends in programs for female offenders: The use of private agencies as service providers. *International Journal of Offender Therapy and Comparative Criminology, 29*: 35–42.

Welch, M. (2007). Immigration lockdown before and after 9/11: Ethnic constructions and their consequences. In M. Bosworth and J. Flavin (eds.), *Race, gender, and punishment: From colonialism to the war on terror* (pp. 149–163). Piscataway, NJ: Rutgers University Press.

Welch, M. (2006). *Scapegoats of September 11th: Hate crimes and state crimes in the war on terror.* New Brunswick, NJ: Rutgers University Press.

Welchans, S. (2005). Megan's Law: Evaluations of sexual offender registries. *Criminal Justice Policy Review, 16*: 123–140.

Wells, D. and Jackson, J. (1992). HIV and chemically dependent women: Recommendations for appropriate health care and drug treatment services. *International Journal of the Addictions, 27*: 571–585.

Western, B. (2002). The impact of incarceration on wage mobility and inequality. *American Sociological Review, 67*: 526–546.

Wiesel, E. (1982). *Night.* New York: Bantam Books.

Wilbanks, W. (1986). Are female felons treated more leniently by the criminal justice system? *Justice Quarterly, 3*: 517–529.

Williams, L. R. (1981). Women, the inmates recreation has passed by. *Parks and Recreation, 16*: 58–63.

Williams, P. J. (1997). *Seeing a color-blind future: The paradox of race.* New York: Noonday Press.

Williams, P. J. (1991). *The alchemy of race and rights.* Cambridge, MA: Harvard University Press.

Williams, S. J. and Torrens, P. R., eds. (2001). *Introduction to health services.* 6th edition. Albany, NY: Delmar.

Wilson, T. P. (1968). Patterns of management and adaptations to organizational roles: A study of prison inmates. *American Journal of Sociology, 74*: 146–157.

Winerip, M. (1999). Bedlam on the streets. *The New York Times Sunday Magazine,* May 23: 41–49, 56.

Winfree, L. T. and Griffiths, C. T. (1975). An examination of factors related to the parole survival of American Indians. *Plains Anthropologist, 20*: 311–319.

Winifred, M. (1996). Vocational and technical training programs for women in prison. *Corrections Today, 58*: 168–170.

Wirtzfeld, R. (1985). New women's jail treats inmates as humans. *Law and Order, 33*: 23, 60.

Woffinden, B. (1985). Innocent women in prison. *New Statesman, 109*: 6.

Women's Prison Association (2004). *A report on the first ten years of the Sarah Powell Huntington House.* New York: Women's Prison Association.

Women's Prison Association (2003). *WPA focus on women and justice: Barriers to reentry.* New York: Women's Prison Association.

Wooldredge, J. D. and Masters, K. (1993). Confronting problems faced by pregnant inmates in state prisons. *Crime and Delinquency, 39*: 195–203.

World Health Organization (2006). Depression. Available at: http://www.who.int/mental_health/management/depression/definition/en/print.html.

Wright, L. E. and Seymour, C. B. (2000). *Working with children and families separated by incarceration: A handbook for child welfare agencies.* Washington, D.C.: CWLA Press.

Yang, S. (1990). The unique treatment needs of female substance abusers: The oblig-ation of the criminal justice system to provide parity services. *Medicine and Law, 9*: 1018–1027.

Young, D. S. (2000). Women's perceptions of health care in prison. *Health Care for Women International, 21*: 219–234.

Young, D.S. (1999). Ethnicity and health service use in a women's prison. *Journal of Multicultural Social Work, 7*: 69–93.

Young, V. D. and Spencer, Z. (2007). Multiple jeopardy: The impact of race, gender, and slavery on the punishment of women in antebellum America. In M. Bosworth and J. Flavin (eds.), *Race, gender, and punishment: From colonialism to the war on terror* (pp. 65–76). Piscataway, NJ: Rutgers University Press.

Young, V. D. (1986). Gender expectations and their impact on Black female offend-ers and victims. *Justice Quarterly, 3*: 305–327.

Young, V. D. (1980). Women, race, and crime. *Criminology, 18*: 26–34.

Zahn, M. and McBride, J. (2000a). Secrecy veils more than 100 deaths. *Milwaukee Journal Sentinel*, October 22: 1A, 14A–16A.

Zahn, M. and McBride, J. (2000b). Changes urged at prisons. *Milwaukee Journal Sentinel*, October 24: 1–6. Available at: wysiwyg://3/http://www.jsonline.com/news/metro/oct00/priz25102400a.asp.

Zaitzow, B. (2001). Whose problem is it anyway? Women prisoners and HIV/AIDS. *International Journal of Offender Therapy and Comparative Criminology, 45*: 686.

Zaplin, R. (1998). *Female offenders: Critical perspectives and effective interventions.* Gaithersburg, MD.: Aspen.

Zedner, L. (1995). Wayward sisters: The prison for women. In N. Morris and D.J. Rothman (eds.), *The Oxford history of the prison.* New York: Oxford University Press.

Ziedenberg, J., R. Gangi and V. Schiraldi (1998). *New York state of mind? Higher edu-cation versus prison funding in the empire state.* Washington, D.C.: Center on Juvenile and Criminal Justice.

Zimbardo, P. (1994). Transforming California's prisons into expensive old age homes: Enormous hidden costs and consequences for California's taxpayers. Center for Juvenile and Criminal Justice, November.

Zingraff, M. T. (1980). Inmate assimilation: A comparison of male and female delin-quents. *Criminal Justice and Behavior, 7*: 275–292.

Zingraff, M. T. and Zingraff, R. M. (1980). Adaptation patterns of incarcerated female delinquents. *Juvenile and Family Courts Journal, 31*: 35–47.

Zinn, M. B. and Dill, B. T., eds. (1994). *Women of color in U.S. society.* Philadelphia: Temple University Press.

Zupan, L. (1992). Men guarding women: An analysis of the employment of male correctional officers in prisons for women. *Journal of Criminal Justice, 20*: 297–309.

Zwerman, G. (1988). Special incapacitation: The emergence of a new correctional facility for women political prisoners. *Social Justice, 15*: 31–47.

INDEX

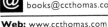